*Life at the Bottom*

# Life at the
# BOTTOM

*The Worldview That Makes the Underclass*

## THEODORE
## DALRYMPLE

*Ivan R. Dee*

CHICAGO

With the exception of the Introduction, the contents of this book first
appeared in *City Journal,* published by The Manhattan Institute.

Library of Congress Cataloging-in-Publication Data:
Dalrymple, Theodore.
    Life at the bottom : the worldview that makes the underclass /
  Theodore Dalrymple.
        p.   cm.
    Includes index.
    ISBN 1-56663-505-5 (alk. paper)      ISBN: 978-1-56663-505-9
    1. Poor—Mental health—Great Britain.   2. Criminals—Mental
  health—Great Britain.   3. Prisoners—Mental health—Great Britain.
    RC451.P6 D35 2001
    362.2'086'9420941—dc21                           2001037221

# Contents

# Introduction

──────────

◈ A SPECTER IS haunting the Western world: the underclass.

This underclass is not poor, at least by the standards that have prevailed throughout the great majority of human history. It exists, to a varying degree, in all Western societies. Like every other social class, it has benefited enormously from the vast general increase in wealth of the past hundred years. In certain respects, indeed, it enjoys amenities and comforts that would have made a Roman emperor or an absolute monarch gasp. Nor is it politically oppressed: it fears neither to speak its mind nor the midnight knock on the door. Yet its existence is wretched nonetheless, with a special wretchedness that is peculiarly its own.

As a doctor who has worked for the past decade in a busy general hospital in a British slum, and also in a nearby prison, I have been in a privileged position to observe the life of this underclass. I have, for example, interviewed some ten thousand people who have made an attempt (however feeble) at suicide, each of whom has told me of the lives of four or five other people around him. From this source alone, therefore, I have learned about the lives of some fifty thousand people: lives dominated, almost without exception, by violence, crime, and degradation. My sample is a selected one, no doubt, as all samples drawn from personal experience must be, but it is not small.

Moreover, having previously worked as a doctor in some of the poorest countries in Africa, as well as in very poor countries in the Pacific and Latin America, I have little hesitation in saying that the mental, cultural, emotional, and spiritual impoverishment of the Western underclass is the greatest of any large group of people I have ever encountered anywhere.

As a doctor I am, of course, committed to treating each patient as an individual. It could hardly be otherwise: when you talk to people about the most intimate details of their lives, it could scarcely occur to you that they are other than fully conscious agents, in essence no different from yourself.

Nevertheless, patterns of behavior emerge—in the case of the underclass, almost entirely self-destructive ones. Day after day I hear of the same violence, the same neglect and abuse of children, the same broken relationships, the same victimization by crime, the same nihilism, the same dumb despair. If everyone is a unique individual, how do patterns such as this emerge?

Economic determinism, of the vicious cycle-of-poverty variety, seems hardly to answer the case. Not only is the underclass not poor, but untold millions of people who were very much poorer have emerged from poverty within living memory—in South Korea, for example. If being poor really entailed a vicious cycle, man would still be living in the caves.

Genetic or racial determinism is no better. It will come as a surprise to American readers, perhaps, to learn that the majority of the British underclass is white, and that it demonstrates all the same social pathology as the black underclass in America—for very similar reasons, of course. Genetics, moreover, can hardly explain such phenomena as the rise of mass illegitimacy, unprecedented in recorded history, since the late 1950s.

The role of the welfare state in the rise (if that is quite the word for it) of the underclass is likewise overstressed. At most it might have been a necessary condition for that rise: it made it possible, not inevitable. Welfare states have existed for substantial periods of time without the development of a modern underclass: an added ingredient is obviously necessary.

This ingredient is to be found in the realm of ideas. Human behavior cannot be explained without reference to the meaning and intentions people give to their acts and omissions; and everyone has a Weltanschauung, a worldview, whether he knows it or not. It is the ideas my patients have that fascinate—and, to be honest, appall—me: for they are the source of their misery.

Their ideas make themselves manifest even in the language they use. The frequency of locutions of passivity is a striking example. An alcoholic, explaining his misconduct while drunk, will say, "The beer went mad." A heroin addict, explaining his resort to the needle, will say, "Heroin's everywhere." It is as if the beer drank the alcoholic and the heroin injected the addict.

Other locutions plainly serve an exculpatory function and represent a denial of agency and therefore of personal responsibility. The murderer claims the knife went in or the gun went off. The man who attacks his sexual consort claims that he "went into one" or "lost it," as if he were the victim of a kind of epilepsy of which it is the doctor's duty to cure him. Until the cure, of course, he can continue to abuse his consort—for such abuse has certain advantages for him—safe in the knowledge that he, not his consort, is its true victim.

I have come to see the uncovering of this dishonesty and self-deception as an essential part of my work. When a man tells me, in explanation of his anti-social behavior, that he is easily led, I ask him whether he was ever easily led to study mathematics or the subjunctives of French verbs. Invariably the man begins to laugh: the absurdity of what he has said is immediately apparent to him. Indeed, he will acknowledge that he knew how absurd it was all along, but that certain advantages, both psychological and social, accrued by keeping the pretense up.

The idea that one is not an agent but the helpless victim of circumstances, or of large occult sociological or economic forces, does not come naturally, as an inevitable concomitant of experience. On the contrary, only in extreme circumstances is helplessness directly experienced in the way the blueness of the sky is experienced. Agency, by contrast, is the common experience of us all. We know our will's free, and there's an end on't.

The contrary idea, however, has been endlessly propagated by intellectuals and academics who do not believe it of themselves, of course, but only of others less fortunately placed than themselves. In this there is a considerable element of condescension: that some people do not measure up fully to the status of human. The extension of the term "addiction," for example, to cover any undesirable but nonetheless gratifying behavior that is repeated, is one example of denial of personal agency that has swiftly percolated downward from academe. Not long after academic criminologists propounded the theory that recidivists were addicted to crime (bolstering their theories with impressive diagrams of neural circuits in the brain to prove it), a car thief of limited intelligence and less education asked me for treatment of his addiction to stealing cars—failing receipt of which, of course, he felt morally justified in continuing to relieve car owners of their property.

In fact most of the social pathology exhibited by the underclass has its origin in ideas that have filtered down from the intelligentsia. Of nothing is this more true than the system of sexual relations that now prevails in the underclass, with the result that 70 percent of the births in my hospital are now illegitimate (a figure that would approach 100 percent if it were not for the presence in the area of a large number of immigrants from the Indian subcontinent).

Literature and common sense attest that sexual relations between men and women have been fraught with difficulty down the ages precisely because man is a conscious social being who bears a culture, and is not merely a biological being. But intel-

lectuals in the twentieth century sought to free our sexual relations of all social, contractual, or moral obligations and meaning whatsoever, so that henceforth only raw sexual desire itself
would count in our decision making.

The intellectuals were about as sincere as Marie Antoinette
when she played the shepherdess. While their own sexual mores
no doubt became more relaxed and liberal, they nonetheless
continued to recognize inescapable obligations with regard to
children, for example. Whatever they said, they didn't want a
complete breakdown of family relations any more than Marie
Antoinette really wanted to earn her living by looking after
sheep.

But their ideas were adopted both literally and wholesale in
the lowest and most vulnerable social class. If anyone wants to
see what sexual relations are like, freed of contractual and social obligations, let him look at the chaos of the personal lives
of members of the underclass.

Here the whole gamut of human folly, wickedness, and misery may be perused at leisure—in conditions, be it remembered,
of unprecedented prosperity. Here are abortions procured by
abdominal kung fu; children who have children, in numbers
unknown before the advent of chemical contraception and sex
education; women abandoned by the father of their child a
month before or a month after delivery; insensate jealousy, the
reverse of the coin of general promiscuity, that results in the
most hideous oppression and violence; serial stepfatherhood
that leads to sexual and physical abuse of children on a mass
scale; and every kind of loosening of the distinction between the
sexually permissible and the impermissible.

The connection between this loosening and the misery of my
patients is so obvious that it requires considerable intellectual
sophistication (and dishonesty) to be able to deny it.

The climate of moral, cultural, and intellectual relativism—
a relativism that began as a mere fashionable plaything for intellectuals—has been successfully communicated to those least

able to resist its devastating practical effects. When Professor Steven Pinker tells us in his best-selling book *The Language Instinct* (written, of course, in grammatically correct standard English, and published without spelling mistakes) that there is no grammatically correct form of language, that children require no tuition in their own language because they are destined to learn to speak it adequately for their needs, and that all forms of language are equally expressive, he is helping to enclose the underclass child in the world in which he was born. Not only will that child's teachers feel absolved from the arduous task of correcting him, but rumors of Professor Pinker's grammatical tolerance (a linguistic version of Pope's dictum that whatever is, is right) will reach the child himself. He will thenceforth resent correction as illegitimate and therefore humiliating. *Eppur si mouve*: whatever Professor Pinker says, the world demands correct grammar and spelling from those who would advance in it. Moreover, it is patently untrue that every man's language is equal to his needs, a fact that is obvious to anyone who has read the pitiable attempts of the underclass to communicate in writing with others, especially officialdom. Linguistic and educational relativism helps to transform a class into a caste—a caste, almost, of Untouchables.

Just as there is said to be no correct grammar or spelling, so there is no higher or lower culture: difference itself is the only recognized distinction. This is a view peddled by intellectuals eager to demonstrate to one another their broad-mindedly democratic sentiment. For example, the newspaper that is virtually the house journal of Britain's liberal intelligentsia, the *Guardian* (which would once honorably have demanded that, in the name of equity and common decency, the entire population should be given access to high culture), recently published an article about a meeting in New York of what it described in headlines as "some of America's biggest minds."

And who were America's biggest minds? Were they its Nobel prize–winning scientists, its physicists and molecular biologists? Were they America's best contemporary scholars or writers? Or perhaps its electronics entrepreneurs who have so transformed the world in the last half-century?

No, some of the biggest minds in America belonged, in the opinion of the *Guardian*, to rap singers such as Puff Daddy, who were meeting in New York (for "a summit," as the *Guardian* put it) to end the spate of senseless mutual killings of East and West Coast rap singers and improve the public image of rap as a genre. Pictures of the possessors of these gigantic minds accompanied the article, so that even if you did not already know that rap lyrics typically espouse a set of values that is in equal part brutal and stupid, you would know at once that these allegedly vast intellects belonged to people indistinguishable from street thugs.

The insincerity of this flattery is obvious to anyone with even a faint acquaintance with the grandeur of human achievement. It is inconceivable that the writer of the article, or the editor of the newspaper, both educated men, truly believed that Puff Daddy *et al.* possessed some of the biggest minds in America. But the fact that the debased culture of which rap music is a product receives such serious attention and praise deludes its listeners into supposing that nothing finer exists than what they already know and like. Such flattery is thus the death of aspiration, and lack of aspiration is, of course, one of the causes of passivity.

Does the fate of the underclass matter? If the misery of millions of people matters, then the answer must surely be yes. But even if we were content to consign so many of our fellow citizens to the purgatory of life in our slums, that would not be the end of the matter. For there are clear signs that the underclass will be revenged upon the whole pack of us.

In the modern world, bad ideas and their consequences cannot be confined to a ghetto. Middle-class friends of mine were appalled to discover that the spelling being taught to their daughter in school was frequently wrong; they were even more appalled when they drew it to the attention of the school's head teacher and were told it did not matter, since the spelling was approximately right and everyone knew anyway what the misspelling meant.

Other institutions have been similarly undermined by the acceptance of ideas that have encouraged and maintained an underclass. When street prostitutes moved in considerable numbers to the street corners of the neighborhood in which I live, the senior local policeman said in response to residents' requests that he do something about it that he would do nothing, since the women came from disadvantaged homes and were probably all addicted to drugs. He was not prepared, he said, to victimize them further. It was therefore our duty as citizens to pick the used condoms from our rose bushes. Such is life under the regime of zero intolerance.

Worse still, cultural relativism spreads all too easily. The tastes, conduct, and mores of the underclass are seeping up the social scale with astonishing rapidity. Heroin chic is one manifestation of this, though no one with any real knowledge of heroin and its effects could find anything chic about either the drug or its effects. When a member of the British royal family revealed that she had adopted one of the slum fashions and had had her navel pierced, no one was in the least surprised. Where fashion in clothes, bodily adornment, and music are concerned, it is the underclass that increasingly sets the pace. Never before has there been so much downward cultural aspiration.

The disastrous pattern of human relations that exists in the underclass is also becoming common higher up the social scale. With increasing frequency I am consulted by nurses, who for the most part come from and were themselves traditionally members of (at least after Florence Nightingale) the respectable lower middle class, who have illegitimate children by men who first abuse and then abandon them. This abuse and later abandonment is usually all too predictable from the man's previous history and character; but the nurses who have been treated in this way say they refrained from making a judgment about him because it is wrong to make judgments. But if they do not make a judgment about the man with whom they are going to live and by whom they are going to have a child, about what are they ever going to make a judgment?

"It just didn't work out," they say, the "it" in question being the relationship that they conceive of having an existence independent of the two people who form it, and that exerts an influence on their lives rather like an astral conjunction. Life is fate.

In what follows I have tried first to describe underclass reality in an unvarnished fashion, and then to lay bare the origin of that reality, which is the propagation of bad, trivial, and often insincere ideas. Needless to say, a true appreciation of the cause of underclass misery is desirable in order to combat it, and even more to avoid solutions that will only make it worse. And if I paint a picture of a way of life that is wholly without charm or merit, and describe many people who are deeply unattractive, it is important to remember that, if blame is to be apportioned, it is the intellectuals who deserve most of it. They should have known better but always preferred to avert their gaze. They considered the purity of their ideas to be more important than the actual consequences of their ideas. I know of no egotism more profound.

This is the excellent foppery of the world, that when we are sick in fortune, often the surfeits of our own behaviour, we make guilty of our disasters the sun, the moon, and stars; as if we were villains on necessity, fools by heavenly compulsion, knaves, thieves, and treachers by spherical predominance, drunkards, liars, and adulterers by an enforced obedience of planetary influence; and all that we are evil in, by a divine thrusting on. An admirable evasion of whoremaster man, to lay his goatish disposition on the charge of a star!

*King Lear*, Act I, scene ii

*Life at the Bottom*

# GRIM REALITY

# The Knife Went In

◈ IT IS A MISTAKE to suppose that all men, or at least all Englishmen, want to be free. On the contrary, if freedom entails responsibility, many of them want none of it. They would happily exchange their liberty for a modest (if illusory) security. Even those who claim to cherish their freedom are rather less enthusiastic about taking the consequences of their actions. The aim of untold millions is to be free to do exactly as they choose and for someone else to pay when things go wrong.

In the past few decades, a peculiar and distinctive psychology has emerged in England. Gone are the civility, sturdy independence, and admirable stoicism that carried the English through the war years. It has been replaced by a constant whine of excuses, complaints, and special pleading. The collapse of the British character has been as swift and complete as the collapse of British power.

Listening as I do every day to the accounts people give of their lives, I am struck by the very small part in them which they ascribe to their own efforts, choices, and actions. Implicitly they disagree with Bacon's famous dictum that "chiefly the mould of a man's fortune is in his own hands." Instead they experience themselves as putty in the hands of fate.

It is instructive to listen to the language they use to describe their lives. The language of prisoners in particular teaches much about the dishonest fatalism with which people seek to explain themselves to others, especially when those others are in a position to help them in some way. As a doctor who sees patients in a prison once or twice a week, I am fascinated by prisoners' use of the passive mood and other modes of speech that are supposed to indicate their helplessness. They describe themselves as the marionettes of happenstance.

Not long ago, a murderer entered my room in the prison shortly after his arrest to seek a prescription for the methadone to which he was addicted. I told him that I would prescribe a reducing dose, and that within a relatively short time my prescription would cease. I would not prescribe a maintenance dose for a man with a life sentence.

"Yes," he said, "it's just my luck to be here on this charge."

Luck? He had already served a dozen prison sentences, many of them for violence, and on the night in question had carried a knife with him, which he must have known from experience that he was inclined to use. But it was the victim of the stabbing who was the real author of the killer's action: if he hadn't been there, he wouldn't have been stabbed.

My murderer was by no means alone in explaining his deed as due to circumstances beyond his control. As it happens, there are three stabbers (two of them unto death) now in the prison who used precisely the same expression when describing to me what happened. "The knife went in," they said when pressed to recover their allegedly lost memories of the deed.

The knife went in—unguided by human hand, apparently. That the long-hated victims were sought out, and the knives carried to the scene of the crimes, was as nothing compared with the willpower possessed by the inanimate knives themselves, which determined the unfortunate outcome.

It might be objected by psychologists, of course, that the deeds of these men were so heinous that it was a natural and perhaps even necessary psychic defense for them to ascribe the deaths of their victims to forces beyond their control: too swift an acknowledgment of responsibility would result in a total collapse of their morale and, possibly, in suicide. But the evasion in their own minds of the responsibility for their deeds was in no way different from that exhibited by lesser criminals: offenders against property or, more accurately, against the owners of property.

A few examples will suffice. A prisoner, recently convicted for the umpteenth time, came to me to complain that he had been depressed ever since his trouble came on him again. And what, I asked, was this trouble that came on him periodically? It was breaking and entering churches, stealing their valuables, and burning them down to destroy the evidence. And why churches? Was it that he had been dragged as a child to tedious services by hypocritical parents and wished to be revenged upon religion, perhaps? Not at all; it was because in general churches were poorly secured, easy to break into, and contained valuable objects in silver.

Oddly enough, he did not deduce from this pragmatic, reasonable, and honest explanation of his choice of ecclesiastical burglary as a career that he was himself responsible for the trouble that mysteriously overtook him every time he was released from prison: he blamed the church authorities for the laxness of their security, which first caused and then reinforced his compulsion to steal from them. Echoing the police, who increasingly blame theft on the owners of property—for failing to take the proper precautions against its misappropriation—rather than on those who actually carry out the theft, the ecclesiastical burglar said that the church authorities should have known of his proclivities and taken the necessary measures to prevent him from acting upon them.

Another burglar demanded to know from me why he repeatedly broke into houses and stole VCRs. He asked the question aggressively, as if "the system" had so far let him down in not supplying him with the answer; as if it were my duty as a doctor to provide him with the buried psychological secret that, once revealed, would in and of itself lead him unfailingly on the path of virtue. Until then he would continue to break into houses and steal VCRs (when at liberty to do so), and the blame would be mine.

When I refused to examine his past, he exclaimed, "But something must make me do it!"

"How about greed, laziness, and a thirst for excitement?" I suggested. "What about my childhood?" he asked.

"Nothing to do with it," I replied firmly.

He looked at me as if I had assaulted him. Actually, I thought the matter more complex than I was admitting, but I did not want him to misunderstand my main message: that he was the author of his own deeds.

Another prisoner claimed to be under so strong a compulsion to steal cars that it was irresistible—an addiction, he called it. He stole as many as forty vehicles a week but nevertheless considered himself a fundamentally good person because he was never violent towards anyone, and all the vehicles he stole were insured, and therefore the owners would lose nothing. But regardless of any financial incentive to do so, he contended, he stole cars for the excitement of it: if prevented for a few days from indulging in this activity, he became restless, depressed, and anxious. It was a true addiction, he repeated at frequent intervals, in case I should have forgotten in the meantime.

Now the generally prevalent conception of an addiction is of an illness, characterized by an irresistible urge (mediated neurochemically and possibly hereditary in nature) to consume a drug or other substance, or to behave in a repetitively self-destructive or anti-social way. An addict can't help himself, and because his behavior is a manifestation of illness, it has no more moral content than the weather.

So in effect what my car thief was telling me was that his compulsive car-stealing was not merely not his fault, but that the responsibility for stopping him from behaving thus was mine, since I was the doctor treating him. And until such time as the medical profession found the behavioral equivalent of an antibiotic in the treatment of pneumonia, he could continue to cause untold misery and inconvenience to the owners of cars and yet consider himself fundamentally a decent person.

That criminals often shift the locus of responsibility for their acts elsewhere is illustrated by some of the expressions they use most frequently in their consultations with me. Describing, for example, their habitual loss of temper, which leads them to assault whomever displeases them sufficiently, they say, "My head goes," or "My head just went."

What exactly do they mean by this? They mean that they consider themselves to suffer from a form of epilepsy or other cerebral pathology whose only manifestation is involuntary rage, of which it is the doctor's duty to cure them. Quite often they put me on warning that unless I find the cure for their behavior, or at least prescribe the drugs they demand, they are going to kill or maim someone. The responsibility when they do so will be mine, not theirs, for I knew what they were going to do yet failed to prevent it. So their putative illness has not only explained and therefore absolved them from past misconduct, but it has exonerated them in advance from all future misconduct.

Moreover, by warning me of their intention to carry out further assaults, they have set themselves up to be victims rather than perpetrators. They told the authorities (me) what they were going to do, and yet the authorities (I, again) did nothing; and so when they return to prison after committing a further horrible crime, they will feel aggrieved that "the system," represented by me, has once again let them down.

But were I to take the opposite tack and suggest preventive detention until they could control their temper, they would be outraged at the injustice of it. What about habeas corpus? What about innocence until guilt is proven? And they deduce nothing from the fact that they can usually control their tempers in the presence of a sufficiently opposing force.

Violent criminals often use an expression auxiliary to "My

head went" when explaining their deeds: "It wasn't me." Here is the psychobabble of the slums, the doctrine of the "Real Me" as refracted through the lens of urban degradation. The Real Me has nothing to do with the phenomenal me, the me that snatches old ladies' bags, breaks into other people's houses, beats up my wife and children, or repeatedly drinks too much and gets involved in brawls. No, the Real Me is an immaculate conception, untouched by human conduct: it is that unassailable core of virtue that enables me to retain my self-respect whatever I do. What I am is not at all determined by what I do; and insofar as what I do has any moral significance at all, it is up to others to ensure that the phenomenal me acts in accordance with the Real Me.

Hence one further expression frequently used by prisoners: "My head needs sorting out." The visual image they have of their minds, I suspect, is of a child's box of bricks, piled higgledy-piggledy, which the doctor, rummaging around in the skull, has the capacity and the duty to put into perfect order, ensuring that henceforth all conduct will automatically be honest, law-abiding, and economically advantageous. Until this sorting out is done, constructive suggestions—learn a skill, enroll in a correspondence course—are met with the refrain, "I will—once my head's sorted out."

At the very heart of all this passivity and refusal of responsibility is a deep dishonesty—what Sartre would have called bad faith. For however vehemently criminals try to blame others, and whatever appearance of sincerity they manage to convey while they do so, they know at least some of the time that what they say is untrue.

That's clear in the habit drug addicts often have of altering their language according to their interlocutors. To doctors, social workers, and probation officers—to all who might prove useful to them either in a prescribing or a testimonial capacity—they emphasize their overwhelming and overpowering craving for a drug, the intolerability of the withdrawal effects from it, the deleterious effects it has upon their character, judgment, and behavior. Among themselves, though, their language is quite different, optimistic rather than abject: it is about where you can obtain the best-quality drug, where it is cheapest, and how to heighten its effects.

I suspect (though I cannot prove, except by anecdote) that it is the same among prisoners. It is hardly a new observation that prisons are the universities of crime. Yet prisoners invariably describe to doctors and psychologists their difficult upbringings (which they bring out for the occasion almost like heirlooms), their violent or absent fathers, their poverty and all the difficulties and disadvantages to which urban flesh is heir. Among themselves, though, what must be the discourse as they establish contacts, learn new techniques, and deride the poor fools who earn an honest living but never grow rich?

That their outlook is dishonest and self-serving is apparent in their attitude towards those whom they believe to have done them wrong. For example, they do not say of the policemen who they allege (often plausibly) have beaten them up, "Poor cops! They were brought up in authoritarian homes and now project the anger that is really directed at their bullying fathers onto me. They need counseling. They need their heads sorted out." On the contrary, they say, with force and explosive emotion, "The bastards!" They assume that the police act out of free, if malevolent, will.

The prisoner's public presentation of himself often takes on a curious resemblance to the portrayal of him by liberals. "You want me to be a victim of circumstance?" he seems to say. "All right, I'll be a victim for you." With repetition of his story, he comes to believe it, at least some of the time and with part of his mind. Denial of guilt—both juridical and moral—thus becomes possible in the presence of the most minute memory of the circumstances of the crime.

Man has always had a capacity for the deceit of others and for self-deception, of course. It was Nietzsche who famously observed that pride and self-regard have no difficulty in overcoming memory; and every psychic defense mechanism known to the modern psychologist makes its appearance somewhere in Shakespeare. Yet one's impression nonetheless is that the ease with which people discard responsibility for what they have done—their intellectual and emotional dishonesty about their own actions—has increased greatly in the last few decades.

Why should this occur just when, objectively speaking, freedom and opportunity for the individual have never been greater?

In the first place, there is now a much enlarged constituency for liberal views: the legions of helpers and carers, social workers and therapists, whose incomes and careers depend crucially on the supposed incapacity of large numbers of people to fend for themselves or behave reasonably. Without the supposed powerlessness of drug addicts, burglars, and others in the face of their own undesirable inclinations, there would be nothing for the professional redeemers to do. They have a vested interest in psychopathology, and their entire therapeutic worldview of the patient as the passive, helpless victim of illness legitimizes the very behavior from which they are to redeem him. Indeed, the tangible advantages to the wrongdoer of appearing helpless are now so great that he needs but little encouragement to do so.

In the second place, there has been a widespread dissemination of psychotherapeutic concepts, in however garbled or misinterpreted a form. These concepts have become the currency even of the uneducated. Thus the idea has become entrenched that if one does not know or understand the unconscious motives for one's acts, one is not truly responsible for them. This, of course, applies only to those acts which someone regards as undesirable: no one puzzles over his own meritoriousness. But since there is no single ultimate explanation of anything, one can always claim ignorance of one's own motives. Here is a perpetual getout.

Third, there has been a widespread acceptance of sociological determinism, especially by the guilt-laden middle classes. Statistical association has been taken indiscriminately as proving causation: thus if criminal behavior is more common among the poorer classes, it must be poverty that causes crime.

Nobody, of course, experiences himself as sociologically determined—certainly not the sociologist. And few of the liberals who espouse such a viewpoint recognize its profoundly dehumanizing consequences. If poverty is the cause of crime, burglars do not decide to break into houses any more than amoebae decide to move a pseudopod towards a particle of food. They are automata—and presumably should be treated as such.

Here the subliminal influence of Marxist philosophy surfaces: the notion that it is not the consciousness of men that determines their being but, on the contrary, their social being that determines their consciousness. If this were so, men would still live in caves; but it has just enough plausibility to shake the confidence of the middle classes that crime is a moral problem, not just a problem of morale.

Into this rich brew of uncertainty and equivocation, social historians are inclined to add their dash of seasoning, pointing out that the middle classes saw crime as a moral problem even in the eighteenth century, when for many malefactors it really was quite another thing, since sometimes the only way for them to obtain food was to steal it. To say this, of course, is to overlook the fundamental change in life chances that has occurred since then. In Georgian London, for example, the life expectancy at birth was about twenty-five years, whereas it is now seventy-five. At the height of the Victorian era, the life expectancy of the royal family was 50 percent lower than that of the very poorest section of the population today. Surely to cling to explanations that might once have held some force but are no longer plausible is, in the most literal sense, reactionary.

The very form of the explanation offered by liberals for

modern crime—from social conditions direct to behavior, without passing through the human mind—offers those who commit crime an excuse in advance, an excuse which with part of their minds they know to be false but which is nonetheless useful and convenient to them in dealing with officialdom.

Finally, consider the effect that the mass media's constant rehearsal of injustices has upon the population. People come to believe that, far from being extremely fortunate by the standards of all previously existing populations, we actually live in the worst of times and under the most unjust of dispensations. Every wrongful conviction, every instance of police malfeasance, is so publicized that even professional criminals, even those who have performed appalling deeds, feel on a priori grounds they too must have been unjustly, or at least hypocritically, dealt with.

And the widespread notion that material inequality is in itself a sign of institutionalized injustice also helps foster crime. If property is theft, then theft is a form of just retribution. This leads to the development of that most curious phenomenon, the ethical thief: the thief who prides himself on stealing only from those who in his estimation can stand the loss. Thus I have had many burglars tell me in a glow of self-satisfaction that they would not steal from the old, from children, or the poor, because that would be wrong.

"In fact, you'd steal only from people like me," I say to them. (A house opposite mine has been burgled four times in two years, incidentally.)

They agree; and strangely enough they expect my approbation of their restrained feloniousness. That's how far things have gone.

*1994*

14

# Goodbye, Cruel World

ONE OF THE WARDS in the hospital in which I work is designated for patients who have poisoned themselves by deliberate overdose. We treat about twelve hundred cases a year there, so each day I go to work firm in the conviction that by now I've heard everything that human foolishness, depravity, fecklessness, and cruelty have to offer by way of narrative. But each day my faith in the ability of human beings comprehensively to ruin their lives is renewed: not for nothing did Tolstoy write at the beginning of *Anna Karenina* that every happy family is happy in the same way, but every unhappy family is unhappy in its own way. Of course, it would be an exaggeration to call the social arrangements in which most of my patients live families, but still the point is made. Truly, the ways of human misery are infinite.

Let us take a snapshot of the ward and examine the previous day's catch from the great ocean of unhappiness that lies all about us.

In the first of the six beds is a young woman of West Indian descent, aged twenty-one, who has dyed her hair orange and painted her nails bright yellow. She tells me that she was once a nursery school teacher but then went "on the sick" with an illness about whose nature it would be indelicate to ask, since it is obviously wholly fraudulent—the product and not the precondition of receiving sickness benefits from the public purse. She has a terrific black eye and a large swelling on her forehead. She tells me that she took her overdose after her ex-boyfriend, aged nineteen, punched her.

"Why did he do that?" I ask.

"I phoned him," she replies. "He said he'd told me he didn't want me to phone him no more."

"So he came round and hit you?"

"Yes."

"Does he hit you often?"

"No," she replies. "Usually, he head-butts me."

In the next bed is a man in his fifties, a former graduate of our ward. Back then, he took to the pills because his brother—his best friend and virtually his only reliable social contact since his own divorce—had died. This time, however, the overdose was precipitated by an entirely different matter.

"Some gypsies was smashing my windows, so I got out my shotgun and shot one of them."

"Was he injured?" I ask.

"No, not serious. A bit in the leg, like. It was only home-made cartridges, see, a bit of powder and scrap metal."

"Are the police involved?"

"No."

After it happened, neither party to the transaction was particularly anxious to seek the protection or interference of the law.

"But now, presumably, you are afraid to return to your flat because they will come for you again, and it won't be only your windows they'll want to smash?"

"That's right."

I arrange for him to be admitted to the psychiatric hospital, the asylum of his choice.

In the next bed is a slender girl, aged fifteen. She wears bright red lipstick and tight-fitting clothes, binges on food and vomits after eating, and has cut her wrists on many occasions. She has taken her stepfather's anti-coagulant pills, which he needs after his heart operation. She is a problem child and was brought to the hospital by her mother as one might deliver a sack of potatoes; her daughter's suicidal gesture had made her late for her bingo. Pouting and eternally on the verge of a temper tantrum, the child says she does not want to return home.

"Because of your mother and stepfather?" I ask.

No, she says. She doesn't want to return home because she was raped three months ago somewhere in the public housing project where she lives, and since then graffiti have appeared there saying that she enjoyed being raped and that she's a "slag" (meaning, a girl of easier virtue than average when adjusted for age, social class, educational background, and so forth). This is a point of view with which her mother wholeheartedly agrees, and so the patient has decided to run away and live on the streets rather than return home.

She doesn't want to go to a municipal children's home either, and in this I can't entirely blame her. She says she wants to be found a foster family, but the social worker informs me that not only is this difficult to arrange in a hurry but that once any prospective family knows her history—her truancy from school, her bulimia, her wrist-cutting—it will not agree to take her. The only possible solution would be for her to live with her aunt (her mother's sister), where she lived once before and was so happy that she behaved herself. But her mother, exercising parental rights if not duties, has specifically forbidden that, precisely because, I surmise, she behaves well there. Her mother wants to be rid of her as much as she wants to be rid of her mother, but her mother also wants to maintain the fiction that this desire stems solely from her daughter's impossible conduct. In order to disguise her own contribution to the situation and her indifference towards her own offspring, it is imperative that no place be found for her daughter that is so agreeable that her behavior improves there.

An impasse results; and so my patient is like the Russia of the old proverb, in which all roads lead to disaster.

On to the next bed. Here is a man in his thirties, of powerful physique and malign countenance—an unfortunate combination, in my experience. He has taken an overdose of his wife's anti-depressant pills, and it does not take Sherlock Holmes to deduce that he is the principal reason she needs them. He took the overdose after he pinned her against the wall by her neck, round which, he says, there are now bruises "no bigger than love-bites." She started it, he says, so it's her fault; she'd been giving him earache about his drinking all day.

"I couldn't take no more, so I had to get out of the house, and she wouldn't let me go. So yes, I did pin her up against the wall." He shows me by mime how he did it. "Everyone's got their breaking point, even you."

He tells me that they argue constantly. "What about?" I ask.

"When I was in prison, she had an affair with a black man, who beat her up, and an abortion."

"How long were you in prison?" I ask.

"Three years."

"Long imprisonment doesn't do much for a marriage," I remark.

"Yeah, but I didn't ask her to lie down and open her legs, did I?"

"Are you staying with her, then?" I ask.

"She's got my children; they're the only thing I've ever had. If she takes them away from me, I'd have to go straight back to crime, because there's nothing else out there for me. I'd blitz the public and the police; they wouldn't know what happened to them. They don't mean no more to me than cockroaches. And I can tell you, I'd soon have money in my pocket, more than you'll ever have."

I point out that history suggests otherwise: he's already spent sixteen years of his life in prison.

"Yeah, well this time I'll do something really big; there's no point in getting a three or a five." His eyes shine with the brilliant, hard light of the purest psychopathy.

"I'm what this society and this government's made me. My father fucked me off to reform school when I was young, and all they learnt me was how to commit more crime. Well, now they've got what they want, so they'd better look out if they take my children from me."

There is not much point in continuing the conversation, so let us now progress to the next bed, which contains a thin twenty-seven-year-old woman of West Indian extraction who has drunk half a bottle of methadone. This she got from a friend, who got it from a friend (the person for whom it was actually prescribed is like a distant ancestor, whom only a diligent genealogist could be expected to uncover). She took the methadone to help her come down from crack cocaine, which she has been taking many times a day for two years. She lives at home with her mother and nine-year-old daughter.

"And the father of your daughter?" I ask delicately, as if I were inquiring about a history of venereal disease.

"I don't see him no more."

"Does he support your daughter in any way?"

"He comes to see her sometimes."

"How often?"

"When he feels like it."

The patient had been a secretary in a law firm until a boyfriend introduced her to crack.

"You didn't have to take it," I tell her.

"It was free," she replies.

"You mean, if I handed you fifty pills now, free of charge, you'd take them?"

"I would if I saw you take them, and they gave you a good time."

The free crack did not last forever, of course, and soon she had to pay for it. And having lost her job, the only way she could do so was by accepting what both the *New England Journal of Medicine* and *The Lancet* now call "sex work."

I ask her whether she currently has a boyfriend.

"He's in prison."

"What for?"

"Burglaries. He's out in two years."

Her mother, who looks after her daughter, arrives on the ward. She is in her fifties, dressed in a blue suit and wearing an old-fashioned hat with a veil and white gloves. As a person of the utmost respectability, a householder and a churchgoer who on Sunday speaks in tongues, she is deeply distressed by the dissolution of her daughter into vice and addiction, though she is at pains to disguise just how deeply. We soon dispatch the daughter to a drug rehabilitation center.

In the last of the six beds in the ward, an eighteen-year-old girl lies looking up at the ceiling. She took her overdose, she tells me, because she hates life. But in my experience people who hate life rarely take quite so much trouble over their appearance, from which I deduce that something more specific is bothering her. She has left home and gone to live with a friend. She took the overdose after a row with her boyfriend, ten years older than she, an ex-soldier dishonorably discharged from the army for smoking marijuana. She has been his girlfriend for nine months now (the whole of her semi-adult life), and so far she has not gone to live with him. But he is very jealous of her, wants to know where she is every minute of the day, accuses her of infidelity, searches through her things whenever she meets him, cross-examines her about her activities in his absence, and searches her purse. Though he has not yet hit her, he has been threatening at times. She is frightened now to go anywhere without him, for fear of his reaction. If they go out together, he never lets her out of his sight.

"Do you know about his previous girlfriends?" I ask.

"He was living with one, but she left him when she found out he was seeing someone else."

"What is your boyfriend interested in, apart from you?" I ask.

"Nothing, really," she replies.

"And what are your interests?" I ask again.

"I don't have any," she says.

She hates her poorly paid job, which requires no skill at all—not that she has any skill to impart. She left school as soon as she could, though I would estimate that she is of above-average intelligence, and in any case she never tried very hard to learn, because it was not socially acceptable to do so. In short, I tell her, she has always taken the line of least resistance, and as it says in Shakespeare, nothing will come of nothing.

"What should I do?" she asks me.

"Your boyfriend will imprison you," I tell her. "He will take over your life completely, and if you go to live with him he will become violent. You will spend several years being ill-treated and abused; eventually you will leave him, but you will not have been a victim. On the contrary, you will have been the co-author of your misery, because I have now told you what to expect, just as your parents and your friends have told you."

"But I love him."

"You are eighteen years old. The law says you are an adult. You must make up your own mind. Here is my telephone number: ring me if you need help."

Our tour of the six beds is complete: nothing unusual or out of the ordinary today, just an average trawl of social pathology, ignorance of life, and willful chasing after misery. Tomorrow is another day, but the same tide of unhappiness will lap at our doors.

Attempted suicide—what is also known as "parasuicide" or "deliberate self-harm," in a vain effort to find the perfect scientific terminology—is the most common cause of emergency admission to the hospital in England among women and the second most common among men. There are more than 120,000 cases a year, and England boasts one of the highest rates of such behavior in the world. Its completed suicide rate, on the other hand, is rather low by international standards. I do not think this merely denotes a general comparative decline in technical competence among the English ("Made in England," after all, no longer indicates quality and reliability, but rather its reverse): it means only that many of those who attempt suicide don't intend to die.

It was not ever thus. Attempted suicide enjoyed, if that is quite the word, an explosive growth at the end of the fifties and the beginning of the sixties. Until then, to attempt suicide had remained a crime in England, and it had also remained a comparatively rare event. But something more than the liberalization of the laws was involved in the opening of the floodgates of self-poisoning, for the floodgates were opened throughout the rest of the Western world also. Within a few years, overdosing was as traditional as Christmas.

Suicide and attempted suicide have attracted the attention of sociologists, psychologists, and psychiatrists ever since the publication in 1899 of Emile Durkheim's great work *Suicide*. Today an academic discipline known as suicidology thrives. The great majority of the published work of these suicidologists is mathematical: their writings overflow with dense statistical tables correlating one factor (the unemployment rate, social class, income, even the phases of the moon) with the act of suicide or attempted suicide.

Try as one might to remember that a correlation does not mean cause and effect, the overall impact of this work is to suggest that, if only enough variables were examined, if only enough data were collected and analyzed with sufficient sophistication, the "cause" of suicide and attempted suicide would be found. The importance of what goes on in the minds of individual human beings is thus implicitly denied, in favor of vast impersonal forces that statistical regularities supposedly reveal and that supposedly determine people's behavior. Thus suicidology joins the other great intellectual movements of the twentieth century—Freudianism, Marxism, and more recently, sociobiology—in denying consciousness any importance in human conduct. On this view, thought is irrelevant to action; and, dimly apprehending the intellectual currents of their time, ordinary people actually begin to experience themselves as unable to affect their own behavior. Many patients have described to me how they took the pills because, like Luther posting his theses on the cathedral doors, they could do no other.

Nevertheless, statistical regularities do exist, and used sensitively they can provide insights into the minds of men. For example, the number of patients admitted to our ward declined precipitously during the first days of the Gulf War and during the European soccer championships. People were too absorbed for a time in affairs other than their own—albeit by the proxy of television—to contemplate suicide. The boredom of self-absorption is thus one of the promoters of attempted suicide, and being attached to a cardiac monitor for a time or having an intravenous infusion in one's arm helps to relieve it. I'm treated, therefore I am.

Patterns are also discernible in the daily flux of a busy overdose ward. There is, for example, the pre-court-appearance overdose, precisely timed to preclude the appearance of the defendant in the dock and calculated to evoke sympathy for him when he finally does appear there, insofar as he now has a psychiatric history. Anyone with a psychiatric history, of course, must be of doubtful responsibility for his own actions and therefore can expect a correspondingly reduced sentence.

And then there is the preemployment overdose. A surprising number of the unemployed who succeed at last in finding a job take an overdose on the evening before they start work: their nonattendance the following morning gets them the sack before they've even begun, and so they join the ranks of the unemployed once more.

And then again there are the young Indian women who take overdoses to avoid arranged marriages or the wrath of their fathers when they discover that, contrary to the community's code of conduct, their daughters have been courting men of their own choice, thus bringing ineradicable shame upon their families.

But patterns and statistical regularities by themselves tell us little unless we are prepared to search for their meaning, and that meaning is always to be found in the minds of men and women.

Why, then, do so many take to the pills? To swallow an overdose without seriously intending to die is a curious thing to do, after all, and is specific to modern Western, or Westernized, society. They don't do it in Senegal or Outer Mongolia.

A gesture in the direction of death, even though only a gesture, is still a powerful signal of distress. But in nine-tenths of the cases (in my experience) the distress is self-inflicted, or at least the consequence of not knowing how to live. The emotions that surround most overdoses are simultaneously intense and shallow.

In modern welfare states, the struggle for subsistence has been abolished. In Africa, where I have also worked, the poor engage in a cruelly demanding battle to obtain water, food, firewood, and shelter for the day, even in the cities. This battle gives meaning to their existence, and another day lived without hunger in, say, Kinshasa, is a personal triumph of a kind. Survival there is an achievement and grounds for celebration.

This is not so in my city, in which subsistence is more or less assured, irrespective of conduct. On the other hand, there are large numbers of people who are devoid of either ambition or interests. They thus have nothing to fear and nothing to hope, and if they work at all it is in jobs that provide little stimulus. Without religious belief to imbue their existence with transcendental meaning from without, they can provide none for themselves from within.

What, then, is left for them? Entertainment and personal relationships.

Entertainment, absorbed passively, informs them, through

television and films, of a materially more abundant and more glamorous way of life and thus feeds resentment. A sense of their own nothingness and failure breeds powerful emotions— especially jealousy and the intense desire to dominate or possess someone else in order to feel in control of at least one aspect of life. It is a world in which men dominate women to inflate their egos, and women want children "so that I can have something of my own" or "someone to love and who'll love me."

Personal relationships in this world are purely instrumental in meeting the need of the moment. They are fleeting and kaleidoscopic, though correspondingly intense. After all, no obligations or pressures—financial, legal, social, or ethical—keep people together. The only cement for personal relationships is the need and desire of the moment, and nothing is stronger but more fickle than need and desire unshackled by obligation.

Unfortunately, the whims of two people rarely coincide, and thus the emotional lives of people—who, remember, have very little else to console or interest them—are repeatedly in crisis. They are the stars of their own soap operas. An overdose—with the secure knowledge that help is at hand—is often the easiest way to relieve the continued crises in their lives. The hospital is warm and welcoming, the staff sympathetic. In the world that I describe, where else can one turn? Parents are frequently hostile, and acquaintances are in the same boat.

Most overdosers—not all, of course—live in an existential void. Theirs are voices calling from an abyss—an abyss created in large part by the idea, peddled by generations of intellectuals, that material security and human relationships unconstrained by any kind of necessity would set mankind free, beyond the dreams of past unenlightened or less fortunate ages. To be or not to be? Overdosers opt for something in between the two.

*1997*

# Reader, She Married Him—Alas

◈ WHEN MULTICULTURALISTS imagine the future, I suspect they have something in mind like the glorious multiplicity of restaurants serving all the cuisines of the world, which is now to be found in most large cities. You can eat Thai on Monday, Italian on Tuesday, Szechuan on Wednesday, Hungarian on Thursday, and so forth, without any strain whatever. Anyone who has withstood the rigors of English cooking is bound to welcome this particular development.

However, the multiculturalist vision of the good society seems to me to be about as profound and realistic as Marx's famous description of what life would be like under communism once society was no longer divided into competing classes. In communist society, wrote Marx, nobody would have one exclusive sphere of activity; instead a man might hunt in the morning, fish in the afternoon, rear cattle in the evening, and criticize after dinner, just as he had a mind to do, without ever becoming a hunter, fisherman, shepherd, or critic. Under multiculturalism, a man might turn towards Mecca in the morning, sacrifice a chicken in the afternoon, and go to Mass in the evening, without ever becoming a Muslim, an animist, or a Catholic.

As a doctor working in a slum area with many immigrant residents, I see multiculturalism from the ground up rather than from the theory down. And it is clear from what I see almost every day that not all cultural values are compatible or can be reconciled by the enunciation of platitudes. The idea that we can all rub along together, without the law having to discriminate in favor of one set of cultural values rather than another, is worse than merely false: it makes no sense whatever.

Let me say at once that I believe immigration to be a healthy phenomenon, particularly for an otherwise insular and inward-looking country such as Britain. Immigrants are generally hard-working and enterprising and enrich cultural life—provided, that is, they are not given victim status *ex officio* and their culture is not subjected to the sort of condescending patronage with which the Soviet state treated minorities.

Very large numbers of immigrants do in fact succeed in living in two cultures at once: not because anyone tells them to do so but because they want to and because they must.

Despite such successes, however, conflicts frequently emerge between individuals and groups because of different cultural standards, beliefs, and expectations. For us, these conflicts can be resolved by appeal to the deeply ingrained higher principle embodied in the law, that individuals have the right (within defined limits) to choose how to live. But this Western notion of individualism and tolerance is by no means a conception in all cultures.

I am consulted by large numbers of young women whose parents came to England from India and Pakistan and remain deeply attached to the values that prevailed in the remote villages from which they emigrated twenty or thirty years ago. It is even possible that, despite the enterprising spirit that brought them from their homeland, they are more culturally conservative than their compatriots who remained at home: for migration across half the world is very stressful and disorienting, and old customs therefore become to some immigrants what soft toys are to children in the dark—a source of great comfort.

Be that as it may, their daughters, having grown up in a different cultural environment, no longer accept the customs to which their parents so tenaciously cling and which seem to them unquestionably right and natural. Conflict usually revolves around matters of education, career, and love.

A sixteen-year-old Muslim girl was referred to me because she had started to wet the bed at night. She was accompanied by her father, an unskilled factory worker of Pakistani origin, and was beautifully dressed in satins and chiffon, her ankles and wrists covered with gold bangles and bracelets. Her father was reluctant to let me speak to her on her own but at my insistence eventually permitted me to do so.

I realized at once that she was both highly intelligent and deeply unhappy. Because of my experience in such cases, it took little time to discover the source of her unhappiness.

Her father had decided that she was to marry in a couple of months' time a man—a cousin—of whom she knew nothing. She, on the other hand, wished to continue her education, to study English literature at university and eventually to become a journalist. Although she controlled herself well—in the circumstances, heroically—there was absolutely no mistaking the passionate intensity of her wishes or of her despair. Her father, though, knew nothing of them: she had never dared tell him, because he was likely then to lock her in the house and forbid her ever to leave, except under close escort. As far as he was concerned, education, career, or choice of husbands was not for girls.

She saw her future life stretch endlessly before her, married to a man she did not love, performing thankless domestic drudgery not only for him but for her in-laws, who, according to custom, would live with them, while always dreaming of the wider world of which she had caught so brief and tantalizing a glimpse at school.

I interviewed her father, also on his own. I asked him what he thought was wrong with his daughter.

"Nothing," he replied. "She is happy, normal girl. Only she is wetting the bed."

There was nothing I could do, other than to prescribe medication. Had I tried to interfere, I could easily have precipitated an extreme reaction on his part. The girl's fears of being locked up were by no means exaggerated or absurd. I have known many instances of girls such as she who were imprisoned in their homes, sometimes for years, by their relatives; there is even a special unit of the local police dedicated to rescuing them, once information has been laid that they are being held at home against their will.

Not that fleeing the parental home is necessarily an answer for a girl in such a situation, for a number of reasons. First, her own feelings towards her parents are likely to be highly ambivalent: family bonds are extremely strong and not easily broken. The daughters love and respect their parents, whom they normally honor and obey, even though the parents inflict upon them a future that will cause nothing but the most prolonged and unutterable misery. The parents are not neglectful and incompetent, like those from the white underclass: according to their lights, they are highly solicitous for what they consider the good of their daughters.

Moreover, the "community" will condemn the girl who runs away and regard her, quite literally, as a prostitute. Since these girls are not fully integrated into the rest of British society and have hitherto led very sheltered lives, they have nowhere to go and nobody to turn to.

In the parents' scale of values, the respect of the community comes higher than the individual happiness of their offspring and indeed is a precondition of it. The need for this respect does encourage a certain standard of conduct, but it depends upon the offspring carrying out without demur the obligations laid upon them by the parents. Thus, once a marriage has been arranged, it is indissoluble—at least by the woman. I have known many young women who have been mercilessly and brutally treated by their husbands, but whose own parents recommended that they put up with the ill-treatment rather than bring public shame upon the whole family by separating from him.

A young patient of mine tried to hang herself. She had had an arranged marriage, but on the wedding night her husband had come to the doubtless mistaken conclusion that she was not a virgin and had administered a severe beating, of which the rest of his family naturally approved. Thereafter he locked her up, beat her regularly, and burned her with a cigarette lighter. She managed to run away, though her husband had said in advance that if ever he caught her doing so, or after having done so, he would kill her, to pay her back for the loss of face she would have caused him in the community. She returned to her mother, who, horrified by her behavior, said she should return to her husband at once (even if he were going to kill her), in order to preserve the good name of the family. Her other daughters would be unmarriageable if it became known in the community that this was the kind of conduct to which the family was prone. If my patient did not return to her husband, she—her mother—would commit suicide. Torn between the threatened suicide of her mother and the prospect of murder by her husband, she took to the rope.

In my quarter of the city there are private-detective agencies that specialize in locating immigrant girls who have run away from their husbands or parents. Once they are found, they are likely to be kidnapped by relatives or vigilantes—an experience which several of my patients have lived through. It is surprising how little reaction bundling someone off the street and driving away with him or her in a car causes nowadays—people do not wish to involve themselves in problems not their own. And the police are generally less than vigorous in their investigation of such cases, for fear of being criticized as racist.

I frequently meet young women whose parents, in flagrant

contravention of the law, prevented them from attending school. The parents resort to a variety of subterfuges to protect their daughters from contamination by Western ideas. Complaisant doctors from the same racial and cultural group, who share the concerns of the parents, provide certificates for bogus illnesses, either of the pupil or of the pupil's mother, which require the girl's presence at home. Another technique is for the girl to be sent to school one week in four, to keep the school inspectors at bay. They too tread warily, for fear of being accused of acting from racial prejudice.

A patient of mine was thus kept away from school after the age of eleven for fear of being contaminated by Western notions. She was sent back to India for months at a time, so that the school lost track of her. Thanks to very superior natural intelligence, however, and surreptitious reading, for which she had a passion, she was now (at the age of twenty-eight) contemplating attending university to study law. But the rest of her story is also instructive and not untypical of what I hear.

At the age of fifteen she had been taken back yet again to India, this time in the company of her parents and a sixteen-year-old boy who until then had been brought up in her house as her brother. When they arrived at the village in Gujurat from which her parents had emigrated, she was told that her "brother" was in fact her first cousin and that she was to marry him the next day. This she said she would not do, whereupon her father beat her black and blue. She still bore the scars of her beating, and her face was still slightly asymmetrical where her cheekbone had been fractured. She maintained her opposition, however, until her father threatened to divorce her mother, casting her out, at the age of forty-five, into the street, unless the daughter consented to the marriage. His threat was not idle.

Reader, she married him. But still it was not enough: the relatives wanted to ensure that the marriage was consummated. Since the happy couple had been brought up as brother and sister, consummation seemed to them rather like incest, but the

relatives would not take no for an answer and locked them together in a room for two weeks. They put a tape recorder under
the bed to ensure that justice was done. When they discovered
that still nothing had happened between them, they threatened
violence: whereupon there was a happy ending, and she became
pregnant.

She lived with her husband for twelve years after their return to England, never loving him as a husband but fearing to
leave him because of her father's reaction. The husband, who
likewise had no love for his wife, feared to leave because of his
own relatives' reaction. Eventually they did separate but maintained the fiction that they still lived together, a fiction whose
verisimilitude it took great expense of effort and ingenuity to
maintain—a true expense of spirit in a waste of shame.

One of the conceits of multiculturalism is that the intolerance against which it is supposedly the sovereign remedy is a
characteristic only of the host society. In the impoverished
imagination of the multiculturalists, all those who do not belong by birth to the predominant culture are engaged in a
united struggle against its oppressive and illegitimate hegemony.

The reality, in my experience, is somewhat different. For example, relations between immigrants from the Indian subcontinent and from Jamaica, at least in my city, are often far from
amicable, the hostility extending to the generation born in England. Indian families are often dismayed (to put it mildly) when
their daughters choose Jamaican lovers. I know of two who
have been killed by their close families to redeem family honor
in the eyes of their community. The first was hanged at home;
the second was taken back to Pakistan, where she was beaten to
death, the local police regarding this as the correct procedure
under the circumstances.

Religious tolerance is not a value universally admired. Not
only is it not emulated or practiced, but the urbane skepticism,
indeed the lack of absolute faith, that it implies is regarded by
many as anathema. Relations between the Hindu Sikhs and the

Muslim Indians, for example, are particularly fraught, and scarcely any greater disaster can befall a family—in the eyes of its respective community—than for one of its own young people to fall in love with a young person of the other religion. The telluric emotions aroused by such liaisons often result in violence. Scarcely a week goes by without a terrible or tragic case coming to my attention.

A pleasant and intelligent Sikh girl, aged eighteen, was asked by her family to accompany her aged grandmother back home in a taxi, in which she was then to return. The taxi firm was run by Sikhs, who not only acted as transporters of the public but as vigilantes and guardians of their community's honor. The driver in this case reported to the girl's brother on her arrival home that, during the return journey through a neighborhood inhabited mainly by Muslims, she had waved to a Muslim boy. The brother, fearing the worst, called her into his room and asked whether she had in fact done so. She denied it, but he did not believe her. He took out a baseball bat (practically no baseball is played in Britain, but plenty of bats are sold as weapons and lie detectors) and tried to beat what he considered the truth out of her. She later appeared in my hospital with a badly fractured skull, but maintained to the police on her recovery that she had been assaulted on her doorstep by person or persons unknown.

A young Sikh boy formed a liaison with a Muslim girl. He was an outgoing lad, a good student and fine athlete who represented his school and his city at several different sports. He used to meet his girlfriend clandestinely, in the flat of a young Muslim friend of his—or someone whom he had considered his friend. The friend, however, telephoned the girl's brothers and asked how long they were going to allow their family to be dishonored.

On his way to his evening work, the Sikh boy was attacked with machetes by the girl's three brothers. They knocked him to the ground, threatened to cut his throat next time, and hacked repeatedly at both his arms. This took place within a hundred yards of my hospital's main entrance. He had a compound fracture of his humerus, and so many of his tendons were cut that he will never recover full use of his hands and arms.

The three brothers were duly caught and tried. Unfortunately, they were granted bail, and when it was clear that the trial was certain to result in a verdict of guilty, they failed to attend the court and were sentenced in absentia to long terms of imprisonment. My patient went into hiding in a city four hundred miles away, fearing to leave his flat there and sleeping always with a knife under his pillow. He had received information from a reliable source that the three brothers were still looking for him and would kill him if they found him. Perhaps the most alarming aspect of the story is that the three brothers were not regarded as delinquents by other members of their community but as having behaved in a thoroughly honorable and decent way. That they had broken the law in pursuing their vendetta, thus risking imprisonment, only added to their honor: they were spirited boys to be proud of.

Of course my work brings me into contact with the most dramatic instances of such caste, religious, and cultural intolerance, but I could tell very many such stories, the protagonists of which also know of many similar instances unknown to me: thus I am seeing the tip of an iceberg, not—to change the metaphor—the last survivors of a rare and endangered species.

I am by no means concluding that the cultures from which these patients come are worthless, that there is nothing to be learned from them (for example, about the role of family solidarity in enabling many children who live in physically poor conditions to achieve at school), or even that there is nothing whatever to be said in favor of the scale of values they espouse. When I talk to the parents who believe in that scale of values, they often speak most eloquently and intelligently of the social devastation they see around them among the white underclass, for whom human relationships are kaleidoscopic in their changeability, and whose lives are built on the most shifting of sands. I can quite understand that what they see only reinforces their determination to live according to their own beliefs, and that they do not want their children to become like that underclass.

Nevertheless, the painful and inescapable fact remains that many aspects of the cultures which they are trying to preserve are incompatible not only with the mores of a liberal democracy but with its juridical and philosophical foundations. No amount of hand-wringing or euphemism can alter this fact. To allow certain groups to refuse to send their girls to school, on the grounds that it is not in their culture to do so, would be to grant such groups the kind of corporate rights that will inevitably result in chronic civil war, with every conceivable group claiming such rights. Individuals will have to forgo altogether the freedoms in which Western liberal democracy believes.

The idea that it is possible to base a society on no cultural or philosophical presuppositions at all, or, alternatively, that all such presuppositions may be treated equally so that no choice has to be made between them, is absurd. Immigrants enrich—have enriched—our culture, but they do so by addition rather than by subtraction or division.

*1995*

# Tough Love

--------

LAST WEEK, a seventeen-year-old girl was admitted to my ward with such acute alcohol poisoning that she could scarcely breathe by her own unaided efforts, alcohol being a respiratory depressant. When finally she woke, twelve hours later, she told me that she had been a heavy drinker since the age of twelve.

She had abjured alcohol for four months before her admission, she told me, but had just returned to the bottle because of a crisis. Her boyfriend, aged sixteen, had just been sentenced to three years' detention for a series of burglaries and assaults. He was what she called her "third long-term relationship"—the first two having lasted four and six weeks, respectively. But after four months of life with the young burglar, the prospect of separation from him was painful enough to drive her back to drink.

It happened that I also knew her mother, a chronic alcoholic with a taste for violent boyfriends, the latest of whom had been stabbed in the heart a few weeks before in a pub brawl. The surgeons in my hospital saved his life; and to celebrate his recovery and discharge, he had gone straight to the pub. From there he went home, drunk, and beat up my patient's mother.

My patient was intelligent but badly educated, as only products of the British educational system can be after eleven years of compulsory school attendance. She thought the Second

36

World War took place in the 1970s and could give me not a single correct historical date.

I asked her whether she thought a young and violent burglar would have proved much of a companion. She admitted that he wouldn't, but said that he was the type she liked; besides which—in slight contradiction—all boys were the same.

I warned her as graphically as I could that she was already well down the slippery slope leading to poverty and misery— that, as I knew from the experience of untold patients, she would soon have a succession of possessive, exploitative, and violent boyfriends unless she changed her life. I told her that in the past few days I had seen two women patients who had had their heads rammed down the lavatory, one who had had her head smashed through a window and her throat cut on the shards of glass, one who had had her arm, jaw, and skull broken, and one who had been suspended by her ankles from a tenth-floor window to the tune of, "Die, you bitch!"

"I can look after myself," said my seventeen-year-old.

"But men are stronger than women," I said. "When it comes to violence, they are at an advantage."

"That's a sexist thing to say," she replied.

A girl who had absorbed nothing at school had nevertheless absorbed the shibboleths of political correctness in general and of feminism in particular.

"But it's a plain, straightforward, and inescapable fact," I said.

"It's sexist," she reiterated firmly.

A stubborn refusal to face inconvenient facts, no matter how obvious, now pervades our attitude towards relations between the sexes. An ideological filter of wishful thinking strains out anything we'd prefer not to acknowledge about these eternally difficult and contested relations, with predictably disastrous results.

I meet with this refusal everywhere, even among the nursing staff of my ward. Intelligent and capable, as decent and dedicated a group of people as I know, they seem, in the matter of judging the character of men, utterly, almost willfully, incompetent.

In my toxicology ward, for example, 98 percent of the thirteen hundred patients we see each year have attempted suicide by overdose. Just over half of them are men, at least 70 percent of whom have recently perpetrated domestic violence. After stabbing, strangling, or merely striking those who now appear in medical records as their partners, they take an overdose for at least one of three reasons, and sometimes for all three: to avoid a court appearance; to apply emotional blackmail to their victims; and to present their own violence as a medical condition that it is the doctor's duty to cure. As for our women patients who've attempted suicide, some 70 percent have suffered domestic violence.

In the circumstances, it isn't altogether surprising that I can now tell at a glance—with a fair degree of accuracy—that a man is violent towards his significant other. (It doesn't follow, of course, that I can tell when a man isn't violent towards her.) In truth, the clues are not particularly subtle. A closely shaven head with many scars on the scalp from collisions with broken bottles or glasses; a broken nose; blue tattoos on the hands, arms, and neck, relaying messages of love, hate, and challenge; but above all, a facial expression of concentrated malignity, outraged egotism, and feral suspiciousness—all these give the game away. Indeed, I no longer analyze the clues and deduce a conclusion: a man's propensity to violence is as immediately legible in his face and bearing as any other strongly marked character trait.

All the more surprising is it to me, therefore, that the nurses perceive things differently. They do not see a man's violence in his face, his gestures, his deportment, and his bodily adornments, even though they have the same experience of the patients as I. They hear the same stories, they see the same signs, but they do not make the same judgments. What's more, they seem never to learn; for experience—like chance, in the famous dictum of Louis Pasteur—favors only the mind prepared. And when I guess at a glance that a man is an inveterate wife beater (I use the term "wife" loosely), they are appalled at the harshness of my judgment, even when it proves right once more.

This is not a matter of merely theoretical interest to the nurses, for many of them in their private lives have themselves been the compliant victims of violent men. For example, the lover of one of the senior nurses, an attractive and lively young woman, recently held her at gunpoint and threatened her with death, after having repeatedly blacked her eye during the previous months. I met him once when he came looking for her in the hospital: he was just the kind of ferocious young egotist to whom I would give a wide berth in the broadest daylight.

Why are the nurses so reluctant to come to the most inescapable of conclusions? Their training tells them, quite rightly, that it is their duty to care for everyone without regard for personal merit or deserts; but for them, there is no difference between suspending judgment for certain restricted purposes and making no judgment at all in any circumstances whatsoever. It is as if they were more afraid of passing an adverse verdict on someone than of getting a punch in the face—a likely enough consequence, incidentally, of their failure of discernment. Since it is scarcely possible to recognize a wife beater without inwardly condemning him, it is safer not to recognize him as one in the first place.

This failure of recognition is almost universal among my violently abused women patients, but its function for them is somewhat different from what it is for the nurses. The nurses need to retain a certain positive regard for their patients in order to do their job. But for the abused women, the failure to perceive in advance the violence of their chosen men serves to absolve them of all responsibility for whatever happens thereafter, allowing them to think of themselves as victims alone rather than the victims and accomplices they are. Moreover, it licenses them to obey their impulses and whims, allowing them to suppose that sexual attractiveness is the measure of all things and that prudence in the selection of a male companion is neither possible nor desirable.

Often their imprudence would be laughable were it not tragic: many times in my ward I've watched liaisons form between an abused female patient and an abusing male patient within half an hour of their striking up an acquaintance. By now I can often predict the formation of such a liaison—and predict that it will as certainly end in violence as that the sun will rise tomorrow.

At first, of course, my female patients deny that the violence of their men was foreseeable. But when I ask them whether they think I would have recognized it in advance, the great majority—nine out of ten—reply, yes, of course. And when asked how they think I would have done so, they enumerate precisely the factors that would have led me to that conclusion. So their blindness is willful.

Today's disastrous insouciance about so serious a matter as the relationship between the sexes is surely something new in history: even thirty years ago, people showed vastly more circumspection in the formation of liaisons than they do now. The change represents, of course, the fulfillment of the sexual revolution. The prophets of that revolution wished to empty the relationship between the sexes of all moral significance and to destroy the customs and institutions that governed it. The entomologist Alfred Kinsey reacted against his own repressed and puritanical upbringing by concluding that all forms of sexual restraint were unjustified and psychologically harmful; the novelist Norman Mailer, having taken racial stereotypes as seriously as any Ku Klux Klansman, saw in the supposedly uninhibited sexuality of the Negro the hope of the world for a more abundant and richer life; the Cambridge social anthropologist Edmund Leach informed the thinking British public over the radio that the nuclear family was responsible for all human discontents (this, in the century of Hitler and Stalin!); and the psychiatrist R. D. Laing blamed the family structure for serious mental illness. In their different ways, Norman O. Brown, Paul Goodman, Herbert Marcuse, and Wilhelm Reich joined in the campaign to convince the Western world that untrammeled sexuality was the secret of happiness and that sexual repression, along with the bourgeois family life that had once contained and channeled sexuality, were nothing more than engines of pathology.

All these enthusiasts believed that if sexual relations could be liberated from artificial social inhibitions and legal restrictions, something beautiful would emerge: a life in which no desire need be frustrated, a life in which human pettiness would melt away like snow in spring. Conflict and inequality between the sexes would likewise disappear, because everyone would get what he or she wanted, when and where he or she wanted it. The grounds for such petty bourgeois emotions as jealousy and envy would vanish: in a world of perfect fulfillment, each person would be as happy as the next.

The program of the sexual revolutionaries has more or less been carried out, especially in the lower reaches of society, but the results have been vastly different from those so foolishly anticipated. The revolution foundered on the rock of unacknowledged reality: that women are more vulnerable to abuse than men by virtue of their biology alone, and that the desire for the exclusive sexual possession of another has remained just as strong as ever. This desire is incompatible, of course, with the equally powerful desire—eternal in the human breast but hitherto controlled by social and legal inhibitions—for complete sexual freedom. Because of these biological and psychological realities, the harvest of the sexual revolution has not been a brave new world of human happiness but rather an enormous increase in violence between the sexes, for readily understandable reasons.

Of course, even before any explanation, the reality of this

increase meets angry denial from those with a vested ideological interest in concealing the results of changes they helped bring about and heartily welcome. They will use the kind of obfuscation that liberal criminologists so long employed to convince us that it was the fear of crime, rather than crime itself, that had increased. They will say (quite rightly) that violence between men and women has existed always and everywhere but that our attitude towards it has changed (perhaps also correct), so that it is more frequently reported than formerly.

Still, the fact remains that a hospital such as mine has experienced in the last two decades a huge increase in the number of injuries to women, most of them the result of domestic violence and many of them of the kind that would always have come to medical attention. The increase is real, therefore, not an artifact of reporting. About one in five of the women aged sixteen to fifty living in my hospital's area attends the emergency department during the year as a result of injuries sustained during a quarrel with a boyfriend or husband; and there is no reason to suppose that my hospital's experience is any different from that of another local hospital, which, together with mine, provides medical attention for half the city's population. In the last five years I have treated at least two thousand men who have been violent to their wives, girlfriends, lovers, and concubines. It seems to me that violence on such a vast scale could not easily have been overlooked in the past—including by me.

And there is very good reason why such violence should have increased under the new sexual dispensation. If people demand sexual liberty for themselves, but sexual fidelity from others, the result is the inflammation of jealousy, for it is natural to suppose that one is being done by as one is doing to others— and jealousy is the most frequent precipitant of violence between the sexes.

Jealousy has always been a feature of the relations between men and women: *Othello*, written four centuries ago, is still instantly comprehensible to us. But I meet at least five Othellos and five Desdemonas a week, and this is something new, if the psychiatric textbooks printed a few years ago were right in claiming that jealousy of the obsessive sort was a rare condition. Far from being rare, it is nowadays almost the norm, especially among underclass men, whose fragile sense of self-worth derives solely from possession of a woman and is poised permanently on the brink of humiliation at the prospect of losing this one prop in life.

The belief in the inevitability of male jealousy is one of the main reasons my violently abused women patients do not leave the men who abuse them. These women have experienced three or four such men in succession, and it hardly makes sense to exchange one for another. Better the abuse you know than the abuse you don't. When I ask whether they'd be better off without any man at all than with a male tormentor, they reply that a single woman in their neighborhood is seen as an easy prey to all men, and, without her designated, if violent, protector, she would suffer more violence, not less.

The jealousy of the men—and the passion is commoner in men, though women are catching up and becoming violent in turn—is a projection onto women of their own behavior. The great majority of the jealous men I meet are flagrantly unfaithful to the object of their supposed affections, and some keep other women in the same jealous subjection elsewhere in the city and even a hundred miles away. They have no compunction about cuckolding other men and actually delight in doing so as a means of boosting their own fragile egos. As a result, they imagine that all other men are their rivals: for rivalry is a reciprocal relationship.

Thus a mere glance in a pub directed at a man's girlfriend is sufficient to start a fight not only between the girl and her lover but, even before that, between the two men. Serious crimes of violence continue to rise in England, many of them occasioned by sexual jealousy. *Cherchez la femme* has never been a sounder guide to explaining attempted murder than it is today; and the extremely fluid nature of relations between the sexes is what makes it so sound a precept.

The violence of the jealous man is not always occasioned by his lover's supposed interest in another man, however. On the contrary, it serves a prophylactic function and helps to keep the woman utterly in thrall to him until the day she decides to leave him: for the whole focus of her life is the avoidance of his rage. Avoidance is impossible, however, since it is the very arbitrariness of his violence that keeps her in thrall to him. Thus when I hear from a female patient that the man with whom she lives has beaten her severely for a trivial reason—for having served roast potatoes when he wanted boiled, for example, or for having failed to dust the top of the television—I know at once that the man is obsessively jealous: for the jealous man wishes to occupy his lover's every thought, and there is no more effective method of achieving this than his arbitrary terrorism. From his point of view, the more arbitrary and completely disproportionate the violence, the more functional it is; and indeed, he often lays down conditions impossible for the woman to meet—that a freshly cooked meal should be waiting for him the moment he arrives home, for instance, though he will not say even to within the nearest four hours when he is arriving home—precisely so that he may have an occasion to beat her. Indeed, so effective is this method that the mental life of many of the violently abused women who consult me has focused for years upon their lovers—their whereabouts, their wishes, their comforts, their moods—to the exclusion of all else.

When finally she leaves him, as she almost always does, he regards it as an act of the utmost perfidy and concludes that he must treat his next female companion with even greater severity to avoid a repetition. Observing the fluidity of the sexual relationships around him and reflecting upon his own recent experience, he falls prey to a permanent sexual paranoia.

Worse still, the social trend to these kinds of relationships is self-reinforcing: for the children they produce grow up supposing that all relationships between men and women are but temporary and subject to revision. From the very earliest age, therefore, the children live in an atmosphere of tension between the natural desire for stability and the emotional chaos they see all around them. They are able to make no assumption that the man in their lives—the man they call "Daddy" today—will be there tomorrow. (As one of my patients put it when talking of her decision to leave her latest boyfriend, "He was my children's father until last week." Needless to say, he was none of the children's biological father, all of the latter having departed long before.)

A son learns that women are always on the point of leaving men; a daughter, that men are not to be relied upon and are inevitably violent. The daughter is mother to the woman: and since she has learned that all relationships with men are both violent and temporary, she concludes that there is not much point in taking thought for the morrow as far as choosing men is concerned. Not only is there little difference between them except in the accidental quality of their physical attractiveness to her, but mistakes can be rectified by the simple expedient of abandoning the man, or men, in question. Thus sexual relationships can be entered into with no more thought than that devoted to choosing breakfast cereal—precisely the ideal of Kinsey, Mailer, *et al.*

But why does the woman not leave the man as soon as he manifests his violence? It is because, perversely, violence is the only token she has of his commitment to her. Just as he wants the exclusive sexual possession of her, she wants a permanent relationship with him. She imagines—falsely—that a punch in the face or a hand round the throat is at least a sign of his continued interest in her, the only sign other than sexual intercourse she is ever likely to receive in that regard. In the absence of a marriage ceremony, a black eye is his promissory note to love, honor, cherish, and protect.

It is not his violence as such that causes her to leave him, but the eventual realization that his violence is not, in fact, a sign of his commitment to her. She discovers that he is unfaithful to her, or that his income is greater than she suspected and is spent outside the home, and it is only then that his violence seems intolerable. So convinced is she that violence is an intrinsic and indispensable part of relations between the sexes, however, that if by some chance she alights next time upon a nonviolent man, she suffers acute discomfort and disorientation; she may, indeed, even leave him because of his insufficient concern for her. Many of my violently abused women patients have told me that they find nonviolent men intolerably indifferent and emotionally distant, rage being the only emotion they've ever seen a man express. They leave them quicker than they leave men who have beaten and otherwise abused them.

The sexual revolutionaries wanted to liberate sexual relations from all but the merest biological content. Henceforth such relations were not to be subject to restrictive bourgeois contractual arrangements—or, heaven forbid, sacraments—such as marriage; no social stigma was to attach to any sexual conduct that had hitherto been regarded as reprehensible. The only criterion governing the acceptability of sexual relations was the mutual consent of those entering upon them: no thought of duty to others (one's own children, for example) was to get in the way of the fulfillment of desire. Sexual frustration that resulted from artificial social obligations and restrictions was the enemy, and hypocrisy—the inevitable consequence of holding people to any standard of conduct whatsoever—was the worst sin.

That the heart wants contradictory, incompatible things; that social conventions arose to resolve some of the conflicts of our own impulses; that eternal frustration is an inescapable concomitant of civilization, as Freud had observed—all these recalcitrant truths fell beneath the notice of the proponents of sexual liberation, dooming their revolution to ultimate failure.

The failure hit the underclass hardest. Not for a moment did the sexual liberators stop to consider the effects upon the poor of the destruction of the strong family ties that alone made emergence from poverty possible for large numbers of people. They were concerned only with the petty dramas of their own lives and dissatisfactions. But by obstinately overlooking the most obvious features of reality, as did my seventeen-year-old patient who thought that men's superior physical strength was a socially constructed sexist myth, their efforts contributed in no small part to the intractability of poverty in modern cities, despite vast increases in the general wealth: for the sexual revolution has turned the poor from a class into a caste, from which escape is barred so long as that revolution continues.

*1999*

# It Hurts,
# Therefore I Am

THE CAUSE OF CRIMINALITY among the white population of England is perfectly obvious to any reasonably observant person, though criminologists have yet to notice it. This cause is the tattooing of the skin.

A slow-acting virus, like that of scrapie in sheep, is introduced into the human body via the tattooing needle and makes its way to the brain, where within a few years it causes the afflicted to steal cars, burgle houses, and assault people.

I first formulated my viral theory of criminality when I noticed that at least nine of ten white English prisoners are tattooed, more than three or four times the proportion in the general population. The statistical association of crime with tattooing is stronger, I feel certain, than between crime and any other single factor, with the possible exception of smoking. Virtually all English criminals are smokers, a fact that sociologists have also unaccountably overlooked.

There are two main schools of tattooing: the do-it-yourself and the professional. They are by no means mutually exclusive; on the contrary, their relationship is rather like that between alternative (or fringe) and orthodox medicine. Devotees of the one often are simultaneously devotees of the other.

The differences between the two schools are very marked.

Home tattooing is monochrome-india-ink colored, while professional tattooing is polychrome. The designs of the first are simple, though no less striking for that. The designs of the latter are elaborate and often executed with exquisite skill, though I am reminded of an old medical dictum that if a thing is not worth doing—a radical mastectomy, for instance—it is not worth doing well. Finally, home tattooing is low-tech; professional tattooing is high-tech.

All over England, lower-class youths aged between fourteen and eighteen indulge in a strange and savage *rite de passage,* in numbers that far exceed those who perform this rite elsewhere in the world. They take an ordinary sewing needle, wrap it in cotton gauze, and dip it into india ink. Then they stab it into their own skins, thus introducing a spot of ink into the dermis. They repeat this until the desired pattern or words form indelibly in their integument.

Like surgical operations before the discovery of anesthetics, this kind of tattooing is often done while the subject is drunk, in front of a crowd of onlookers who encourage him to withstand the pain of the process. In any case, this pain is inclined to diminish to mere numbness after a few stabs of the needle, or so I am told by my auto-tattooed patients. The redness of inflammation subsides within a few days.

What messages do these young men wish to communicate to the world? Generally, they are quite short and to the point: and they all too pithily express the violent nihilism of their lives. The most common consists of two words, with one letter on each of four knuckles: LOVE and HATE. Another fairly common tattoo consists of a dot on four knuckles of one hand, with or without the letters A C A B. These letters stand for ALL COPPERS ARE BASTARDS.

The anti-police theme is one that I have seen represented in a more explicit way, in the form of a gallows from which was suspended a dangling policeman. In case the meaning of this was insufficiently clear to onlookers, the words HANG ALL COP-

PERS were appended beneath. Alas, this frank and manly expression of sentiment did not always stand the bearer in good stead, inasmuch as he was frequently in the custody of the constabulary, and the tattoo, being on his forearm, was not easily hidden from their eyes. I shall return later to the several disadvantages of being tattooed.

A surprisingly large number of auto-tattooists choose for the exercise of their dermatographical art the chief motto of British service industries, namely FUCK OFF. Why anyone should want these words indelibly imprinted in his skin is a mystery whose meaning I have not yet penetrated, though my researches continue, but I recall a patient who had the two words tattooed in mirror writing upon his forehead, no doubt that he might read them in the bathroom mirror every morning and be reminded of the vanity of earthly concerns.

It isn't only in the service industries that Britain limps behind, of course. The former workshop of the world has come to manufacture so little that nowadays one rarely sees the words MADE IN ENGLAND anywhere—except, that is, tattooed around the nipple or umbilicus of some of the less cerebral alumni of our least distinguished schools.

Naturally, this kind of tattoo can also serve romantic ends. Men, it is well known, are frequently prepared to endure agonies for love, and so it is not altogether surprising that the name of a girlfriend is recorded not on pen and paper but in ink and dermis. Unfortunately, romantic affections tend to be rather fluid in the age of auto-tattooing, and it is not unusual to see an entire romantic history inscribed, list-wise, upon an arm, sometimes with a name crossed through when the parting of the ways has been particularly bitter.

One youth I met had tattooed his romantic aspirations, rather than his romantic history, upon himself. The fingers of one hand bore the crude letters L T F C; those of the other, E S U K. When he folded his hands together—in an emblem of the message he wished to convey, that one alone is incomplete, but two together make a whole—the letters spelled out LETS FUCK. Did this ever work? I asked with some skepticism. "Well, yes," he replied with great complaisance. "Sometimes."

Often a tattoo acts as a membership badge. For example, a little blue spot on one cheekbone indicates that the bearer has been to Borstal, a correctional institution for wayward youth named after a village in Kent, the garden of England, site of the first such institution. The blue badge of rebellion is worn in the manner of the old school tie, that Old Borstalians may recognize one another—and be recognized. For in the circles in which they move, the meaning of the blue spot is well known and understood: *Noli me tangere.*

But like those peculiar moths and butterflies about which naturalists delight to tell us, which imitate the colorful plumage of poisonous species without being poisonous themselves, that potential predators on lepidoptera might leave them alone, so do certain young people tattoo themselves with the blue spot without ever having been to Borstal. They wear the spot both as protection and as a means of gaining the admiration of their peers; but, to change the metaphor slightly, the coinage is soon debased, and what was once a sign of considerable value is now almost emptied of it.

And thus the study of a seemingly minor social phenomenon such as tattooing affords us a little glimpse into the Hobbesian moral world inhabited by a section of the population with whom we normally have little contact: they actually want to be considered psychopathic. Not their eyes but their tattoos are the windows of their souls.

Another popular pattern—though it makes one shudder to think of the process by which it is inscribed upon the skin, or the consequences if a mistake is made—is the spider's web on the side of the neck. Occasionally this is spread over the whole of the face, even over the scalp. At first I assumed this design must have a symbolic meaning, but having inquired of many bearers of it, and having been assured by them that there is no such meaning, I am now satisfied that it is its intrinsic beauty, and a certain vaguely sinister connotation attached to spiders' webs, that attracts people to the design and induces them to adorn themselves with it. Moreover, I vividly recall the scene at a murder trial in which I testified. The judge and counsel were embroiled in a learned discussion of the finer points of *mens rea*, watched by the prisoner in the dock and his family in the public gallery—all of whom, down to the $n$th generation, had spiders' webs prominently tattooed on their necks. Never was the class basis (as the Marxists used to call it) of British justice more clearly visible: two classes separated by, among other things, a propensity on the part of one of them to self-disfigurement.

A considerable number of the auto-tattooed inject themselves with swastikas. At first I thought this was profoundly nasty, a reflection of their political beliefs, but in my alarm I had not taken into consideration the fathomless historical ignorance of those who do such things to themselves. People who believe (as one of my recent patients did) that the Second World War started in 1918 and ended in 1960—a better approximation to the true dates than some I have heard—are unlikely to know what exactly the Nazis and their emblem stood for, beyond the everyday brutality with which they are familiar, and which they admire and aspire to.

About one in twenty of English auto-tattooists adorn themselves with dotted lines around their neck or their wrists, with the instruction to onlookers to CUT HERE, as if they were coupons in a newspaper or magazine—an instruction that many of their acquaintances are perfectly equipped to obey, inasmuch as they routinely carry sharp knives with them.

Such tattoos can have serious consequences. Not long ago a prisoner with the words NO FEAR tattooed prominently on the side of his neck came before me with a medical complaint, and I inquired into his medical history. He wore his hair shaved, and his scalp reminded me of that of the old, one-eyed, half-eared tomcat in the garden next door to me at home, whose scalp is a mass of scars.

"Have you ever had any serious injuries?" I asked.

"No," he replied.

"And have you ever been in the hospital for anything?" I continued.

"Yes, four times." "What for?"

"Broken skull."

I should explain in parentheses that the tattooed classes of England do not consider fractures of the skull to be serious injuries, even when they result in operations, steel plates inserted into the remainder of the skull, and prolonged sojourns in the hospital. It is difficult for them to conceive of everyday occurrences as being serious: for example, one patient had his skull staved in with a baseball bat but said of the incident that "it was just a usual neighborly row," and therefore nothing for the police or doctors to get too worried about.

"And how did you come by these fractures of your skull?" I asked my patient.

It was his tattoo that was responsible. Everyone assumed that NO FEAR meant precisely that, so that whenever he walked into a pub he would be challenged to a fight by those who felt entitled to be feared, and who regarded a lack of fear as a personal insult. Moreover, he had often been glassed (the verb to glass meaning to smash a glass into someone's face or over his head, usually in a pub) because of his tattoo.

When asked why they inflict these marks of Cain upon themselves, the tattooed cite pressure from their peers and boredom. Perhaps the pain of it reassures them they are alive: it hurts, therefore I am.

"I was bored," said one man whose hands were covered in scores of such tattoos, and who claimed that they had kept him unemployed for many years. "It was either tattooing myself, or going out robbing." No other possibility presented itself to his ill-furnished mind; but in any case, the distraction caused by the tattooing soon wore off, and he went out robbing just the same.

Just as many who start with marijuana go on to crack, so do most who tattoo themselves go on to be tattooed by professionals. It is illegal in Britain to tattoo anyone under the age of eighteen (though of course if the government were really serious about restricting the numbers of the tattooed, it would make tattooing compulsory). The parlors of those whom I suppose I must call the ethical tattooists—who refuse to tattoo their clients' penises, for example—are inspected regularly by the Health Department for cleanliness and sterile technique. The tattooists display their licenses upon the wall, as well as their membership in various organizations of tattoo artists, as doctors in America do.

The tattoo and body-piercing parlors—and I have now visited several—are all very much the same in both layout and atmosphere. In the reception area are posters illustrating the patterns from which most of the clients choose, bespoke tattooing being considerably more expensive. The patterns seem inspired mainly by sub-Wagnerian Norse mythology, the female figures deriving in equal measure from Brünnhilde and Ursula Andress, the male from Siegfried and Arnold Schwarzenegger. Snakes winding their way round skulls, saber-toothed tigers, and bulldogs baring their fangs are also popular.

The owners are themselves heavily tattooed, though some of them, in the privacy of our conversation, admitted that they would not tattoo themselves, at any rate so extensively, if they had their time again. But business is business, and the demand is more than sufficient to keep them in work. I estimate that in our city of one million inhabitants, about three thousand are tattooed by professionals each year: a high proportion of what epidemiologists call "the population at risk," that is to say, young men between the ages of eighteen and thirty.

Indeed, the popularity of tattooing in some quarters seems

to be growing rather than declining. It is a curious characteristic of our age that cultural influences now seem to flow from the lower social classes upward, rather than from the upper classes downward, so that middle-class people are having themselves tattooed in greater numbers than ever before. And what used to be an all-male preserve is no longer so: along with banking and gentlemen's clubs, another bastion of patriarchy has fallen.

And just as Britain is the most culturally degraded country in Europe, so does its cultural influence grow. Tattooing used to be uncommon in France, for example, and discreet at that; but (or so several tattoo artists have told me) it is becoming ever more popular there. And one of the parlors has opened a branch in Spain, mainly—but, alas, not entirely—for the drunken British oaf market.

It doesn't take long or cost much to have a small tattoo done, though an hour or two of the process is the most people can stand at any one session. You can stigmatize yourself thoroughly in an hour for a mere fifty dollars. But those who want to cover their entire integuments (85 percent coverage of the body surface being by no means rare) may spend years of their life in the tattooing parlor. Watching as yet untattooed young men browsing through the patterns in the parlor reception areas, I felt like a Victorian evangelist or campaigner against prostitution, an impulse rising within me to exhort them to abjure evil; but their adoption of the characteristic expression of the urban underclass (a combination of bovine vacancy and lupine malignity) soon put paid to my humanitarian impulse.

But few are the tattooed who do not eventually come to regret their youthful folly, for both aesthetic and practical reasons. A patient of mine described how his tattoos had always prevented him from getting a job: at interviews he was able to cover up the dotted lines around his neck with a high collar, as the ruff in the sixteenth and seventeenth centuries covered up the scrofula, but those around his wrist always let him down.

Well, perhaps he wasn't all that keen on work anyway; but

the last straw—the precipitant of his despair—came when he was refused entry to a nightclub because of his tattoos. On seeing them, the bouncer at the door stepped in front of him and kept him out: even in a world where distinctions are few and crude, his tattoos put him beyond the pale.

The follies of the foolish are the opportunities of the wise, of course. I learned from the Yellow Pages that for every five professional tattoo parlors, there are three clinics for the removal of tattoos by laser treatment (thus is our gross domestic product increased). The most sophisticated of these clinics has several lasers to deal with different colors, which are susceptible to different wavelengths. The lasers shatter the particles of pigment, and the body's own macrophages can then remove the tiny fragments. Many tattoo parlors offer a removal service as well, but the method they most commonly use, the injection of a dissolving acid into the tattoo, has scarring effects on the skin tissue, so the results are not good.

The principal drawbacks of laser treatment are its cost and duration. A single session lasting ten minutes costs $160. The skin will not tolerate more prolonged treatment, and between each session a period of six or eight weeks should elapse. An average tattoo on the biceps muscle, three inches by three, requires between five and eight such sessions for full removal. Since many people have a much larger area than this adorned with tattoos, they must invest many thousands in their removal. And in general such people are drawn from the poorer segments of society.

Nevertheless, demand for treatment outstrips supply, and one company that already operates four clinics throughout the country is opening two more. The treatment is not generally available under the National Health Service (Britain's system of socialized medicine), except for those patients in whom their tattoos cause serious psychological or psychiatric disturbance. Despair over tattoos can lead to suicide attempts, even to efforts to carve them out of the skin with kitchen knives. A patient who had tried to cut hers out with a razor blade told me that for years she could think of nothing else. Her obsession with her tattoos (incidentally, they had been done under duress by other inmates in an all-female orphanage) sapped her will to live, and only after they had been removed was she able to start a normal life.

That the Health Service makes exception in these cases (subcontracting the actual work to private clinics) is not generally known, and is certainly not advertised, for fear of provoking a wave of money-saving psychological disturbance among the tattooed. It is a regrettable fact that psychological distress expands to meet the supply of publicly funded services available to reduce it.

It occurred to me, however, albeit in a moment of uncharacteristic weakness, that the prison in which I work should offer a tattoo-removal service for its involuntary guests. After all, even recidivists would be better placed to find honest employment without their marks of Cain.

But then I remembered that every policy has its unintentional consequences. If tattoos were removed free of charge in prison, then people with tattoos might commit crimes specifically to avail themselves of this opportunity. And then the association of tattooing with criminality would be even stronger than it already is.

*1995*

# Festivity, and Menace

◈ THE ENGLISH, it was observed by an aristocratic French-man as long ago as the eighteenth century, take their pleasures sadly. Nowadays they also take them passively, like a drug addict who seeks happiness and oblivion simultaneously by the simplest means possible.

I do not mean that the English make no effort to seek out entertainment; on the contrary, like the addict's search for his drug, this pursuit is often the only serious business of their lives. But the entertainment, once found, should require—for it to be truly entertaining—as little active mental contribution from the entertained as possible.

*Primum inter pares* is, of course, television. The average English adult now watches twenty-seven hours of it per week, it is said, twice as much as two decades ago. In this the English are no different from many other nations; indeed, the Americans while away about the same proportion of their lives in front of the small screen as the island race.

In any case, the figure could be misleading; experience from doing medical house calls convinces me that a television switched on is not necessarily a television watched. It flickers in the background, competing for fragments of divided attention with a radio and perhaps a domestic quarrel or two. And even when it is watched, there is no guarantee that anything gets much farther than the optic nerves: I have many times asked patients whom I have visited at home while they were sitting in front of a television to describe what they were watching, only to be met with the blank silence of inability or incomprehension. One might as well have asked an habitué of an opium den for the contents of his consciousness as ask modern viewers of television for theirs.

When I was young and inexperienced, I used to ask the patient or his relatives to turn the television off; but in England that means (at best) only a slight reduction in its volume. It is disconcerting to conduct a medical examination with a moving picture casting a changing light over the room, and the patient trying to peer over one's shoulder, or round one's side, to catch a glimpse of it, while confusing one's questions with the dialogue of a soap opera. Once I went to a paralyzed old lady's house and found the television on. I asked the daughter, who was present, to turn it off.

"I don't know how," she said. And she didn't.

Nowadays I march into a house and turn the television off myself. It is the only way to get the patient's full attention— even if he or she is seriously ill and likely to die without medical treatment.

In the hospital it is now regarded as cruel to deprive the patients of their daily screen: so much so that watching it has become virtually compulsory for them, or at least inescapable for those not in a position to remove themselves. Gone are the days when the hospital was a place of quiet (insofar as possible) and repose: no one dies nowadays without benefit of chat-show.

I have many times tried the following simple experiment: in a ward full of incapacitated patients, I have turned off the television or televisions and then left the ward for five minutes. Unfailingly, the television or televisions are switched on again by the time I return; but who has turned them on again, I have never been able to discover. The patients could not have done so, and the nurses deny it; it is a mystery as complete as that of the Turin shroud. But the nurses always say, "The patients want it on," and will continue to say it even though a straw poll usually reveals precisely the opposite.

It seems to me prima facie unlikely that an eighty-year-old lady with a right-sided hemiplegia after a stroke, and with difficulty swallowing her own saliva, really wants to watch Mr. Motivator, a keep-fit fanatic in a body-hugging Lycra outfit of fluorescent colors, demonstrating to the insistent beat of disco music the exercises by means of which the viewer may rid herself of the cellulite on her thighs. There is someone in the ward, however (a postmodernist, perhaps), who believes otherwise, who believes that a moment unentertained is a moment wasted, and that a mind unfilled by someone else's drivel is a vacuum of the kind Nature abhors.

But it is on Saturday night, provincial downtown, that the unquenchable English thirst for entertainment—at least among the young—is seen to best advantage. To reach Saturday night is the summit of ambition of much of English youth. Nothing fills their minds with such anticipation or eagerness. No career, no pastime, no interest, can compete with the joys of Saturday night, when the center of the city turns into a B-movie Sodom and Gomorrah, undestroyed by God only because (it must be admitted) there are worse places on earth, which call for more immediate elimination.

On Saturday night the center of the city has a quite distinct atmosphere. It is crowded, but gone are the shoppers, browsing at shop windows like sheep on grass; almost no one over thirty is to be seen on the streets. It is as if a devastating epidemic had swept over the country and left alive no one who has reached middle age.

There is festivity in the air, but also menace. The smell of cheap perfume mingles with that of take-out food (fried and greasy), stale alcohol, and vomit. The young men—especially those with shaved heads and ironmongery in their noses and eyebrows—squint angrily at the world, as if they expect to be attacked at any moment from any direction, or as if they have been deprived of something to which they were entitled. It is, indeed, dangerous to look them in the eye for longer than a fraction of a second: any more prolonged eye contact would be construed as a challenge, inviting armed response.

Even some of the young women seem aggressive. Two of them pass me in the street, eloquently discussing their rivalry for the affections of Darren.

"You fancy him," snarled the first.

"No I fucking don't," snarled back the second.

"You fucking do."

"Oh fuck off."

I recall a recent patient of mine, her eyesight permanently damaged by a group of girls in a club who glassed her (that is to say, broke some glasses and pushed the jagged edges into her face and neck) because she looked for too long and with too intense an interest at the boyfriend of one of her assailants.

Outside the Ritzy club, as I walk past, there is a pool of as yet uncongealed blood, next to which lies a broken bottle of beer. The weapon is self-evident, if not the motive. Some unfortunate person has not even got as far as being glassed: he has been bottled.

The people in the line to get into the Ritzy are untroubled by the blood, however; it will not spoil their evening. The flashing pink neon bulb casts an intermittently lurid light on them as the bouncers frisk them two by two, checking them for the knives that, in other circumstances, at least half of them carry.

All the cars that go by relay the insistent beat of quadraphonic music via the stones of the sidewalk into the legs of people walking or standing there. My own legs tingle with the vibrations. Sometimes I wonder whether those who play their music so loudly do so with the idea that they are performing a public service.

I walk on. A group of young men stagger out of the Newt and Cucumber, drunkenly chanting—one couldn't call it singing—an obscene song. This is the sound that terrifies the cheap coastal resorts of Europe and any Continental city unfortunate enough to play host to an English football team.

I enter the Newt and Cucumber. Everyone is shouting, but still no one can make himself heard (which perhaps is just as well). Twenty televisions blare: eight each playing two different songs (one rock and one reggae), and four relaying a wrestling match. Ten seconds of this and one feels one has a food mixer inside one's skull working at full speed on one's brain: I too stagger out. The base of a lamppost nearby has been fertilized with vomitus during my brief visit to the pub.

I walk on, marveling at the wonderful vulgarity of English girls. Is this a country, I wonder, without mirrors? Or is it merely eyes that young English females lack? They have evidently chosen their clothes with great care, for such gaudy slatternliness is not natural. They squeeze their fat and suety figures—too much junk food consumed in front of the television—into tight iridescent outfits, which leave no contour unstated, or into extra-short skirts that they pull down by half an inch when a gust of autumn wind blows and they start to shiver. The only thin girls are those who smoke more than fifty a day or who have anorexia.

I find a pedestrianized passage in which every doorway enters a club. The passage is closed to all cars except for the scarlet BMW of a chief bouncer, who makes a point of scattering the crowd. He parks it ostentatiously where he shouldn't and swaggers out to greet his underlings.

Six feet tall and a yard and a half wide, he is a fine example of the species. Hitting him would be like trying to punch your way into a locked safe. He has three days' stubble (how do they always manage to keep it at three days, I wonder?) and an earring. A gold chain ripples round his bull neck. There are scars on his shaven scalp. He oozes anabolic steroids and obviously spends more time in the gym than most Englishmen spend in front of the television. The lord of all he surveys—and he surveys his surroundings constantly—he engages in an elaborate handshaking ritual with his underlings, which would be of interest to anthropologists who study the ceremonies of primitives.

The truth is that nightclub bouncing is part job, part protection racket. I was told by a psychiatric nurse who was a club bouncer during his off-duty hours that the smaller clubs—those not owned by large corporations—are staked out by gangs of bouncers, who offer to keep the customers in order but who also threaten to turn the club over and destroy it if they are not thus employed. They then protect the clubs that employ them against other gangs of bouncers. The gangs recruit their staff in prisons, where grievous bodily harmers and armed robbers hone their skills and their physiques in the prison gymnasium.

Saturday night in provincial England belongs to the bouncers. For some reason, looking at them reminds me of my childhood, when the BBC ran an educational radio program for children in which correspondents were sent back sixty million years to report on the appearance and behavior of dinosaurs. How small and vulnerable the correspondents said they felt among the threatening saurian giants! Just like I feel this Saturday night, in fact.

I pick my club: it looks a little more respectable than the others (no jeans, no leather), and the bouncers seem calmer and more confident than elsewhere, though their musculature still bulges through their tuxedos. I am later told by one of them that my choice was wise; there is serious trouble here only once every two weeks or so.

So this is the Mecca of all those young people who have told me that their only interest in life is going out to clubs! This is the cynosure of a million English lives!

The music is loud, but at least there is only one song playing at a time. The lights flash kaleidoscopically. The dance floor is upstairs, the main bar downstairs. This is where the wallflowers (all women) sit, staring disconsolately into their drinks as in the painting by Degas. Two young girls, one fat and one so drunk that she must surely throw up soon, gyrate to the music, but without reference to its rhythm.

On the dance floor itself, a great seething mass of people move like maggots in a tin. With so large a number of people crammed into so small a space, it is astonishing that there is no social contact among them. Most of the pairs do not even look into each other's eyes; because of the noise, verbal communication is out of the question. They dance solipsistically, each in a world of his or her own, literally entranced by the rhythm and the continual physical activity. They dance the way Scotsmen go to bars: to blot out the memory of their lives.

Some of the bouncers patrol the club, gripping walkie-talkies; some stay at lookout posts. I approach two of them—one white and one black—and ask them about their work: we have to shout to make ourselves heard. They love their work and are proud to do it well. They are doormen, not bouncers. They have certificates in first aid and in fire prevention. They are students of human nature (their words, not mine).

"We know who's going to be trouble, even before they come in," the black doorman says.

"We try to prevent trouble, not deal with it afterwards," says the white.

"You don't use words," explains the black. "You don't discuss with them. That only spreads the trouble, because if you stand there discussing it, everyone notices and joins in."

"A quick surgical operation, and they're out. You use the minimum force possible."

I ask what kind of serious trouble they expect.

"Well, there's a gang in the city called the Zulus that gets its fun from wrecking clubs," says the black. "There's too many of them: we can't handle them."

"Mind you," adds the white, looking on the bright side, "they know us, so they wouldn't kill us or nothing."

"No, they'd only give us a good kicking, no more than that."

If I tried to kick either of them—and I'm not a dwarf—I should be more likely to break my toe than to injure them.

"And what do you do if you get a good kicking?" I ask. "Surely, you want to find other work?"

"No, you just got to go back the next night, or you lose your respect," says the black, grinning but serious.

There is a scuffle on the dance floor. My two bouncers are called to assist with the ejection of a troublemaker. They move with surprising agility, in unison. I have seen such coordination before, among men who are like them in many ways: prison wardens, who deal with disturbances in the cells in a similar fashion.

A small young man, who resembles a pilot fish among sharks, is escorted off the premises by eight doormen. I notice as he goes by that he too is a bodybuilder: his biceps threaten to split the short sleeves of his shirt. He is drunk, but not so drunk that he does not recognize overwhelming force when he sees it.

I follow him out. Nearby, a girl in short cream satin pants, with fat lily-white legs and black velvet high-heeled shoes, is draped like a sack over the shoulder of her boyfriend, the St. Christopher who carries her across the road because she is incapable of making it herself. She is drunk and vomits, fortunately missing his back but definitely hitting the sidewalk. The vomit will be cleared up by morning: it makes you proud to pay your local taxes.

It is two o'clock. A little farther on, a small crowd gathers below a first-floor window. A blowsy woman with peroxided hair and a cigarette stuck by dried saliva to the corner of her mouth shouts the name of a district of the city at the crowd below. This is a taxi office, and she shouts out the destination of taxis as they arrive. Some of the would-be passengers are too drunk to recognize the destinations of the taxis they themselves have ordered, and so she has to repeat them.

Only taxi drivers in desperate financial straits work Saturday nights. They've all been robbed, of course, mostly at knifepoint, and an informal survey I once carried out revealed that about a third of them have had their cars stolen. I remember one driver—working Saturday night to pay for his divorce—who had had seven of his ribs broken by passengers who were incensed by being asked to pay for their ride. Like the doormen after a good kicking, the driver returned at once to work.

The following Monday morning, I walk into my ward of the hospital. In the first bed there sits an eighteen-year-old girl, dressed in a gold satin bathrobe, staring blinklessly into space. Her blood pressure is high, her heartbeat too fast, her pupils dilated. When I speak to her, she does not hear me, or at least does not respond. I try three simple questions, and then she leans forward, shrieks "Help!" and sinks back against her pillows, exhausted and terrified.

She has been to the XL Club on Saturday night, a large barn of a dance hall where everyone takes Ecstasy—methylenedioxymethamphetamine, of very variable purity—and enters a trance. We have a steady flow of patients from the XL: not long ago, one of them was DOA (dead on arrival), and his friend who came with him suffered permanent brain damage. This girl, though, had begun to act strangely after leaving the XL—gesturing wildly at something that was not there—and had been brought to the hospital by a friend.

Next to her is another product of the XL Club. She made it home on Saturday night but then tried to jump out of the window because she thought her boyfriend's enemies were coming to kill her. She had taken Ecstasy every Saturday night for six months, and it had made her paranoid for most of that time. In fact, she had given up her work in an office because she felt the other workers there were plotting against her. Strangely enough, she knows that Ecstasy is not good for her, that it has nearly ruined her life.

"Then why do you take it?"

"I want to get through the night."

In another part of the hospital lies a sixteen-year-old girl who has taken an overdose to force the local authorities to give her an apartment. Such apartments are allocated on the basis of need and vulnerability, and a young girl who attempts suicide could hardly stand in greater need of help. She hates her mother because they argue all the time, and she has left home to live on the street; she doesn't know who her father is, and she doesn't care. She hated school, of course, and left sooner than the law allowed—not that the law cares much.

"What are your interests?" I ask.

She doesn't know what I mean, and pouts. I rephrase the question.

"What are you interested in?"

She still doesn't know what I mean. All the same, she is of good intelligence—very good, in fact.

"What do you like doing?"

"Going out."

"Where to?"

"Clubs. Everything else is shit."

*1996*

# We Don't Want
# No Education

◆ EDUCATION HAS ALWAYS BEEN a minority interest in England. The English have generally preferred to keep the bloom of their ignorance intact and on the whole have succeeded remarkably well, despite a century and a quarter of compulsory schooling of their offspring.

In the past their ignorance was purely passive: the mere absence of knowledge. Of late, however, it has taken on a more positive and malign quality: a profound aversion to anything that smacks of intelligence, education, or culture. Not long ago there was a popular song whose first lines successfully captured this widespread mood of hostility: "We don't need no education,/We don't need no thought control." And a couple of months ago I noticed some wall posters advertising a new song: "Poor, White, and Stupid."

I wish I could say that some irony was intended, but the cult of stupidity has become in England what the cult of celebrity is in the United States. To call someone clever has never been an unequivocal compliment in England, but it takes a special kind of perversity for students at the high school situated four hundred yards from my hospital to say to one of their colleagues, who took an overdose because of the constant bullying to which she was subject: You're stupid because you're clever.

What did they mean by this apparent paradox? They meant that anyone who tried hard at school and performed well was wasting his time, when he could have been engaged in the real business of life, such as truanting in the park or wandering downtown. Furthermore, there was menace in their words: If you don't mend your ways and join us, they were saying, we'll beat you up. This was no idle threat: I often meet people in their twenties and thirties in my hospital practice who gave up at school under such duress and subsequently realize that they have missed an opportunity which, had it been taken, would have changed the whole course of their lives much for the better. And those who attend the few schools in the city that maintain very high academic standards risk a beating if they venture to where the poor white stupids live. In the last year I have treated two boys in the emergency room after such a beating, and two others who have taken overdoses for fear of receiving one at the hands of their neighbors.

Just as it was impossible to go broke underestimating the taste of the American public, so it is impossible to overstate the abysmal educational depths to which a large proportion of the English have now sunk, boding ill for the country's future in the global market. Very few of the sixteen-year-olds whom I meet as patients can read and write with facility; they do not even regard my question as to whether they can read and write as in the least surprising or insulting. I now test the basic literacy of nearly every such youth I meet, in case illiteracy should prove to be one of the causes of his misery. (I had a patient recently whose brother committed suicide rather than face the humiliation of public exposure in the social security office of his inability to read the forms he was required to fill in.) One can tell merely by the way these youths handle a pen or a book that they are unfamiliar with these instruments. Even those who are under the impression that they can read and write adequately are utterly defeated by words of three syllables, and while they can sometimes read the words of a text, they no more understand them than if they had been in Church Slavonic.

I cannot recall meeting a sixteen-year-old white from the public housing estates that are near my hospital who could multiply nine by seven (I do not exaggerate). Even three by seven often defeats them. One boy of seventeen told me, "We didn't get that far." This after twelve years of compulsory education (or should I say, attendance at school).

As to knowledge in other spheres, it is fully up to the standards set in mathematics. Most of the young whites whom I meet literally cannot name a single writer and certainly cannot recite a line of poetry. Not a single one of my young patients has known the dates of the Second World War, let alone of the First; some have never heard of these wars, though recently one young patient who had heard of the Second World War thought it took place in the eighteenth century. In the prevailing circumstances of total ignorance, I was impressed that he had heard of the eighteenth century. The name Stalin means nothing to these young people and does not even evoke the faint ringing of a bell, as the name Shakespeare (sometimes) does. To them, 1066 is more likely to mean a price than a date.

Thus are the young condemned to live in an eternal present, a present that merely exists, without connection to a past that might explain it or to a future that might develop from it. Theirs is truly a life of one damned thing after another. Likewise, they are deprived of any reasonable standards of comparison by which to judge their woes. They believe themselves deprived, because the only people with whom they can compare themselves are those who appear in advertisements or on television.

Mere semi-literacy and ignorance do not necessarily disqualify young people from passing public examinations, at least lower-level exams. Since failure is now regarded as fatally damaging to self-esteem, anyone who actually presents himself at an examination is likely to emerge with a certificate. I recently encountered a boy aged sixteen in my clinic who wrote Dear Sir as deer sur, and I'm as ime (and whose grammar was fully consonant with his orthography), who had passed a public examination—in English.

Clearly, something very strange is happening in our schools. Our educational practices are now so bizarre that they would defy the pen of a Jonathan Swift to satirize them. In the very large metropolitan area in which I work, for example, the teachers have received instructions that they are not to impart the traditional disciplines of spelling and grammar. Pettifogging attention to details of syntax and orthography is said to inhibit children's creativity and powers of self-expression. Moreover, to assert that there is a correct way of speaking or writing is to indulge in a kind of bourgeois cultural imperialism; and to tell children that they have got something wrong is necessarily to saddle them with a debilitating sense of inferiority from which they will never recover. I have met a few teachers who disobey these instructions in an atmosphere of clandestinity, in fear for their jobs, rather reminiscent of the atmosphere that surrounded those who secretly tried to propagate truth behind the late Iron Curtain.

I was told of one school where the teachers were allowed by the headmaster to make corrections, but only five per piece of work, irrespective of the number actually present. This, of course, was to preserve the *amour propre* of the children, but it seemed not to have occurred to this pedagogue that his five-correction rule was likely to have unfortunate consequences. The teacher might choose to correct an error in the spelling of a word, for example, and overlook precisely the same error in the next piece of work. How is a child to interpret correction based on this headmaster's principle? The less intelligent, perhaps, will regard it as a species of natural hazard, like the weather, about which he can do very little; while the more intelligent are likely to draw the conclusion that the principle of correction as such is inherently arbitrary and unjust.

Alarmingly, this arbitrariness reinforces precisely the kind of discipline that I see exercised around me every day by parents whose philosophy of child-rearing is laissez-faire tempered by insensate rage. A small child rushes about noisily, creating havoc and wreaking destruction about him; the mother (fathers scarcely exist, except in the merest biological sense) first ignores the child, then shouts at him to stop, then ignores him, pleads with him, ignores him again, laughs at him, and then finally loses her temper, screeches abuse at him, and gives him a clout on the ear.

What is the child supposed to learn from this? He learns to associate discipline not with principle, and punishment not with his own behavior, but with the exasperated mood of his mother. This mood will itself depend upon many variables, few of them under the control of the child. The mother may be irritable because of her latest row with her latest boyfriend or because of a delay in the arrival of a social security payment, or she may be comparatively tolerant because she has received an invitation to a party or has just discovered that she is not pregnant after all. But what the child certainly never learns is that discipline has any meaning beyond the physical capacity and desire of the mother to impose it.

Everything is reduced to a mere contest of wills, and so the child learns that all restraint is but an arbitrary imposition from someone or something bigger and stronger than himself. The ground is laid for a bloody-minded intolerance of any authority whatever, even should that authority be based upon patently superior and benevolent knowledge and wisdom. Authority of any kind is experienced as an insult to the self, and must therefore be challenged because it is authority. The world is thus a world of permanently inflamed egos, trying to impose their wills on one another.

In the schools, young children are no longer taught in whole classes but in little groups. It is hoped that they will learn by discovery and play. There is no blackboard and no rote learning. Perhaps the method of teaching by turning everything into a game can work when the teacher is talented and the children are already socialized to learn; but when, as is usually the case, neither of these conditions obtains, the results are disastrous, not just in the short term but probably forever.

The children themselves eventually come to know that something is wrong, even if they are not able to articulate their knowledge. Of the generations of children who grew up with these pedagogical methods, it is striking how many of the more intelligent among them sense by their early twenties that something is missing from their lives. They don't know what it is, and they ask me what it could be. I quote them Francis Bacon: "It is a poore Center of a Mans Actions, Himselfe." They ask me what I mean, and I reply that they have no interests outside themselves, that their world is as small as the day they entered it, and that their horizons have not expanded in the least.

"But how do we get interested in something?" they ask.

This is where the baleful effect of education as mere entertainment makes itself felt. For to develop an interest requires powers of concentration and an ability to tolerate a degree of boredom while the elements of a skill are learned for the sake of a worthwhile end. Few people are attracted naturally by the vagaries of English spelling or by the rules of simple arithmetic, yet they must be mastered if everyday life in an increasingly complex world is to be negotiated successfully. And it is the plain duty of adults, from the standpoint of their superior knowledge and experience of the world, to impart to children what they need to know so that later they may exercise genuine choice. The demagogic equation of all authority, even over the smallest child, with unjustifiable political authoritarianism leads only to personal and social chaos.

Alas, the age of twenty is not the age at which to learn either to concentrate or to tolerate effort which is in itself not enjoyable. Never having experienced the pleasures of mastering something through disciplined effort, and with minds pro-

foundly influenced by the swiftly moving and superficially ex-
citing images of television, these young adults find that a sustained interest in anything is now beyond them. And in the
modern urban world, anyone who cannot concentrate is truly a
lost soul, for the only communities in such a world are those
which grow up around interests that people hold in common.
Moreover, in an age of increasing technological change, those
without the ability or inclination to learn will be left farther and
farther behind.

The gimcrack pedagogical notion that education should be
"relevant" to children's lives gained currency in England in the
sixties. The thought that this would confine children to the
world that they already knew—and a pretty dismal world it
was, too, as anyone with the slightest acquaintance with English working-class life will testify—apparently never occurred
to those educationists who claimed such exceptional sympathy
with the relatively disadvantaged. The result was that a route—
perhaps the one most frequently traveled—to social advancement was substantially closed to them.

Unfortunately, it is extremely difficult to overturn these educational (or anti-educational) developments even now, when the
central government has belatedly realized their disastrous consequences. Why? First, the teachers and the teachers of the
teachers in the training colleges are deeply imbued with the
kinds of educational ideas that have brought us to this pass.
Second, a huge educational bureaucracy has grown up in England (one bureaucrat per teacher, pullulating like admirals in a
South American navy) which uses every subterfuge to prevent
change, from falsification of figures to willful misinterpretation
of government policy. The minister of education may propose,
but the bureaucracy disposes. Thus it happens that Britain
spends a higher percentage of its GDP on education than any of
its competitors and ends up with a catastrophically ill-educated
population, whose lack of intelligence is evident from their ru-

minant gaze to be seen on every street in the country, and which is remarked upon by all my foreign friends.

Bad as educational policy has been, however, there remains an important and refractory cultural dimension to the problem. It is easy—conceptually at least—to see what should be done on the plane of policy, but the English disdain for education is not easily overcome even in principle.

In the neighborhood in which I work, there are many immigrant groups. The largest are those from northwest India, Bangladesh, and Jamaica. There is also a large and settled white working class. The children from all these groups go to the same bad schools with the same bad teachers, but the results are dramatically different. The children of poor and unemployed immigrants from northwest India are never illiterate or semi-literate; a very respectable number go on to further education, even at the highest level, despite overcrowding in the home and apparent poverty. The other groups vie with each other to achieve the lowest educational level.

The lamentable fact is that a considerable proportion of the English population is simply unaware of the need for education. It seems stuck with the Victorian idea that England is by right and divine providence the workshop of the world, that Englishmen by virtue of their place of birth come into the world knowing all that it is necessary for them to know, and that if there are no jobs to employ their unskilled (and, it must be said, rather reluctant) labor, it is the fault of the government in league with the plutocrats in top hats and tails who have conspired to exploit cheap Japanese labor. One thing an unemployed young Englishman is definitely not going to do is to make a concerted effort to equip himself with a salable skill.

I have had the following conversation on innumerable occasions with young men of about twenty who have been unemployed since leaving school, and whose general educational level is outlined above:

"Have you thought of improving your education?"

"No."

"Why not?"

"There's no point. There are no jobs."

"Could there be any other reason to get educated?"

"No." (This after puzzlement as to what I could possibly mean.)

There are two things to notice in this conversation. The first is that the unemployed young person considers the number of jobs in an economy as a fixed quantity. Just as the national income is a cake to be doled out in equal or unequal slices, so the number of jobs in an economy has nothing to do with the conduct of the people who live in it but is immutably fixed. This is a concept of the way the world works that has been assiduously peddled, not only in schools during "social studies" but in the media of mass communication.

The second thing worthy of remark is the complete absence of the idea that mental culture is a good in itself, that it has a value irrespective of one's employment prospects. Just as patients' responses to the same illness and disability vary according to their predisposition and character, so does a man's response to unemployment. A man with an interest to pursue, or at least with the mental equipment to pursue an interest, is not in such dire straits as a man obliged by the tabula rasa of his mind to stare vacantly at the four walls for weeks, months, or years on end. He is more likely to come up with an idea for self-employment, or at the very least to seek work in places and in fields that are new to him. He is not condemned to stagnation.

There is one great psychological advantage to the white underclass in their disdain for education: it enables them to maintain the fiction that the society around them is grossly, even grotesquely, unjust, and that they themselves are the victims of this injustice. If, on the contrary, education were seen by them as a means available to all to rise in the world, as indeed it could be and is in many societies, their whole viewpoint would naturally have to change. Instead of attributing their misfortunes to others, they would have to look inward, which is always a painful process. Here we see the reason why scholastic success is violently discouraged, and those who pursue it persecuted, in underclass schools: for it is perceived, inchoately no doubt, as a threat to an entire Weltanschauung. The success of one is a reproach to all.

And a whole way of life is at stake. This way of life is akin to drug addiction, of which crime is the heroin and social security the methadone. The latter, as we know, is the harder habit to kick, and its pleasures, though less intense, are longer lasting. The sour satisfaction of being dependent on social security resides in its automatic conferral of the status of Victim, which in itself simultaneously explains one's failure and absolves one of the obligation to make something of oneself, *ex hypothesi* impossible because of the unjust nature of society which made one a victim in the first place. The redemptive value of education blows the whole affecting scene apart: no wonder we don't want no education.

In one sense (and in one sense alone), however, the underclass has been victimized, or perhaps betrayed is a better word. The educational absurdities foisted on the lower orders were the idea not of the lower orders themselves but of those who were in a position to avoid their baleful effects: that is to say, middle-class intellectuals. If I were inclined to paranoia (which fortunately I am not), I should say that the efforts of educationists were part of a giant plot by the middle classes to keep power for themselves and to restrict competition, in the process creating sinecures for some of their less able and dynamic members—namely the educationists. But if these middle classes have maintained their power, it is in an increasingly enfeebled and impoverished country.

*1995*

# Uncouth Chic

---

◈ LAST JUNE IN PARIS, a young Englishman walked into a bar frequented by Britons, having agreed to meet his girlfriend there. A row had been brewing between them all day, and he asked her to leave with him. She was enjoying herself, however, and demurred; whereupon he dragged her into the adjoining room, punched her to the ground, and kicked her so viciously that he left her head and stomach covered in bruises. The bar staff pulled him off and threw him out, but not before he had received a Glasgow kiss—a head-butt—from a chivalrous patron of the bar.

Only two months earlier, a court had acquitted the young Englishman of an assault on his previous girlfriend, the mother of his two-year-old child. The pair had quarreled over access to the child, and the woman alleged that, as his clinching argument, he had beaten her. On learning of his lucky and probably undeserved acquittal, his new girlfriend—the one he assaulted in Paris—said, "For any dad, what [he] has gone through is a nightmare, but the case won't affect our relationship." (Presumably, as the mother of a three-year-old by a previous liaison, she had special insight into the parental heart.) But when his former girlfriend, the mother of his child, heard about the assault on her successor in Paris, she was less sentimental. "Frankly," she said, "I am not surprised that someone [else] has found themselves on the receiving end of something like this."

# Uncouth Chic

When the young Englishman had had time to reflect on the incident, he said, "I totally regret everything that happened"— as if what had happened were a typhoon in the East Indies, over which he could have been expected to exert no influence.

Apart from its Parisian setting, every aspect of the story seems familiar to the student of English underclass life: the easily inflamed ego, the quick loss of temper, the violence, the scattering of illegitimate children, the self-exculpation by use of impersonal language. But the young Englishman was not a member of the underclass, nor was the woman he assaulted. His salary alone was $1.25 million a year, and she was a well-known weather-girl-turned-talk-show-host. Poverty was not the explanation of their behavior.

The young Englishman was a famous professional soccer player. True, soccer players are usually drawn from the class adjacent to the underclass, into which downward slippage is all too easy. But in the past, those who managed to escape their lowly origins usually aspired to be taken for bona fide members of the middle or upper classes by conforming their conduct to middle-class standards.

The young soccer player felt no such impulse: and why should he have, when his public behavior resulted neither in legal sanction, social ostracism, or even strong disapproval? For the truth is that in modern Britain, the direction of cultural aspiration has reversed: for the first time in history, it is the middle and upper classes that aspire to be taken for their social inferiors, an aspiration that (in their opinion) necessitates misconduct. No wonder, therefore, that the young soccer player didn't feel that his newfound wealth imposed any obligation upon him to change his ways.

The signs—both large and small—of the reversal in the flow of aspiration are everywhere. Recently a member of the royal family, a granddaughter of the queen, had a metal stud inserted into her tongue and proudly displayed it to the press. Such body piercing began as a strictly underclass fashion, though it has spread widely to the popular culture industry—into a branch of which, of course, the monarchy is fast being transformed.

Middle-class girls now consider it chic to sport a tattoo—another underclass fashion, as a visit to any British prison will swiftly establish. The idea that a girl should have herself tattooed would have horrified the middle classes as recently as ten years ago. But young middle-class women now proudly wear tattoos as badges of antinomian defiance, of intellectual independence, and of identification with the supposedly downtrodden—if not of the entire world, then at least of our inner cities.

Advertising now glamorizes the underclass way of life and its attitude towards the world. Stella Tennant, one of Britain's most famous models and herself of aristocratic birth, has adopted almost as a trademark the stance and facial expression of general dumb hostility to everything and everybody that is characteristic of so many of my underclass patients. A recent advertisement for a brand of casual shirt featured a snarling young man demanding to know, What you looking at?—precisely the words that spark so many knife-fights between young underclass men of exquisitely tender ego. A new style has been invented: uncouth chic.

Diction in Britain has always been an important marker, to some extent even a determinant, of a person's place in the social hierarchy. Whether this is a healthy phenomenon may be debated, but it is an indisputable fact. Even today, social psychologists find that the British almost universally associate what is known as received pronunciation with high intelligence, good education, and a cultured way of life. Rightly or wrongly, they see it as a marker of self-confidence, wealth, honesty, even cleanliness. Regional accents are generally held to signify the opposite qualities, even by people who speak with them.

So it is a development worthy of remark that, for the first time in our modern history, people who would, by upbringing, use received pronunciation as a matter of course, now seek to suppress it. In other words, they are anxious not to appear intelligent, well educated, and cultured to their fellow country-men, as if such attributes were in some way shameful or dis-advantageous. Where once the aspiring might have aped the diction of their social superiors, the upper classes now ape the diction of their inferiors. Those who send their children to ex-pensive private schools, for example, now regularly report that they emerge with diction and vocabulary little different from the argot of the local state school.

The BBC, which until a few years ago insisted with very few exceptions on received pronunciation by its announcers, is now falling over itself to ensure that the speech that comes over the airwaves is demographically representative. The political ideol-ogy underlying the decision to make this change is a crude and simple one, a hangover from Marxism: that the upper and mid-dle classes are bad; that what has traditionally been regarded as high culture is but a fig leaf for middle- and upper-class oppres-sion of the working class; and that the working class is the only class whose diction, culture, manners, and tastes are genuine and authentic, valued for their own sake rather than as a means to maintain social hierarchy. Communist utopianism may be dead in Russia, but it molders on at the BBC—exclusively among people of the upper and middle classes, of course.

Symbolic of the sea change in the direction of cultural influ-ence brought about by liberal middle-class self-hatred is the contrast between two recent prime ministers, Mrs. Thatcher and Mr. Blair. Mrs. Thatcher, of lowly origin, taught herself to speak like a grandee; Mr. Blair, nearer to the grandee class by birth, now toys (not altogether convincingly) with the glottal stop and other vocal mannerisms of the lower classes, such as the short *a* in words like class and pass. And the only clubs of which Mr. Blair admits membership in his entry in Who's Who are the Trimdon Colliery and Deaf Hill Working Men's Club and the Fishburn Working Men's Club. Indeed, the most exclu-sive social organization to which any of his cabinet admits membership in Who's Who is the Covent Garden Community

Centre. Otherwise the cabinet appears to confine its socializing to the Jewel Miners' Welfare Club and the Newcraighall Miners' Welfare Club: a curious phenomenon for a group of people distinguished chiefly for their wealth.

After his election, Mr. Blair lost little time in establishing that his tastes were thoroughly demotic, contrary to the impression created by the recent sale of his house for $1 million. He invited one of the Gallagher brothers, of the pop group Oasis, to his first party at Downing Street, seemingly as a matter of national urgency.

The Gallagher brothers are notorious for their crudity. Their antics might be a mere publicity stunt, of course, and it is possible that in private they are charm itself, but it was as a public figure that one of them was invited to Downing Street. I saw their act for myself when a newspaper asked me to attend one of their concerts, an event I would otherwise have been at some pains to avoid. Nine thousand young fans (at thirty dollars a ticket) crowded into an exhibition hall; they were mainly people at the lower end of the social and educational spectrum. The group's publicity agents gave me earplugs, surely a strange way of currying favor for a musical act. Not that there was any danger that I wouldn't be able to hear it: for despite the plugs, the sound waves were so strong that I felt a vibration in my throat, detectable even with my hand.

The Gallaghers dressed exactly as the underclass dresses; their mannerisms were precisely those of my underclass patients. Between songs, one of them spoke a few words, among which *fuck* and its various derivatives were frequent, uttered not so much to convey a meaning as a general mood of egotistical defiance. About halfway through the concert, one of the brothers asked the audience, "Any of you fuckers out there got any fucking drugs?"

His attitude of untouchable snarling insolence was not lost on his audience, of course; and neither will have been its effective endorsement by the prime minister's invitation. What is the point of restraint and circumspection if such stream-of-consciousness vulgarity can win not merely wealth and fame but complete social acceptance? For the hundreds of thousands of young men and women who have been to Oasis concerts, what is good enough for the Gallaghers and the prime minister will be good enough for them.

By so ostentatiously inviting one of the Gallaghers, the prime minister also endorsed a belief about music that is now general in England: that there is no better and no worse, only popular and unpopular. Difference is held to inhere not in the quality of the music but in the size and social composition of the audience: so that the easy and the popular that might once have been considered worse is now considered not merely equal but better. Even people one might have expected to defend high culture have surrendered abjectly to populism—indeed, have fanned its flames with multicultural fervor. I recently heard an Oxford classics don aver that in point of quality there was nothing to choose between Mozart and the productions of the latest rap group (though I wouldn't mind betting what his deeply held preferences were, under all the posturing and bad faith). When anyone mentions great songwriters, it is now obligatory to bracket the Beatles with Schubert to establish one's broad-minded, democratic bona fides; and the Midland Bank has just withdrawn its subsidy of the Royal Opera House, Covent Garden—on the grounds that opera is a minority interest—and will now give the money to a pop festival instead. Patronage of the arts, therefore, has become mere polling and pandering.

Even in behavior, the new orthodoxy for all classes is that, since nothing is better and nothing is worse, the worse is better because it is more demotic. Everyone knows that British soccer crowds are the worst-behaved in Europe, if not the world. But what is less well known is that these crowds are not made up solely, or even mainly, of people at the bottom of the social ladder—and, in fact, solid middle-class citizens perpetrate much of the worst behavior. What was once a proletarian entertainment is now distinctly bourgeois, and far from having improved the conduct at matches, the change in the social composition of the audience has caused a deterioration.

I saw this for myself in Rome, where I went to report for a newspaper on British soccer hooliganism at a match between Italy and England. For the duration of the English invasion, Rome had the atmosphere of a city under siege (though the barbarians were truly within the gates). Thousands of police were on duty throughout the city to prevent the drunken riot and looting to which an English crowd, left to its own devices, now almost always degenerates.

At the match itself, in the Olympic Stadium, the English crowd behaved with typical unpleasantness. For about three hours—before, during, and after the game—it hurled insults in unison at the Italian crowd. It chanted, *Who the fuck do you think you are?* and *You're shit and you know you are,* with scarcely a break. As far as I could tell, I was the only person in the English section of the stadium who did not join in. It was precisely for this that the thousands had come to Rome. Even worse, this mob of free-born Englishmen accompanied the chanting by what looked unconscionably like the fascist salute—taking the adage, "When in Rome, do as the Romans do," a step beyond urbanity.

The ten thousand Britons who went to Rome—a notoriously expensive city—had well-paid jobs, requiring education and training. The man next to me, for example, was a computer programmer, in charge of the information technology of a city council. All those I asked were employed in skilled capacities; a Sotheby's auctioneer, I was told, was in the crowd.

I asked a few people around me why they behaved like this. Did they not think it unseemly to go a thousand miles just to shout obscenities at strangers? They all claimed that it was both fun and a necessary release for them. A release from what, exactly? Frustration, they replied, if they replied anything. It had occurred to none of them that the petty drama of their internal lives did not provide a justification for anti-social activity. They thought that frustration was like pus in an abscess, better out than in: and I was reminded of a murderer who once said to me that he had had to kill his victim, otherwise he didn't know what he might have done.

At the Rome airport I witnessed an extraordinary instance of the desire for the appearance, if not the reality, of downward social mobility. An Englishwoman in her thirties ahead of me, unmistakably upper middle class, spoke politely, with the received pronunciation, at the check-in counter. A little later I saw her again in the bus that took us to the plane. Now that she was among the soccer-fan friends with whom she had come to Rome, she adopted a lower-class accent and larded her speech liberally with four-letter words.

Soccer fans are by no means the only prosperous Britons who affect underclass hooliganism abroad, however. Recently the British vice-consul on the island of Ibiza resigned because he no longer wished to rescue the citizens of his country from the legal consequences of their own incontinent behavior.

Why should the British have become such total and shameless vulgarians in a matter of three or four decades? Why should a kind of Gresham's Law of behavior now operate, such that bad conduct drives out good?

Like so many modern ills, the coarseness of spirit and behavior grows out of ideas brewed up in the academy and among intellectuals—ideas that have seeped outward and are now having their practical effect on the rest of society. The relativism that has ruled the academy for many years has now come to rule the mind of the population. The British middle class has bought the multiculti cant that, where culture is concerned, there is only difference, not better or worse. As a practical matter, that means that there is nothing to choose between good manners and bad, refinement and crudity, discernment and lack of discernment, subtlety and grossness, charm and boorishness.

To refrain from urinating in doorways, say, is thus no better than not refraining: it is merely different, and a preference for doorways free of the smell of urine is but a bourgeois prejudice without intellectual or moral justification. Since it is easier and more immediately gratifying to behave without restraint than with it, and there is no longer any generally accepted argument or even prejudice in favor of the restraint that leads to public decorum, there is no standpoint from which to criticize vulgarity.

British society and culture were additionally vulnerable to attack from the intellectuals, for historically they were openly elitist and therefore supposedly undemocratic. That its cultural productions were magnificent, that Newton and Darwin, Shakespeare and Dickens, Hume and Adam Smith did not speak to or for a national elite but to and for all mankind, has been conveniently forgotten. Nor did it matter for ideological purposes that, though elitist, British society and culture were never closed, but that anyone of talent was able to make his contribution: that Britain absorbed outsiders into its inner circle with ease, from Sir Anthony Van Dyck to Joseph Conrad, from Sir William Herschel to Sir Karl Popper, from George Frideric Handel to Sir Ernst Gombrich. A simplified account of British history has been peddled, according to which it was nothing but a tale of oppression, exploitation, and snobbery (all of which, of course, existed). A rejection of the traditions of British high culture was therefore in itself a meritorious political act, a sign of solidarity with those whom history had oppressed and exploited.

An early avatar of this rejection was the metamorphosis of Viscount Stansgate into Tony Benn, the left-wing politician, via the intermediate or pupal stage of Anthony Wedgwood-Benn. He was obliged to forgo his hereditary peerage to continue to sit in the House of Commons, but the plebeian contraction of his family name was his own invention. Left-wing in everything except his finances, he sent his children in well-publicized fashion to the local state school, omitting to mention the extensive private tutoring they received. A perfect solution to the moral dilemma facing every left-leaning parent of the upper and middle classes: the moral high ground of having self-denyingly rejected private education while simultaneously having avoided the disastrously low educational standards in the state system that have left at least a quarter of the British population virtually illiterate.

The combination of relativism and antipathy to traditional culture has played a large part in creating the underclass, thus turning Britain from a class into a caste society. The poorest people were deprived both of a sense of cultural hierarchy and of the moral imperative to conform their conduct to any standard whatever. Henceforth what they had and what they did was as good as anything, because all cultures and all cultural artifacts are equal. Aspiration was therefore pointless: and thus they have been as immobilized in their poverty—material, mental, and spiritual—as completely as the damned in Dante's *Inferno*.

Having in large part created this underclass, the British intelligentsia, guilty about its own allegedly undemocratic antecedents, feels obliged to flatter it by imitation and has persuaded the rest of the middle class to do likewise. And so, just as in Russia under the tsars every town and village had its Holy Fool for Christ's Sake, whose selfishness and misconduct were taken as signs of his deep attachment to Christian principle, we in Britain now have hundreds of thousands, perhaps millions, of middle-class people whose willingness to shout *Fuck off* for hours at Italians is living proof of the purity of their democratic sentiments.

For anyone who does not want to see the lowest common cultural denominator triumph, but who also remains attached to the ideal of liberal democracy, the spectacle of British vulgarity is very disturbing. There are more votes in the flattery of vulgarity than in the denunciation of it.

Does that mean it is destined to be ever victorious?

*1998*

# The Heart of a
# Heartless World

OPPOSITE MY HOUSE, in the center of the square, stands a Victorian Gothic church, a building of some grandeur, which soars upward with immense confidence. Its interior is unspoiled, its stained-glass windows magnificent. It is almost always empty.

The architect, when he built it, could only have supposed that he was expressing in stone a faith that would endure forever. He could not have imagined that, a century and a quarter later, the established church that commissioned his splendid building would be on the verge of extinction, its bishops straining vainly after modernity by signing on to the fashionable sociological untruths of a couple of decades ago or by suggesting variously that Jesus was a homosexual or that he was not resurrected in any corporeal sense. Still less could he have imagined that members of the Synod of the Church of England would one day express more interest in Third World Indebtedness or Global Warming than in Sin. In its characteristically lukewarm and timorous fashion, the church has adopted (and diluted) the liberation theology that has so hastened the erosion of Catholic hegemony in Latin America.

But the Church of England is a broad church, and the vicar

is a survivor of the days when God was still on the side of the upper classes. An ex-army man, he wears a monocle and has a twinkle in his other eye. He is a most amusing dinner guest, far too urbane to bring religion into the conversation. He won't have anything to do with his Bolshevik of a bishop; and he still believes in good works at the prompting of a kind heart, now deemed a most retrograde, even reactionary, conception of charity. He once found a job in the church for a patient of mine, an alcoholic ex-prisoner who wanted at last to go straight: he said, with an amiable laugh, that if the church couldn't give reformed sinners a chance, who on earth could?

Still, the vicar's tolerant and restrained kind of religion is not the kind to spark a revival, and he knows he is almost the last of his breed. The hold of a church over its society is like the bloom of a grape: once gone, it is gone for good.

Belief in the supernatural, however, has not necessarily gone the same way as attendance at the Church of England. Until quite recently I had rather casually supposed that the English, being among the least religious of people, had somehow become indifferent to the superlunary world of angels, devils, evil spirits, and so forth. I was disabused of my too-easy assumptions by a television discussion program on the practice of exorcism, in which I was asked to participate on the panel, representing Science—or at least Rationality.

The other participants included a self-proclaimed bishop who had set up a Catholic church in opposition to the one ruled by the impostor in Rome and an active member of the British Humanist Association of the type who spends wet Sunday afternoons at Speakers' Corner, preaching fiercely anti-God sermons to a congregation of one.

Next to me in the studio sat a man who had served several prison sentences for crimes of violence, obviously a psychopath who, however, had reformed ever since his exorcism, in the course of which he had vomited up a little green devil into a plastic bucket. He had served no sentences since, and I was asked—as the sole legitimate representative of Reason in the studio—to comment.

Of course I found myself unwilling to humiliate the exorcised psychopath in front of ten million viewers. The argument went by default; and what surprised me was the reaction of the audience, bused in from a local factory for the evening. It regarded the little green devil theory of this man's former misconduct as perfectly plausible, not as inherently absurd. I was surprised.

Since then I have taken more notice of the symptoms of religious revival in the city. Large (and competitive) signs exhort the passerby to read the Holy Quran, God's Last Testament, or to Read the Bible Before Christ Comes. In the Yellow Pages there are, amazingly enough, half as many places of worship listed as pubs—including the President Saddam Hussein Mosque, to which the city council recently granted $75,000 to extend its parking lot, which is now, presumably, the mother of all parking lots. The Eternal Sacred Order of Cherubim and Seraphim, on the other hand, is omitted from the list because it has no telephone—though the Chief Apostle has a portable one. The Eternal Sacred Order's chapel, as it happens, is not more than two hundred yards from the church opposite my house, and though the building somewhat lacks grandeur, still displaying architectural features of the cold, Gradgrindian school hall it once was, there is no mistaking the warmth of feeling that suffuses it during a service.

I first encountered the Eternal Sacred Order in eastern Nigeria, near the city of Port Harcourt, where the order was founded. Every Sunday large numbers of the faithful, dressed in long white seraphic robes, trooped down a path of beaten red earth through the lush undergrowth to a large church built of cinder block, where they sang and prayed lustily, forgetting for a while the insecurities of life in a country in which the police

and soldiers hired out their weapons by the night to armed robbers, and where at least one of the Four Horsemen was never
far off.

Two hundred yards, then, from the church where the religion of the English upper class genteelly sighs its last, an assem-
bly of Nigerian immigrants (all from Rivers State in eastern
Nigeria) don their robes (now satin), sing, and shout hallelujah.
The air in the chapel is thick with incense and rent by urgent
prayer. The police in England don't hire out their weaponry to
armed robbers, at least not yet, but life is still full of insecurities
for these immigrants. By no means welcomed with open arms
by the local population, they find the climate cold, the cost of
living unexpectedly high, and the moral dangers for their children manifold and pervasive.

"Oh, Lord," sighs the Junior Apostle (the Senior Apostle is
away in Jerusalem), "many are widout jobs, many are widout
mudders and farders, many are widout homes. We pray thee,
Lord, to find dem work, to find dem homes, to bring comfort to
dem dat are widout mudders and farders."

The congregation is on its knees, facing in all directions, and
unanimously utters a heartfelt amen, with some banging of
heads on the ground for added emphasis. Then one of the
women in the congregation—which is two-thirds female—
comes forward and prays in distinctly biblical language, King
James version, for the sick of the world, especially for Sister
Okwepho, who is in the hospital with abdominal pain. She asks
the Lord to guide the doctors and scientists who are trying to
rid the world of diseases, and from thence she moves by natural
progression to the Second Coming, when there will be no more
suffering or abdominal pain, when there will be no more
disease or hunger, no more injustice or war, no more unemployment or poverty, but only goodness, brotherhood, and content-
ment. Now the congregation is standing, its hands upraised,
and it begins to sway rhythmically, eyes closed, already bathed

in the bliss of a world without grey hostile skies, a suspicious immigration department, or temptations for adolescents to fall into the wrong company.

The ability to give meaning to the everyday vexations of existence and to overcome them, at least in the imagination, is one of the characteristics that unite the myriad churches that flourish, unseen except when looked for, among the poor. A hundred yards from the prison where I work is another church unlisted in the Yellow Pages, a large octagonal building (an ecclesiastical Benthamite panopticon to match the penal one close by) with a seating capacity of eight hundred, built by subscription of its impoverished members.

They are either Jamaicans or of Jamaican parentage, and they live at the heart, both physically and socially, of the inner-city maelstrom. What remain for me mere events to observe and theorize about are to them the daily problems of life; and two days before I attended a service in the church, a young crack dealer had been shot dead twenty yards from the prison gate in a drive-by assassination, while a few minutes later another dealer was shot dead not a quarter of a mile away. In all, five young men had been shot dead during the previous month, a small tally by Washington standards, perhaps, but still enough to instill fear into the local population.

I had met the suspected killers in the prison the day before I attended the service, three young blacks in their early twenties, to whom killing was no more problematical, morally, than making a telephone call: men who, when I spoke to them, were so convinced of the gross injustice of the world that they were convinced also that nothing they did themselves could add significantly to its sum.

The congregation—perhaps four hundred strong and, again, two-thirds female—was all black. The congregants were dressed in all their finery, immaculately turned out in elegant hats and dazzling dresses; the older among them wore veils and gloves.

Some might be inclined to laugh at this quaint sartorial echo of the respectability of a bygone age; but I learned long ago, when I practiced briefly in the townships of South Africa, that the yearning of poor people for respectability, their desire to appear clean and well-dressed in public, is not laughable in the least but is, on the contrary, something noble and inspiring. It is the prerogative of the unthinkingly prosperous to sneer at the bourgeois virtues, and I now recall my own adolescent gestures and affectations in that direction with distaste.

The shootings were much on the mind of the congregation, for the victims and perpetrators alike could have been the sons, brothers, or consorts (I hardly dare speak of husbands anymore, for fear of being thought implicitly intolerant) of the women who now sobbed their impromptu prayers facedown on their pews. The preacher, a young woman, called the congregation for testimony to the Lord, and an old lady with a limp, whom I had passed several times in the street, came forward. She thanked the Lord in trembling voice for all the blessings that He had showered upon her, His servant, among which was the great gift of life itself.

"We thank Thee, Lord! We thank Thee, Lord! We thank Thee, Lord!"

It was extraordinary to hear this lady, who in other circumstances appeared retiring and undemonstrative, whip a large congregation into a frenzy of emotion by the repetition of a simple phrase, with a constantly rising intonation. And then, with an instinctive mastery of crowd psychology (which she shared with many others who later came forward), she waited for the hubbub of excited gratitude to die down, choosing precisely the right moment to resume her testimony.

"We thank Thee, Lord, for the gift of healing."

"Amen!" muttered the congregation. "Praise the Lord!"

"Last week I fell down on the stair and cut my leg. I went to the hospital [the one in which I work, several of whose nurses were in the congregation], and the doctor came, and he saw that I was bleeding. And he said to me that he would sew it up, and he sewed it up, but still it was bleeding." (That sounds like my hospital all right, I thought.) "So the doctor said, 'I will bind it up with a bandage,' but still it bled right through the bandage. So I prayed a little to the Lord Jesus to stop the bleeding, and do you know? The bleeding stopped."

The congregation was profoundly moved.

"Doctor Jesus! Doctor Jesus! Doctor Jesus!" exclaimed the old lady.

An excited young man to the right of me—a bit of an exhibitionist, I thought—stood up and spoke in tongues. "Garabalaga ingerolipola singapatola hamagaruga!" he said (more or less). The old lady let him have his say until he ran out of steam, and when he had finished she resumed her testimony.

"But we are all sinners, Lord. Therefore we pray for forgiveness. We do not always follow Your ways, Lord; we are proud, we are stubborn, we want to go our own way. We think only of ourselves. That is why there is so much sin, so much robbery, so much violence, on our streets."

I recalled the faces of the young men in the prison now accused of murder: their hard, glittering, expressionless eyes—young men who recognized no law but their own desire of the moment. The old lady described (and explained) their radical egotism in a religious way.

Murmurs of assent were heard everywhere. It wasn't the police's fault, or racism's, or the system's, or capitalism's; it was the failure of sinners to acknowledge any moral authority higher than their personal whim. And in asserting this, the congregation was asserting its own freedom and dignity: poor and despised as its members might be, they were still human enough to decide for themselves between right and wrong. And they offered hope to others, too: for if a man chose to do evil, he could later elect, by an act of will, to do good. No one had to wait until there was perfect justice in the world, or all the circumstances were right, before he himself did good.

A few hundred yards away is yet another Pentecostal church. On its side wall, in letters three feet high, are painted the words GOD'S LOVE IS NOT A LOTTERY. Inside, as if to emphasize that God helps him who helps himself, a notice advises congregants not to park in the street but in the church parking lot, where a security camera is in operation.

How necessary, alas, is that advice! The curbsides of all the local streets are sprinkled with the sparkling shards of glass from a thousand thefts of (or from) cars parked there. But such theft is the least of it around here, as I know from my patients. One of them lives in a house within sight of the church, where she is virtually imprisoned by crime. Her car has been stolen, her house broken into three times in the past year, and her daughter, who visits her every day, has bought a mobile telephone in order to call her mother from the bus when she is about to get off at the bus stop. Her mother looks from an upstairs window for potential muggers and gives her the all clear, but even so she runs the two hundred yards between the bus stop and her mother's front door. She has been mugged at knifepoint once before; and just as a French victim of the German concentration camps observed that once you have been tortured you remain tortured for the rest of your life, likewise once you have been mugged at knifepoint you remain mugged at knifepoint for the rest of your life.

Also overlooking the church—towering above it, in fact—is a twenty-story block of public housing, to which the ironists of the Housing Department have assigned a name full of rural connotations (the more rural the name given to such blocks, I have discovered, the larger the surrounding area of concrete). I know this particular block quite well, having paid two house calls as a doctor there—accompanied by the riot police to protect me, a very necessary precaution as it transpired. Another of my patients who lives there has repeatedly stabbed herself in the abdomen (five times so far) in an attempt, so far unavailing, to get the Housing Department—whose concern for its tenantry makes the average aristocratic landlord of the eighteenth century look positively sentimental—to move her somewhere less violent. The department has so far stuck to its opinion that she is adequately housed, by which it means that she has four walls and a roof that is impermeable to water, if not to noise or intruders.

So I think I know what Marx meant when he wrote that religion is the sigh of the oppressed, the heart of a heartless world, the opium of the people. Of course, he misidentified the oppressor: in present-day England it is not the bloated plutocrat; it is your drug-dealing, rock-music-playing, baseball-bat-wielding neighbor. And inside this Pentecostal church the pastor addresses a large congregation that knows only too well what it is to live in the shadow of lawlessness, where psychopathy rules. He quotes the case of a seven-year-old girl, placed on a table in a pub by her mother and sold to the highest bidder to abuse as he liked for the night—a story I should be inclined to dismiss as apocryphal were I not to hear equivalently dreadful tales every day in my hospital.

This congregation has one striking feature: it is half black and half white. This is all the more remarkable because, within a few hundred yards, there are pubs that are racially segregated, where a man of the wrong race is as welcome as a blasphemer in Iran. But in the church the races are united by their mutual experience of the moral squalor that surrounds them and by the failure of the public authorities to tackle it in any way, or even to acknowledge its existence.

Once more they seek assurance that their suffering is not without meaning. Congregant after congregant speaks of delinquency and drug taking, of illegitimacy and domestic violence, of criminality and cruelty. They all pray for the conversion of the world and, exulting in its imminent prospect, speak in tongues. This paralinguistic gibberish is uttered with the deepest feeling: it is a catharsis, a release.

The desperate search for order in the midst of anarchy often renders people vulnerable to self-proclaimed authorities who rush in to fill the moral vacuum. A patient of mine recently revealed to me the world of religious cults that flourishes, anonymously and unseen by the rest of us, in the modern city.

My patient was brought to the hospital having very nearly succeeded in a suicide attempt. Suicide was the only means, he thought, by which he could escape the cult that he had embraced and that had embraced him in his times of trouble.

"If I couldn't take the church out of my life," he said, "at least I could take my life out of the church."

He was an intelligent man who had left college to marry young. A few years later his wife left him for another man. He began to drink heavily, and before long he was in a desperate state. He had lost not only his wife and child but his home and his job. His parents disowned him because of his inclination to aggression while drunk. He slid down the social scale very fast and soon found himself in a hostel for men with similar stories.

He was contemplating suicide when he met a young missionary from a cult called the Jesus Army on the street. She took him to a meeting at one of the Army's many communal homes in the city.

The people there seemed deeply contented, happy and laughing all the time; they clapped and sang at their daily meetings. They displayed a profound interest in his welfare and seemed to offer him their unconditional love, which only later was he to recognize as highly conditional, manipulative, and false. When asked to join one of the Army's communal homes, he thought he had found his salvation, and he readily agreed.

Most of the other inmates of the homes had been in similar situations, caused by drink or drugs. And there was no doubt that by joining the Jesus Army they overcame their addictions (thus demonstrating that, pace what many experts aver, addiction is a moral, or at least an existential, question). But life-saving as the Army undoubtedly was, life-enhancing it certainly wasn't.

It attempted to re-create primitive Christian communities in the modern world, taking the Acts of the Apostles as its fundamental text. All goods were held in common, their use determined by the church hierarchs. No one was allowed any money, and even the most minimal expenditure, such as bus fare, had to be justified in theological terms. A request for a bar of chocolate, for instance, would be greeted with the unanswerable question, "What use is it to the redemptive work of the church?" And thus the meaninglessness of precult existence was replaced by the equally dispiriting deep meaningfulness of the most trivial of desires and actions, and the request for a bar of chocolate made the occasion of a battle between the forces of Good and Evil. No entertainment was permitted: no radio, no television, no games, no magazines or books. The church was called the Kingdom, and everything that was not of the church was called the World. Each member had his Shepherd, one stage higher up the hierarchy, who acted as a spy for the church authorities, and from whom nothing was to be hidden. In the Kingdom, no secrets were allowed.

The Army ran its own businesses, including law and medical practices, which outwardly appeared perfectly normal. A patient of the Army's medical practice (funded by the National Health Service) would not notice any difference from any other practice. But the wages paid to the staff of all such businesses and practices, including to doctors and lawyers, went directly into the cult's coffers: the wage bills shown in the accounts were purely nominal. And if an employee of one of the cult's businesses should backslide and opt to leave the Kingdom for the World, he would at once lose his job. Considered by the state to have made himself voluntarily unemployed, he would be offered the most minimal assistance in the way of unemployment benefits, an arrangement that suited the Army's purposes admirably.

Of course, those who enter the Kingdom are encouraged to sever ties with any members of their family who remain in the World. Within a few months, therefore, the new entrant into the Kingdom is enmeshed more thoroughly than any fly in a spider's web. With no money, belongings, job, or family to call his own, it is difficult for a member of the church to leave the Kingdom, whatever his reservations about it. Moreover, if his desire to leave becomes known, he is immediately subject to Chinese thought-reform methods to make him change his mind. He is made to feel a member of Iscariot's party. No one is freed of the cult's power at a stroke: there is always a lingering doubt that perhaps the cult really is the Way, the Truth, and the Life, after all. And the backslider has to believe that the cult is not all bad; otherwise he is forced to conclude that he has been a gullible fool—which all of us understandably are reluctant to do.

Several hundred people live in Jesus Army communities in my city. The most visible signs of the Army's existence are the large buses in which its missionaries trawl the streets for the vulnerable. And it is by no means the only such cult in the city, or the most extreme. Another cult sends its Shepherds directly into the sheep pens themselves: a Shepherd is sent to live at a new adherent's house, and the family is held virtually prisoner by him until adjudged sufficiently indoctrinated to be let out on their own.

Despite its appearance of religious indifference, then, our city has an unexpectedly intense religious life. In an age of relativism, people seek certainty; when violence strikes at random, they seek transcendent meaning; when crime goes unpunished by the secular power, they seek refuge in divine law; when indifference to others reigns, they seek community. Everyone to whom I spoke thought there was some kind of subterranean religious revival in our slums. And as far as the Jesus Army is concerned, the more degraded the World, the richer the harvest for the Kingdom. Like Lenin and Mao, it knows the contradictions should be heightened. As Lenin so charmingly put it, the worse the better.

*1996*

# There's No Damned
# Merit in It

◆  THE BRITISH have a curious attitude towards wealth:
they desire it for themselves but wish to deny it to others. And
so, not surprisingly, there are very few methods of acquiring
wealth of which they approve. Among them is gambling.

When in 1991 the government instituted a National Lottery,
Britons were hooked at once. It seemed to them that buying a
winning ticket was a perfectly legitimate—perhaps the only perfectly legitimate—way of acquiring a lot of money. After all,
everyone who buys a ticket has an equal chance: the effort and
talent usually necessary to accumulate wealth are redundant. A
mental defective has as much chance of winning as a genius, a
slothful spendthrift as an industrious saver. This is what the
British now mean when they talk of equality of opportunity—
though they have not yet quite descended to the level of the
Nigerian author of a self-help manual who, illustrating the need
for hard work as a prerequisite for success, asked rhetorically,
"How can you win a lottery if you do not fill the ticket in?"

Full-page ads in the British press recently trumpeted the immense success of the National Lottery. In its short existence (the
ad boasted) it had raised more money than its longer-estab-
lished equivalents in Japan, France, and Spain, adding that this
success was "not by chance."

No, indeed not: for the British population is universally acknowledged to be the worst-educated of any Western country and, as one commentator wrote, any National Lottery may be construed as a tax on stupidity. In fact, it is as much a tax on hopelessness and impatience as stupidity. The poorest and worst-educated section of the population spends the most, both relatively and absolutely, on lottery tickets. Those who feel that there's no way to escape their predicament through their own efforts are most inclined to resort to the lottery; and every week—soon to be twice a week—the selection of random numbers fans the embers of hope among innumerable people in despair.

The National Lottery is both a form of gambling and a true tax, by means of which the poor pay for the pleasures of the rich. A committee awards the profits to orchestras, art galleries, dance companies—even a theater group composed of radical feminist ex-prisoners. The largest beneficiary so far has been the Royal Opera House, Covent Garden, where a heavily subsidized seat can still cost four hundred dollars. But like all gamblers, lottery ticket buyers think not of where their lost stakes go but of how they will dispose of their winnings.

If the British happily accepted inequalities of wealth as being in the nature of things, indeed as both a precondition and a consequence of a free society, the pernicious effect of the National Lottery upon the morals of the nation would not be so great. It would merely be a bit of fun. But most Britons equate inequalities of wealth with inequity and injustice, and explain away their own urge for sudden enrichment as a kind of poor man's revenge upon a system that allows men to accumulate an unfairly large portion of the world's goods by talent and hard work. Even so, there is more rejoicing in Britain over the bankruptcy of one self-made millionaire than over the enrichment of ninety-nine poor men.

The social legitimacy of gambling in Britain is of relatively recent origin. When I was a child, I heard dark hints that an uncle of mine had wasted his substance upon the ponies; he had also gone, in the words of *Nicholas Nickleby*'s Mr. Mantalini, to the demnition bow-wows and had wagered—and lost—a fortune upon them. Off-track betting offices (delicately called Turf Accountants in the early days of their legality to give them an air of professional respectability) were illegal until 1963. Indeed, my first contact with gambling as a child was in my local barber shop, which ran an illegal book. The barber would interrupt the progress of the clippers down my neck (I can feel the tingling still) to rush to the telephone, down which, sotto voce, he spoke an incomprehensible jargon—nine to four on, the going's soft, three to one each way, and so forth.

Meanwhile, I was left to contemplate the mysterious little purple-and-cream envelopes on the shelf in front of me, which my older and wiser brother later explained to me contained condoms. Thus sex and gambling came alike to symbolize for me the illicit and the forbidden. Even now, sex and gambling have a connection in my mind: many of my younger female patients, explaining the existence of an illegitimate child or two, use expressions universally current hereabouts: "I caught pregnant," or "I caught for a boy." Unavoidably, an image rises to my mind's eye of a spinning roulette wheel revolving ever more slowly, until the ball settles in a compartment that bears not a number but the word "boy" or "girl."

Few social inhibitions against gambling remain: the Yellow Pages now list casino and bingo halls in the same category as veterans' associations, political clubs, and voluntary societies to provide amusement for the elderly. Bookmakers, however, have a section to themselves: a considerably longer section than the one immediately next to it listing booksellers.

Apart from the National Lottery and scratch cards, which have turned every supermarket, convenience store, and gasoline station in the country into a gambling hall, there are three main types of establishments for gambling in the city, each with its own clientele, which I list in ascending order of unsociability: the bingo hall, the betting shop, and the casino.

The bingo industry expanded in the sixties, and what had formerly been a game played once a year at the seaside while on holiday became the focal point of the social lives of hundreds of thousands of Britons. No town of any size is without several bingo halls, almost always converted cinemas with names like Ritzy, Rex, or Roxy. Like raspberries, which today are imported year-round from the uttermost parts of the earth so that we should never be without them, bingo is now perennial. Come rain or shine, the players may be seen arriving at the bingo hall as punctually as alcoholics arriving at the bars for opening time.

Pink and apple-green neon lights festoon the buildings on the outside, lending an air of cheap and gaudy gaiety. But the atmosphere inside, in the Art Deco auditorium, is quite different. Demographically the crowd resembles the Russian Orthodox congregations of Khrushchev's day: preponderantly elderly women, with a high concentration of widows and walking sticks. All the men—not more than a fifth of the total—are old; a glance shows that many suffer from that former bane of the English working class, chronic bronchitis.

No wonder: the air is thick with cigarette smoke, so thick that I feel the back of my throat seizing up, as if in a gas attack. My eyes begin to sting. I haven't seen or breathed air like this since my childhood, when the London November pea-souper meant that men had to walk in front of buses to guide them on their way, and it was too dark for me to go to school.

Medical correctness hasn't reached the bingo hall yet. It is with a certain pleasure—no, joy—that I watch women with the physiques and mobility of beached whales refresh themselves constantly (as they mark their cards) with large piles of cholesterol-raising fried foods and large volumes of tepid, watery English beer. Tomorrow, of course, they'll go to their doctors and tell them that, however hard they try, they just can't seem to lose weight: they only have to look at food, and the pounds go on.

I'm recognized at once as someone who doesn't belong here, both because of my comparative youth and my ignorance of what to do and how to play. An elderly man, a widower, takes me under his wing and shows me the ropes. He advises me to take only two cards at a time: a tyro like me couldn't manage more. He is happy to induct the younger generation into the bingo culture, content that bingo will live after him.

To my shame, I see around me old ladies of the type I would normally test for Alzheimer's disease were they to appear in my hospital sitting, with eight, ten, and twelve cards that they mark simultaneously and with aplomb. They even have time for humorous remarks to their neighbors. They take in up to 180 numbers at a single glance, and mark off the numbers as they are called with so little effort that they must have memorized to perfection all the cards. Could it be that the mental exercise, hour after hour and day after day, of marking the cards keeps old brains young? Could it be that the hope, repeated every day, of winning tonight's jackpot—an all-expenses-paid week for two in Tenerife or a complete set of Le Creuset saucepans—is what keeps neuronal degeneration at bay?

The young man, dressed in a golden satin tuxedo, who calls out the numbers randomly generated by the computer tries desperately to infuse the process with human interest: some numbers seem to surprise and others to amuse him. A few of the numbers are known by their nicknames: legs 11, for example. The contestants greet them with murmurs of appreciation, as if they were old friends.

Before long, someone calls "Bingo!" I and all the others have lost, but the winner's triumph seems to arouse no envy, only genuine pleasure and even congratulation: after all, it could have been any one of us, and next time it probably will be. As Lord Melbourne, the nineteenth-century British prime minister, put it when explaining the advantages of the Order of the Garter, the highest British chivalric order, which was then awarded exclusively to members of the upper aristocracy, "There's no damned merit in it." Triumph without merit: surely the dream of half of mankind and three-quarters of the British.

The first couple of rounds of bingo just about hold my interest, but the charm soon wears thin and will evaporate into tedium. As if sensing my incipient boredom after the completion of the second round, the man who calls the numbers declares that he has an important announcement to make: it is Beryl's birthday. Applause breaks out, and the man leads us all in singing "Happy Birthday" to Beryl. He asks Beryl to come forward and collect the champagne—actually, a cheap imitation—with which the ever-solicitous management is pleased to present her on this auspicious occasion. More applause.

Everyone is touched. Beryl takes a bow, as if she had achieved something. In fact, the bingo hall celebrates at least one birthday every day, sometimes as many as five or six, because to join the club (you cannot by law walk straight off the street into a bingo hall) you have to have given the management your date of birth. The computer spews out birthday invitations to members to come celebrate in the hall; since the club has more than three thousand members, it finds at least one celebrant per day. Yet each birthday, like each bottle of fake champagne, kindles not just delight but surprise, and every birthday can be applauded with gusto because there is no damned merit in it: everyone has a birthday.

Beryl slides back into anonymity after her cometlike blaze across the firmament of the bingo hall, and the serious business of the day is resumed. I am now completely bored.

"How often do you come?" I ask my bingo mentor. "Three or four times a week," he replies. "But I'm not a fanatic, like some of them."

"Is that common?" I ask. "Yes," he replies. "It's somewhere to go for them and something to do."

Life, in this view, is seventy years of tedium sandwiched between two eternities of oblivion. I leave the bingo hall with a strange amalgam of thoughts and feelings: for the hall offers many elderly people the simulacrum, at least, of a social life, and bingo, apart from those few who become so obsessed with it that they waste their entire income upon it, is harmless. The atmosphere in the hall is warm, welcoming, reassuringly womb-like, and the players are decent folk intent on a little fun. But the repetitious mindlessness of the game seems to speak of a mental and spiritual void that, given the age of the players, has evidently been present in England for many years. We have a land not of bread and circuses but of potato chips and bingo.

The betting shop, by contrast, is as exclusively a male pre-serve as London clubs used to be. My hospital being in an area of high unemployment (24 percent, in fact), there are several betting shops within a few hundred yards of its main entrance. I have never seen a female customer in any of them, and most of the customers are poor and unemployed. You would hardly have to be a revolutionary Marxist to observe how the poor are fleeced—with their own eager cooperation, of course—of what little money they have by the possessors of capital, in this case the owners of the betting shops, which are affiliated with one of two large chains. The poor, as a sixteenth-century German bishop once remarked, are a gold mine—though curiously, among my patients I meet only those who claim to win on the horses, never to lose.

Inside the betting shop, whose windows onto the street are always opaque (a residuum of the old taboo against betting), knots of men gather to discuss local gossip and hot racing tips of the day. Arguments break out about the relative merits of Kevin's Slipper and Aladdin's Cave for the 3:30 at Utoxeter. They are the kind of men I know well from my medical prac-tice: men whose chronic backaches prevent them from ever again undertaking gainful employment, but who are capable of surprising feats of physical endurance in the right circum-stances, such as a pub brawl.

Attached to the walls are today's racing papers. Middle-aged men read them with a studious air, peering at them with donnish half-moon spectacles. I find it rather difficult to follow the technical language, as in this description of a horse: "Dancing Alone: Out of a winning sprinter but no sign of ability for Pip Payne at two when well beaten in maidens and a seller (well backed for the latter); off track since and first run for a new stable." The dog-racing language, terser, is almost as opaque: "Well-placed on the stagger, sees out the trip," or "Operates well enough from 'red,' must respect."

Even the forms on which the bets are placed require technical knowledge of the different types of bet: the Round Robin, the Patent, the Yankee and Super Yankee, the Tricast, and the Alphabet. The betting shop is not so much a form of entertainment as what American social anthropologists would call a culture. It is a way of life: up and down the country thousands of people spend the entire day, the entire week, in the betting shop. There are never fewer than fifteen people in the shops I have been into, and, since there are at least two hundred such shops in the city, there must be at least three thousand people in betting shops at any given moment in our city of just under a million, or about 1 percent of the adult male population.

Overhead televisions relay the races as they happen: a cacophony of competing commentaries, mixed with announcements over the public address system advertising new types of bets—not just on horses or dogs—with prizes of $150,000 for a stake of only $1.50. You can bet on anything, it seems: the results of individual soccer and boxing matches, the forthcoming election, the outcome of a debate in the House of Commons, the number of winners on track number 3 this evening at Small Heath Dog Racing Stadium, and even on the likelihood of the end of the world happening by the year 2000, though presumably collection in the event of being right would in this instance prove difficult.

A man in a camel hair coat and with a spiv's greased mus-

tache approaches me and points to one of the television screens:
a horse is winning the race by a mile. My interlocutor holds
himself as a cut above the rabble in the corner who are smoking
dope (the center of crack dealing in a nearby area is the local
betting shop). That is why he has approached me.

"That's a good horse," he says, with an air of profound cog-
itation. "He won like that last time out. I'm thinking of backing
him for the Classic. What do you think?"

"I . . . er . . ." I'm not sure what to say: he's being friendly
and wants to start a long and learned conversation about White
Admiral's chances in the Classic, but it won't take him long to
discover that I know nothing about it, that I am a complete
stranger, a foreigner, in his country. "Personally, I bet at random," I reply and wish him good luck—probably considered
the height of ill taste in these circles. A winning ticket in the lottery is good luck; a win on the horses is the result of long study
of the form and superior perspicacity. The study of the form is
the betting man's philology, philosophy, science, and literary
criticism all rolled into one. Such a betting man invests immense
effort and long periods of time in cogitating permutations of
variables—the going, the handicaps, past performance, the
jockeys, the position at the start, and so forth—as alchemists
devoted themselves with useless pedantry to the transmutation
of base metal into gold. And how many betting widows do I
meet in the hospital, who hardly see their husbands while the
betting shops are open!

The third type of gambling establishment in our city is the
casino. There are two within walking distance of my house, and
I am now a member of the more salubrious of them. Sometimes,
when I go for a walk, I pass the prostitutes who solicit nightly
on my street corner, and I continue past the casino, a renovated
Victorian building with a decor of bordello pink with a minor
Turkish pasha's chandeliers. In the parking lot, at all times of
the day and night, Jaguars and BMWs congregate, and their
owners always seem to have one last conversation on the mo-

bile phone before going in to the roulette tables. They are businessmen with money to throw away: to lose a few thousand in front of their peers and retain their sangfroid brings them prestige. They must be doing well if losing a sum like that within a few minutes hardly affects them.

They are not the only customers. Smaller fry abound also, dressed usually with a shabby gentility, who come to stake their barely disposable income on the tables. No one is excluded: the casino is a democratic institution.

There are five casinos in our city, and the law says you must have been a member for forty-eight hours before you enter one of them. I show my passport and am told the following rules of membership: 1) No T-shirts; 2) No trainers (i.e., sneakers).

I promise to comply, and two days later I receive my membership card and a letter from something called the Membership Committee, which sounds like an invention by G. K. Chesterton: "The Membership Committee is pleased to inform you that you have been elected to life membership of the . . . Club." I can't help feeling flattered: though, as I discover later, more than 3 percent of the population of our city, or thirty thousand people, are likewise life members of this one casino alone. As the manager of another casino put it to me, however, the real question is, how many of the members are active? This is precisely the question churches ask: baptisms and funerals are all very well, but what happens in between?

Casinos haven't changed very much down the ages. Everything to be observed in the casino of which I am a life member is to be found in a novella by Dostoevsky written in 1866. Casino gambling is a solitary vice, asocial and atomistic: I watch a man despairingly fling sixty dollars to the croupier, who picks it up and inserts it into the bowels of the table with lizard quickness, returning him some chips. Within two minutes he has won—and lost—sixteen hundred dollars. Like Grandmama in Dostoevsky's *The Gambler*, he has won twice in succession on a single number; and like the onlookers when the protagonist of *The Gambler* wins an immense sum, I want desperately to urge the man to go, to leave while he is winning. But no; in another minute he has lost everything. And, as Dostoevsky remarks, no other human activity provides so many and such strong emotions in so short a space of time: fevered hope, despair, elation, joy, misery, excitement, disappointment. This is crack cocaine without the chemicals.

Widows with large solitaire diamond rings walk round the tables with their little notepads, supplied by the casino, recording numbers and trying to work out a system. There is no system, of course, and never has been, not since the women in *The Gambler* walked round the tables with their little notepads, supplied by the casino, trying to work out a system. . . .

The best customers of casinos have changed: they used to be Jews, then Greeks, then Chinese, and now increasingly they are Indian. But the roulette table dissolves all racial and social barriers: the Muslim and the Hindu, the businessman and the unskilled worker, are rendered brothers and equals by the spin of the wheel. If the lion and the lamb could play roulette, they'd lie down together in perfect peace.

I watch a man in his fifties, obviously not rich and dressed shabbily, buy chips for forty dollars. He loses them all in a few minutes. He takes twenty dollars from his pocket and loses it even quicker. He searches his pockets and comes up with ten dollars. When he has lost that, he is penniless. Despair and disgust—with himself, with the world—are written on his face: but he'll be back, probably tomorrow, or whenever his pension arrives.

I went to a meeting of Gamblers Anonymous, held in a dismal and cold community center. There are five such groups in the city, the same number as casinos. Most of the gamblers there had been in trouble with the law: they had diverted funds from the companies for which they worked; they had lied, cheated, stolen, and defrauded even their own relatives and loved ones to fund their habits. There was practically no depth to which they had not sunk, that they might recover their losses with one last coup.

"As an organization, Gamblers Anonymous has no position on gambling," said one of them, a man "addicted" to slot machines. He had played them up to eight hours a day before coming—or being forced by the threat of prosecution for embezzlement—to his senses. "Millions of people gamble without coming to harm."

"But should gambling be officially encouraged or discouraged?"

Silence.

*1997*

# Choosing to Fail

⬧ THE CHILDREN OF IMMIGRANTS from the Indian subcontinent make up a quarter of all British medical students,
twelve times their proportion in the general population. They
are likewise overrepresented in the law, science, and economics
faculties of our universities. Among the Indian immigrants who
arrived in the country with next to nothing, moreover, there are
now reportedly some thousands of millionaires.

Despite its reputation for being ossified and class-ridden,
then, Britain is still a country in which social mobility is possible—provided, of course, that a belief that Britain is an ossified
and class-ridden society doesn't completely stifle personal effort. It is the mind, not society, that forges the manacles that
keep people enchained to their misfortunes.

But where there can be upward social mobility, there can be
mobility in the opposite direction. And the children of Indian
immigrants are dividing into two groups: a segment that
chooses the upward path, and a segment that chooses descent
into the underclass.

Sometimes this division occurs within the very same family.
For example, last week I met two prisoners of Indian origin, all
of whose siblings had gone to college and become either professional or business people. Their brothers and sisters had chosen
law, medicine, or commerce: they had chosen heroin, burglary,

and the intimidation of witnesses. The financial status of their parents could not explain their choices: the father of one was a bus driver, the second a successful travel agent, and both fathers had been not only willing and able but longing to fund their higher education, had they wanted it.

I first noticed signs of a developing Indian underclass a few years ago in the prison in which I work, where there has been an inexorable rise in both the absolute and relative numbers of prisoners of Indian origin. In the last eight years the proportion of Indian prisoners has more than doubled, and if it continues to rise at the same rate for the next eight years, prisoners of Indian origin will have surpassed their proportion in the general population. As the proportion of Indians in the age group most likely to be imprisoned has not increased, demography doesn't explain this shift.

Eight years ago, most of the Indian prisoners were guilty of white-collar crime, such as tax evasion: not the kind of thing to make you fear to walk the streets at night. All that has changed now. Burglary, street robbery, car theft, and drug-dealing, with their attendant violence, have become so commonplace among them that mention of their seriousness elicits only a bored shrug of incomprehension. Why make a fuss over anything so ordinary as a street robbery? Everyone does it. Liberals to whom I have mentioned the phenomenon applaud it as representing the assimilation and acculturation of an ethnic minority into the wider society.

They are right to view this development as a cultural phenomenon. There are many other outward signs of the acculturation of Indians into the lower depths. Although their complexions are by no means well adapted to it, tattooing is fast on the increase among them. Other adornments—a ring through the eyebrow or the nose, for example—are membership badges of the clan. Gold in the front teeth, either replacing an entire incisor or framing it with a rim of gold, is virtually diagnostic of heroin addiction and criminality. Such decorative dentistry is imitative of the black underclass and is intended as a signal of both success and dangerousness.

Young Indians have adopted, too, the graceless manners of the class to which they aspire to belong. They now walk with the same self-assured vulpine lope as their white compatriots, not merely as a way of locomotion but as a means of communicating threat. Like the whites, they shave their heads to reveal the scars upon their scalps, the wounds of the underclass war of each against all.

They have made the gestures and postures of their white and black mentors their own. When a member of the developing Indian underclass consults me, he slouches in the chair at so acute an angle to the floor that I would not have thought it possible, let alone comfortable, for a man to retain the position. But it isn't comfort he is after: he is making a statement of disrespect in the face of what he supposes to be authority. His fragile ego demands that he dominate all social interactions and submit to no convention.

He also adopts a facial expression unique to the British underclass. Asked a question, he replies with an arching and curling of half his upper lip, part snarl, part sneer. Expressive both of disdain and of menace, it is by no means easy to achieve, as I proved to myself by trying it without success in the mirror. It simultaneously demands, "Why are you asking me that?" and warns: "Don't push me too far." It is the response to all questions, no matter how innocuous: for in a world in which every contact is a jostling for power, it is best to establish straightaway that you are not to be trifled with.

The growing Indian underclass adheres to the values of the white underclass—values that are at once shallow and intensely held. For example, I was once a witness in a murder trial of four young Indians accused of killing their companion in the course of a quarrel over the brand of sneakers he wore. They mocked him because his footwear was not of the latest fashionable brand, and eventually he lashed out at them in frustration. In the ensuing fight, they killed him and left his body at the entrance to his apartment building.

Illegitimate birth has now made its appearance among Indians. Where once it was almost unknown for an Indian to have a child out of wedlock, it is no longer even rare. The Indians have reached the 5 percent level from which the rate of illegitimacy in the home population grew exponentially in the 1960s, and there is no reason why, in a few years' time, they should not reach the national average of 33 percent, for when history repeats itself, it is usually at an accelerated pace.

At first, only Indian men produced illegitimate children; some of those who had submitted to an arranged marriage kept a woman, usually white but sometimes black, in concubinage elsewhere in the city. Often the concubine—knowing nothing of the man's background, biography, or culture—had no idea that he was married. She would then have his child under the disastrously mistaken impression that it would bind his hitherto inconstant attention more firmly to her.

More recently, however, the bearing of illegitimate children has spread to young Indian women. An Indian girl runs away from home after a long period of conflict with her parents over makeup, dress, the hour at which she may return from nightclubs, and so on. She soon falls into the embrace of a young man—white, black, or Indian—all too willing to prove his masculinity by impregnating her and then, of course, abandoning her.

From this experience she learns nothing. She is lonely, in need of male company and—in the predatory world in which she now finds herself—male protection. The cycle repeats itself until she has three children by three different fathers, though by the end of her reproductive career she remains as isolated and friendless as the day she left home. One might have supposed that young Indian women would go to almost any lengths to avoid so terrible and predictable a fate. Not so: they are increasingly embracing it as if it were enviable. Though their numbers are as yet small, they are the party of the future.

How has an Indian underclass formed so quickly? And why has a proportion of the Indian population embraced the life of the underclass with such apparent enthusiasm? These are important questions: the answers we give to them both reflect and determine our entire social philosophy.

The liberal would no doubt argue that the formation of an Indian underclass is the inevitable response to poverty and prejudice and the despair they evoke. With the path to advancement blocked by a racist society, young Indians drop out of school, shave their heads, tattoo their skin, inject themselves with heroin, father children out of wedlock, and commit crimes.

But if they are caught in a vicious cycle of poverty and prejudice, why do so many of their compatriots succeed, and succeed triumphantly? Why do the children of successful Indian parents also choose the underclass way of life? And why may stunning success and abject failure so often occur in the same family?

The explanation must surely involve conscious human choice. Young Indians do not join the underclass through inadvertence or by force of parental example, as young whites—now into the third generation of this way of life in England—often do. In no case known to me have the parents of young Indians approved of their children's choices or been other than horrified by them.

Such parents frequently consult me after they have watched with growing dismay one or all of their children take the primrose path to urban perdition. For example, a taxi driver who sometimes drives me home begged me to talk to his son. The driver was, of course, exactly the kind of petit bourgeois who, when not actually hated by intellectuals, is despised as an uninteresting and unimaginative menial, whose dream is what they have mocked for so long—respectable independence. He is therefore beyond the pale of sympathetic understanding: for the

small man is to be defended only so long as he consents to remain a victim, in need of publicly funded ministrations.

The driver's son (alone of his five children) had taken to the
needle, and in doing so had caused him grief beyond his powers
to express it in English. His son now stole from the family
home, lied, cheated, cajoled, threatened, and even used violence
to extract enough money from his parents and siblings for his
drugs. The father didn't want to turn him out of his house or
over to the police; but neither did he want to work his long
hours merely to supply his son with the drugs that might one
day kill him.

I asked the son—complete with gold front dentistry, baggy
trousers, baseball cap worn backward even in my consulting
room, and the latest sneakers—why he had started to take
heroin.

"There's nothing else to do on the street," he replied.
"That's society, what it puts you in." His attribution of his own
choice to society was not unusual. I asked him whether he had
not known the dangers of heroin before he took it.

"Yes," he replied.

"But you took it all the same?"

"Yes."

"Why?"

"No offense, doctor, but the people who gave it to me know
more about life than you do. They know what it's about, what
it's like on the street. And they're not prejudiced or racists."

He was under the influence of the idea that some aspects of
reality are more real than others: that the seedy side of life is
more genuine, more authentic, than the refined and cultured
side—and certainly more glamorous than the bourgeois and respectable side. This idea could be said to be the fundamental
premise of modern popular culture. As for his reference to racism, it was clearly intended as an all-purpose self-justification,
since his own brother was now a tolerably successful lawyer.

Another set of parents consulted me about their son, eighteen, who had chosen a similar path. Both his parents had white-collar jobs and were neither rich nor poor. At about thirteen, their son had started to play hooky from school, smoke marijuana, drink alcohol, stay out all night, and brush against the law. On the few occasions he attended school, he argued with the teachers and was eventually expelled for attacking one of them. He left home at sixteen to live with his pregnant girlfriend, whose name he tattooed on his forearm as a preliminary to abandoning her altogether, having discovered that he was not yet ready for a life of domesticity. Falling in with drug dealers, he now lived an itinerant life, dodging the law, indulging in crack, and occasionally ending up in the hospital with an overdose, taken not so much to kill himself as to seek temporary sanctuary or asylum from the consequences of his own style of life.

The father said that his son had now become exactly what he had hoped he would never be: a member of the English underclass. He had watched him descend into barbarism, acutely aware of his own impotence to prevent it. The Spanish Inquisition could hardly have invented a worse torture for him.

His son was of high intelligence and had once been expected to do well by his teachers. I asked him why he had had such a rooted objection to school.

"I wanted to earn some money."

"What for?"

"To have a good time. And clothes."

The clothes he wanted were the inelegant but expensive (and ever changing) uniform of slum youth. The good time consisted entirely of attendance at clubs with thousands of like-minded young people. There was nothing in his conception of the Good Life other than constant excitement and instant gratification. His idea of paradise was life as MTV.

"Did you not think you had something still to learn?"

"No."

In other words, he considered himself perfectly formed and

complete at thirteen. Precociously adolescent, he was trapped in immaturity. In a sense he was a victim: not of poverty or racism or a vicious cycle of deprivation but of a popular culture that first attracted and then engulfed him, but always through the mediation of his own choices.

There is a dreadful predictability to the explanation the young Indians give for their descent into the underclass, identical to those their white counterparts give. "I was easily led," they say. "I fell in with the wrong crowd." I have heard these things said hundreds of times. They pretend not to notice the self-exculpatory nature of these answers, whose truth they expect me to accept without further examination.

"Why, if you are so easily led," I ask them, "were your parents not able to lead you? And did you not choose the wrong crowd rather than fall into it like a stone?"

As to why they started to take heroin, their standard reason is the one that Sir Edmund Hillary gave when asked why he climbed Everest: "Because it was there." But in the case of heroin, "there" is "everywhere": "Heroin's everywhere," they say, as if it were the air they could not help but breathe in.

"Are you telling me that every last person in your area takes heroin?"

"No, of course not."

"Then you chose to, didn't you?"

"Yes, I suppose so."

"Why?"

Like the whites, they go to some length to provide an answer other than that they liked it and found pleasure in doing what they knew they ought not to do.

"My grandfather died," or "My girlfriend left me," or "I was in prison": never do they avow a choice or a conscious decision. And yet they know that what they are saying is untrue: for they grasp the point immediately when I tell them that my grandfather, too, died, yet I do not take heroin, as indeed the great majority of people whose grandfathers have died do not.

In fact, they have assimilated to the local cultural and intellectual climate: a climate in which the public explanation of behavior, including their own, is completely at variance with all human experience. This is the lie that is at the heart of our society, the lie that encourages every form of destructive self-indulgence to flourish: for while we ascribe our conduct to pressures from without, we obey the whims that well up from within, thereby awarding ourselves carte blanche to behave as we choose. Thus we feel good about behaving badly.

This is not to deny that social factors in upbringing influence the way people think and make decisions. If the negligent and sometimes brutal incompetence of so much white British parenting (solicitously justified by liberal intellectuals and subsidized by the welfare state) explains the perpetuation and expansion of the white British underclass, if not its origins, could it be that the severity and rigidity of Indian upbringing, combined with British culture's siren song of self-gratification, explain the development of an Indian underclass? The fact that the Muslim population has a crime rate six times that of the Hindu and three times that of the Sikh suggests that it could, for the Muslim culture of the subcontinent has in general much greater difficulty compromising creatively with Western culture than the other two religions have. This startling difference is a further argument against those who would see in the development of an Indian underclass an inevitable response to racial prejudice: for it is surely unlikely that the racially prejudiced would trouble themselves to distinguish between Muslims, Sikhs, and Hindus. Muslim parents are more reluctant than Sikh and Hindu parents to recognize that their children, having been brought up in a very different cultural environment from that in which they grew up, inevitably depart from their own traditional ways and aspire to a different way of life. While many Muslim parents send their daughters out of the country at the age of twelve to prevent them from becoming infected with local ideas (but as the Jesuits would tell them, it is already too late—they should send their daughters away at seven), very few Sikhs do so and no Hindus at all.

Parental inflexibility is an invitation to adolescent rebellion, and so it is hardly surprising that, in the developing Indian underclass, Muslims should predominate so strongly. But there are more ways of rebelling than one, and alas, rebellious Indian adolescents have an antinomian example to hand in the shape of the preexisting British underclass. The popular culture tells them that to spit in the eye of everyone they can reach is a sign of moral election—insofar as it is possible to be morally elect in a world without moral judgment. The underclass life offers them the prospect of freedom without responsibility, whereas their parents offer them only responsibility without freedom. They are left to discover for themselves that the exercise of liberty requires virtue if it is not to turn into a nightmare.

The development of an Indian underclass in Britain is a matter of greater significance than the numbers involved might suggest. For it is not a quasi-mechanical response to economic conditions, to racial prejudice, or to any other form of oppression of the kind beloved of liberal social engineers. It is a refutation of the infinitely pernicious Marxist maxim, which has corrupted so much of intellectual life, that "it is not the consciousness of men that determines their being, but on the contrary, their social being that determines their consciousness." Men—even adolescent boys—think: and the content of what they think determines in large part the course of their lives.

*2000*

# Free to Choose

LAST WEEK a middle-aged man was brought to my hospital in a desperate condition. He had discharged himself from a mental hospital against medical advice three weeks before; arriving home, he had found the prospect of life with his wife no more inviting than that of life in the wards of an asylum. He had taken himself to the center of the city, where he camped out in the open in a small public garden next to a luxury hotel. There he stayed, eating nothing and drinking little, until he was eventually found unconscious and so dehydrated that the blood had thickened and clotted in one of his legs, which was gangrenous and therefore had to be amputated.

What story could better illustrate the supposedly callous indifference and cruel individualism of our society than that of a man left nearly to die in the middle of the city, next to a hotel with rooms at two hundred dollars a night, in the full gaze not only of the guests but of thousands of his fellow citizens, all for the lack of a little water?

But other interpretations of the story are possible. Perhaps the thousands of passersby who saw the unfortunate man as he declined slowly towards the verge of death were so accustomed to the idea that the state would (and should) step in that they felt no personal duty to do something on the man's behalf. One does not, after all, pay half one's income in taxes in order to assume individual responsibility for the welfare of one's neighbors. One's taxes are supposed to ensure not only oneself, but everyone else, against neglect. Just as no one is guilty when everyone is, no one is responsible when everyone is.

Then again, perhaps the passersby thought the man was only exercising his right to live as he chose, as championed by those early advocates for deinstitutionalization of the insane, psychiatrists Thomas Szasz and R. D. Laing. Who are we to judge in a free country how people should live? Apart from a slight measure of untidiness, the man created no public nuisance. Perhaps the passersby thought, as they tolerated him nearly to death, that he was merely doing his own thing, and in the conflict between the imperative to act the good Samaritan and the imperative to respect the autonomy of others, the latter prevailed. In the modern climate, after all, rights always trump duties.

Still, the existence of people who live on the street, or who are of no fixed abode, is generally taken, at least by liberals, as an indication not of our society's commitment to freedom but of its injustice, inequity, and indifference to human suffering. There is no subject more likely than homelessness to produce calls for the government to intervene to put an end to the scandal; and no subject is better suited to that most pleasurable of human activities, compassionate handwringing.

Yet as is so often the case with social problems, the precise nature and location of the alleged injustice, inequity, and indifference to suffering become unclear when things are looked at close up rather than through the lens of generalizations, either ethical ("no one in an affluent society should be homeless") or statistical ("homelessness rises in times of unemployment").

In the first place, it is far from evident that our society in the abstract is indifferent to homelessness. Indeed, homelessness is the source of employment for not negligible numbers of the middle classes. The poor, wrote a sixteenth-century German bishop, are a gold mine; and so, it turns out, are the homeless.

For example, in one hostel for the homeless that I visited, located in a rather grand but disused and deconsecrated Victorian church, I discovered that there were ninety-one residents and forty-one staff members, only a handful of whom had any direct contact with the objects of their ministrations.

The homeless slept in dormitories in which there was no privacy whatever. There was a rank smell that every doctor recognizes (but never records in the medical notes) as the smell of homelessness. And then, passing along a corridor and through a door with a combination lock to prevent untoward intrusions, one suddenly entered another world: the sanitized, air-conditioned (and airtight) world of the bureaucracy of compassion.

The number of offices, all computerized, was astonishing. The staff, dressed in smart casual clothes, were absorbed in their tasks, earnestly peering into their computer screens, printing documents, and rushing off for urgent consultations with one another. The amount of activity was impressive, the sense of purpose evident; it took some effort to recall the residents I had encountered as I entered the hostel, scattered in what had been the churchyard, who were swaying if upright and snoring if horizontal, surrounded by empty cans and plastic bottles of 9 percent alcohol cider (which permits the highest alcohol-to-dollar ratio available in England at the moment). Nero fiddled while Rome burned, and the hostel administrators made pie charts while the residents drank themselves into oblivion.

There are twenty-seven hostels listed in the Yellow Pages of our city's telephone directory, and many known to me are unlisted. Some of the hostels are smaller and have fewer staff members than the one I have described; but clearly, some hundreds of people—and possibly as many as a couple of thousand—owe their jobs to the homeless. Besides the employees of the hostels themselves, there are social workers and housing officers for them; there is a special clinic with doctors and nurses for them; and there is a psychiatric team of five, headed by a doctor at a salary of $100,000, that cares for the mentally ill homeless. The doctor is an academic and spends half his time on research; I would personally be prepared to bet quite a lot of money that the scale of the problems of the mentally ill homeless in our city will not decline in proportion to the number of papers he writes or the number of academic conferences he attends.

Since our city is in no way untypical and contains approximately 2 percent of the British population, it is a fair assumption that not far short of fifty thousand people earn their living from the homeless in these islands. This may be a sign of inefficiency, of incompetence, and even of profligacy, but scarcely of indifference in the liberal's sense of the word; and compassion for some is undoubtedly a good career move.

Still, it might be argued that all this activity is but a Band-Aid to a fracture or aspirin to malaria. By the work of charitable and governmental agencies, society assuages its conscience and turns a blind eye to the fundamental causes of the plight of the homeless.

It is accepted as axiomatic, of course, that the plight of the homeless is a desperate one. Who can look at the physical surroundings of most hostels without revulsion, or contemplate the food from their soup kitchens without nausea? Does it not follow that those who spend their lives in these conditions are the most hapless of beings and ought to be rescued?

As a child, whenever I saw a gentleman of the road who dressed a little like Tolstoy playing at peasantry, with his tangled grey beard, muttering his imprecations and calling down his curses upon the world, I did not pity him but on the contrary thought of him as a superior kind of being, a little like God of the Old Testament, in fact, or at least like His prophets. These men were schizophrenic, no doubt, and I soon enough lost the preposterous idea that their strange behavior was the consequence of esoteric wisdom available to them but not, say, to my parents. And even in these days of community care, so called, of the mad, the schizophrenic make up only a minority of the homeless; but I have learned by another route that the homeless are not merely to be pitied, like injured hedgehogs or birds with broken wings, to be healed by a little well-meaning intervention by professional helpers, *de haut en bas*. The homeless suffer, all right, but not always in the way or for the reasons we imagine.

A fifty-five-year-old man who had spent half a lifetime traveling from hostel to hostel round the country was admitted to my ward suffering from delirium tremens. His condition then was indeed pitiable; he was terrified of the small animals that he saw crawling from the bedclothes and the walls, his tremor was so profound that he could not stand, for him to hold a cup or cutlery was out of the question, and looking at his bed one might have supposed that a prolonged and serious earthquake was taking place. He was incontinent of urine and had to have a catheter inserted; sweat poured from him as rain drips from the foliage of a rain forest. It took a week of baths to clear him of the smell of homelessness and a week of tranquilizers to calm him. Surely, you would have thought, any way of life was preferable to the way of life that led to this.

Once restored to health, however, he was by no means the pitiful creature he had been only shortly before. On the contrary: he was a man of intelligence, wit, and charm. There was a roguish twinkle in his eye. Nor had he emerged from the kind of family background commonly (but erroneously) supposed to necessitate a dismal future without prospects: his sister was a senior nurse, and his brother was a director of a large public company. He himself had done well at school but had insisted upon leaving at the earliest opportunity, running away to sea. After an early marriage, the birth of a son, and the irksome assumption of a mortgage, he longed for the restoration of his premarital freedom and rediscovered the joys of irresponsibility: he deserted his wife and child and worked no more but rather spent his days drinking.

Before long he had descended the housing scale from apartment to rented room to hostel bed. But he regretted nothing: he said his life had been fuller of incident, interest, and amusement than if he had kept to the narrow path of virtue that leads straight to a pension. I asked him when he was fully recovered to write a short article describing an incident from his past, and he chose his first night ever at a hostel. It was raining hard, and a line of bums waited outside the Salvation Army for admittance. A fight broke out, and one man pulled another by the hair. There was a ripping sound, and the assailant was left holding his victim's scalp.

Far from so appalling him that he resolved at once to reform, my patient was intrigued. His temperament was that of a sensation seeker; he hated boredom, routine, and being ruled by others. He joined the large fraternity of wanderers who live on the margins of the law, ride trains without tickets, taunt the burghers of small towns with their outrageous behavior, infuriate magistrates by confronting them with their own impotence, and frequently wake a couple of hundred miles from where they started out in the evening, without any recollection of how they got there. In short, the life of the chronic homeless is one of ups as well as downs.

Of course, the longer it is lived, the harder it is to give up, not only because of habit but because it grows progressively more difficult for the person who lives it to reinsert himself into normal society. A fifty-five-year-old man might have some difficulty explaining to a prospective employer what he had been doing for the last twenty-seven years. With age, however, the physical hardships of the existence grow more difficult to sustain, and my patient said to me that he thought that unless he gave up the wandering, he might not have very long to live. I agreed with him.

I found him a hostel for alcoholics who had dried out and who had undertaken not to drink again. At first he did very well: he kept his appointments with me and was neatly turned out. He even appeared happy and contented. He was surprisingly well read, and we had pleasant literary conversations together.

After about three months of this stable existence, my patient confessed that he was growing restless again. Yes, he was happy, and yes, he felt physically well—much better, in fact, than he had felt in years. But something was missing from his life. It was the excitement: the chases down the street by policemen, the appearances in the magistrates' courts, the sheer warmth and companionship of the barroom. He even missed that important question with which he used to wake each morning: Where am I? Waking in the same place each day was not nearly as much fun.

And sure enough, he missed his next appointment, and I never saw him again.

This is not by any means an isolated case: far from it. People like this patient are the most numerous category among the hostel dwellers. At least two of them are admitted to my ward each week. Today, for example, I spoke to a forty-five-year-old man who had once held a responsible job as a store manager but who was admitted a couple of days ago in delirium tremens. He agreed that his wandering life, now of twelve years' duration, had not been an entirely miserable one. The patient, who drank as much as any patient I have ever encountered, was proud of the fact that he had not been in trouble with the police for the past seven years, though not for lack of breaking the law. His social security check was totally inadequate to his consumption of spirits, and he had become a practiced thief, "though only for what I need, doctor." It was evident that the craft of stealing without getting caught gave him much pleasure. He admitted that he wasn't driven to theft by necessity: he told me that he was an accomplished portraitist and could earn enough money in a few hours by his skill to keep himself drunk for a week.

"I've had plenty of money in my time, doctor. Money's no problem to me. I could get plenty again. But the more I get, the longer I binge."

This patient, too, knew that he would return to the life he had been leading, whatever we did for him, whatever we offered him.

These homeless men, then, have made a choice, which one might even dignify as an existential one. The life they have chosen is not without its compensations. Once they have overcome their initial revulsion at the physical conditions in which they have decided to live, they find themselves secure: more secure, in fact, than most of the population engaged in a struggle to maintain its standard of living and by no means guaranteed of success. These men know, for example, that there are hostels everywhere, in every town and city, that will take them in, feed them, and keep them warm, whatever may happen and whether the market is bullish or bearish. They have no fear of failure and are utterly without the constraint of routine: their only daily task is to appear on time for a meal, and their only weekly task is to collect their social security. Moreover, they are automatically part of a fraternity—quarrelsome and occasionally violent, perhaps, but also tolerant and often amusing. Illness goes with the territory, but a general hospital is never far away, and treatment is free.

It is difficult for most of us to accept that this way of life, so unattractive on the surface, is freely chosen. Surely, we think, there must be something wrong with those who choose to live like this. Surely they must be suffering from some disease or mental abnormality that accounts for their choice, and therefore we should pity them. Or else, as the social workers who arrive periodically in the hostels believe, all who lodge there are by definition the victims of misfortune not of their own making and quite beyond their control. Society, as represented by social workers, must therefore rescue them. Accordingly, the social workers select a few of the longest-standing residents for what they call rehabilitation, meaning rehousing, complete with grants of several hundred dollars to buy those consumer durables the lack of which nowadays is accounted poverty. The results are not hard to imagine: a month later, the rent of the apartment remains unpaid and the grant has been spent, but not on refrigerators or microwave ovens. Some of the most experienced among the homeless have been rehabilitated three or four times, securing them brief but glorious periods of extreme popularity in the pub at taxpayers' expense.

To say, however, that a choice is a free one is not to endorse it as good or wise. There is no doubt that these men live entirely parasitically, contributing nothing to the general good and presuming upon society's tolerance of them. When hungry, they have only to appear at a hostel kitchen; when ill, at a hospital. They are profoundly anti-social.

And to say that their choice is a free one is not to deny that it is without influences from outside. A significant part of the social context of these homeless men is a society prepared to demand nothing of them. It is, in fact, prepared to subsidize them to drink themselves into oblivion, even to death. And all of them, without exception, consider it part of the natural and immutable order of things that society should do so; they all, without exception, call collecting their social security "getting paid."

These gentlemen of the road are being joined in their homelessness by increasing numbers of young people, fleeing their disastrous homes, where illegitimacy, a succession of abusive stepfathers, and a complete absence of authority is the norm. We are constantly told by those liberals whose nostrums of the past have contributed so richly to this wretched situation that society (by which is meant government) should do yet more for such pitiable people. But is not homelessness, at least in modern-day society, a special instance of a law first enunciated by a British medical colleague of mine, namely, that misery increases to meet the means available for its alleviation? And does not anti-social behavior increase in proportion to the excuses that intellectuals make for it?

*1996*

# What Is Poverty?

WHAT DO WE mean by poverty? Not what Dickens or Blake or Mayhew meant. Today no one seriously expects to go hungry in England or to live without running water or medical care or even TV. Poverty has been redefined in industrial countries, so that anyone at the lower end of the income distribution is poor ex officio, as it were—poor by virtue of having less than the rich. And of course by this logic, the only way of eliminating poverty is by an egalitarian redistribution of wealth—even if the society as a whole were to become poorer as a result.

Such redistribution was the goal of the welfare state. But it has not eliminated poverty, despite the vast sums expended, and despite the fact that the poor are now substantially richer—indeed are not, by traditional standards, poor at all. As long as the rich exist, so must the poor, as we now define them.

Certainly they are in squalor—a far more accurate description of their condition than poverty—despite a threefold increase in per capita income, including that of the poor, since the end of the last war. Why they should be in this condition requires an explanation—and to call that condition poverty, using a word more appropriate to Mayhew's London than to today's reality, prevents us from grasping how fundamentally the lot of "the poor" has changed since then. The poor we shall always have with us, no doubt, but today they are not poor in the traditional way.

## What Is Poverty?

The English poor live shorter and less healthy lives than their more prosperous compatriots. Even if you didn't know the statistics, their comparative ill health would be obvious on a casual observation of rich and slum areas, just as Victorian observers noted that the poor were on average a head shorter than the rich, due to generations of inferior nourishment and hard living conditions. But the reasons for today's difference in health are not economic. By no means can the poor not afford medicine or a nourishing diet; nor do they live in overcrowded houses lacking proper sanitation, as in Mayhew's time, or work fourteen backbreaking hours a day in the foul air of mines or mills. Epidemiologists estimate that higher cigarette consumption among the poor accounts for half the difference in life expectancy between the richest and poorest classes in England—and to smoke that much takes money.

Notoriously, too, the infant mortality rate is twice as high in the lowest social class as in the highest. But the infant mortality rate of illegitimate births is twice that of legitimate ones, and the illegitimacy rate rises steeply as you descend the social scale. So the decline of marriage almost to the vanishing point in the lowest social class might well be responsible for most of its excess infant mortality. It is a way of life, not poverty per se, that kills. The commonest cause of death between the ages of fifteen and forty-four is now suicide, which has increased most precipitously precisely among those who live in the underclass world of temporary step-parenthood and of conduct unrestrained either by law or convention.

Just as it is easier to recognize ill health in someone you haven't seen for some time rather than in someone you meet daily, so a visitor coming into a society from elsewhere often can see its character more clearly than those who live in it. Every few months, doctors from countries like the Philippines and India arrive fresh from the airport to work for a year's stint at my hospital. It is fascinating to observe their evolving response to British squalor.

At the start they are uniformly enthusiastic about the care that we unsparingly and unhesitatingly give to everyone, regardless of economic status. They themselves come from cities—Manila, Bombay, Madras—where many of the cases we see in our hospital would simply be left to die, often without succor of any kind. And they are impressed that our care extends beyond the merely medical: that no one goes without food or clothing or shelter, or even entertainment. There seems to be a public agency to deal with every conceivable problem. For a couple of weeks they think this all represents the acme of civilization, especially when they recall the horrors at home. Poverty—as they know it—has been abolished.

Before very long, though, they start to feel a vague unease. A Filipina doctor, for example, asked me why so few people seemed grateful for what was done for them. What prompted her question was an addict who, having collapsed from an accidental overdose of heroin, was brought to our hospital. He required intensive care to revive him, with doctors and nurses tending him all night. His first words to the doctor when he suddenly regained consciousness were, "Get me a fucking roll-up" (a hand-rolled cigarette). His imperious rudeness didn't arise from mere confusion: he continued to treat the staff as if they had kidnapped him and held him in the hospital against his will to perform experiments upon him. "Get me the fuck out of here!" There was no acknowledgment of what had been done for him, let alone gratitude for it. If he considered that he had received any benefit from his stay, well, it was simply his due.

My doctors from Bombay, Madras, or Manila observe this kind of conduct open-mouthed. At first they assume that the cases they see are a statistical quirk, a kind of sampling error, and that, given time, they will encounter a better, more representative cross section of the population. Gradually, however, it dawns upon them that what they have seen is representative. When every benefit received is a right, there is no place for good manners, let alone for gratitude.

Case after case causes them to revise their initial favorable opinion. Before long they have had experience of hundreds, and their view has changed entirely. Last week, for example, to the amazement of a doctor recently arrived from Madras, a woman in her late twenties entered our hospital with the most common condition that brings patients to us: a deliberate overdose. At first she would say nothing more than that she wanted to depart this world, that she had had enough of it.

I inquired further. Just before she took the overdose, her ex-boyfriend, the father of her eight-month-old youngest child (now staying with her ex-boyfriend's mother), had broken into her apartment by smashing down the front door. He wrecked the apartment's contents, broke every window, stole $110 in cash, and ripped out her telephone.

"He's very violent, doctor." She told me that he had broken her thumb, her ribs, and her jaw during the four years she was with him, and her face had needed stitching many times. "Last year I had to have the police out to him."

"What happened?"

"I dropped the charges. His mother said he would change."

Another of her problems was that she was now five weeks pregnant and didn't want the baby.

"I want to get rid of it, doctor."

"Who's the father?"

It was her violent ex-boyfriend, of course.

"Did he rape you, then?"

"No."

"So you agreed to have sex with him?"

"I was drunk; there was no love in it. This baby is like a bolt out of the blue: I don't know how it happened."

I asked her if she thought it was a good idea to have sex with a man who had repeatedly beaten her up, and from whom she said she wished to separate.

"It's complicated, doctor. That's the way life goes sometimes."

137

What had she known of this man before she took up with him? She met him in a club; he moved in at once, because he had nowhere else to stay. He had a child by another woman, neither of whom he supported. He had been in prison for burglary. He took drugs. He had never worked, except for cash on the side. Of course he never gave her any of his money, instead running up her telephone bills vertiginously.

She had never married but had two other children. The first, a daughter aged eight, still lived with her. The father was a man whom she left because she found he was having sex with twelve-year-old girls. Her second child was a son, whose father was "an idiot" with whom she had slept one night. That child, now six, lived with the "idiot," and she never saw him.

What had her experience taught her?

"I don't want to think about it. The Housing'll charge me for the damage, and I ain't got the money. I'm depressed, doctor; I'm not happy. I want to move, to get away from him."

Later in the day, feeling a little lonely, she telephoned her ex-boyfriend, and he visited her.

I discussed the case with the doctor who had recently arrived from Madras and who felt he had entered an insane world. Not in his wildest dreams had he imagined it could be like this. There was nothing to compare with it in Madras. He asked me what would happen next to the happy couple.

"They'll find her a new flat. They'll buy her new furniture, television, and refrigerator, because it's unacceptable poverty in this day and age to live without them. They'll charge her nothing for the damage to her old flat, because she can't pay anyway, and it wasn't she who did it. He will get away scot-free. Once she's installed in her new flat to escape from him, she'll invite him there, he'll smash it up again, and then they'll find her somewhere else to live. There is, in fact, nothing she can do that will deprive her of the state's obligation to house, feed, and entertain her."

I asked the doctor from Madras if poverty was the word he

would use to describe this woman's situation. He said it was not: that her problem was that she accepted no limits to her own behavior, that she did not fear the possibility of hunger, the condemnation of her own parents or neighbors, or God. In other words, the squalor of England was not economic but spiritual, moral, and cultural.

I often take my doctors from the third world on the short walk from the hospital to the prison nearby. It is a most instructive eight hundred yards. On a good day—good for didactic purposes, that is—there are seven or eight puddles of glass shattered into fragments lying in the gutter en route (there are never none, except during the most inclement weather, when even those most addicted to car theft control their impulses).

"Each of these little piles of smashed glass represents a car that has been broken into," I tell them. "There will be more tomorrow, weather permitting."

The houses along the way are, as public housing goes, quite decent. The local authorities have at last accepted that herding people into giant, featureless, Le Corbusian concrete blocks was a mistake, and they have switched to the construction of individual houses. Only a few of their windows are boarded up. Certainly by comparison with housing for the poor in Bombay, Madras, or Manila, they are spacious and luxurious indeed. Each has a little front yard of grass, surrounded by a hedge, and a much larger back yard; about half have satellite dishes. Unfortunately the yards are almost as full of litter as municipal garbage dumps.

I tell my doctors that in nearly nine years of taking this walk four times a week, I have never seen a single instance of anyone attempting to clean his yard. But I have seen much litter dropped; on a good day I can even watch someone standing at the bus stop dropping something on the ground no farther than two feet from the bin.

"Why don't they tidy up their gardens?" asks a doctor from Bombay.

A good question: after all, most of the houses contain at least one person with time on his or her hands. Whenever I have been able to ask the question, however, the answer has always been the same: I've told the council (the local government) about it, but they haven't come. As tenants, they feel it is the landlord's responsibility to keep their yards clean, and they are not prepared to do the council's work for it, even if it means wading through garbage—as it quite literally does. On the one hand, authority cannot tell them what to do; on the other, it has an infinitude of responsibilities towards them.

I ask my third-world doctors to examine the litter closely. It gives them the impression that no Briton is able to walk farther than ten yards or so without consuming junk food. Every bush, every lawn, even every tree is festooned with chocolate wrappers or fast-food packaging. Empty cans of beer and soft drinks lie in the gutter, on the flower beds, or on top of the hedges. Again, on a good day we actually see someone toss aside the can whose contents he has just consumed, as a Russian vodka drinker throws down his glass.

Apart from the anti-social disregard of the common good that each little such act of littering implies (hundreds a week in the space of eight hundred yards alone), the vast quantity of food consumed in the street has deeper implications. I tell the doctors that in all my visits to the white households in the area, of which I've made hundreds, never—not once—have I seen any evidence of cooking. The nearest to this activity that I have witnessed is the reheating of prepared and packaged food, usually in a microwave. And by the same token, I have never seen any evidence of meals taken in common as a social activity—unless two people eating hamburgers together in the street as they walk along is counted as social.

This is not to say that I haven't seen people eating at home; on the contrary, they are often eating when I arrive. They eat alone, even if other members of the household are present, and never at the table; they slump on a sofa in front of the television. Everyone in the household eats according to his own whim and timetable. Even in so elementary a matter as eating, therefore, there is no self-discipline but rather an imperative obedience to impulse. Needless to say, the opportunity for conversation or sociality that a meal taken together provides is lost. English meals are thus solitary, poor, nasty, brutish, and short.

I ask the doctors to compare the shops in areas inhabited by poor whites and those where poor Indian immigrants live. It is an instructive comparison. The shops the Indians frequent are piled high with all kinds of attractive fresh produce that, by supermarket standards, is astonishingly cheap. The women take immense trouble over their purchases and make subtle discriminations. There are no precooked meals for them. By contrast, a shop that poor whites patronize offers a restricted choice, largely of relatively expensive prepared foods that at most require only the addition of hot water.

The difference between the two groups cannot be explained by differences in income, for they are insignificant. Poverty isn't the issue. And the willingness of Indians to take trouble over what they eat and to treat meals as important social occasions that impose obligations and at times require the subordination of personal desire is indicative of an entire attitude towards life that often permits them, despite their current low incomes, to advance up the social scale. Alarmingly, though, the natural urge of the children of immigrants to belong to the predominant local culture is beginning to create an Indian underclass (at least among young males): and the taste for fast food and all that such a taste implies is swiftly developing among them.

When such slovenliness about food extends to all other spheres of life, when people satisfy every appetite with the same minimal effort and commitment, no wonder they trap themselves in squalor. I have little trouble showing my doctors from India and the Philippines that most of our patients take a fast-food approach to all their pleasures, obtaining them no less fleetingly and unstrenuously. They have no cultural activity they can call their own, and their lives seem, even to them, empty of purpose. In the welfare state, mere survival is not the achievement that it is, say, in the cities of Africa, and therefore it cannot confer the self-respect that is the precondition of self-improvement.

By the end of three months my doctors have, without exception, reversed their original opinion that the welfare state, as exemplified by England, represents the acme of civilization. On the contrary, they see it now as creating a miasma of subsidized apathy that blights the lives of its supposed beneficiaries. They come to realize that a system of welfare that makes no moral judgments in allocating economic rewards promotes anti-social egotism. The spiritual impoverishment of the population seems to them worse than anything they have ever known in their own countries. And what they see is all the worse, of course, because it should be so much better. The wealth that enables everyone effortlessly to have enough food should be liberating, not imprisoning. Instead it has created a large caste of people for whom life is, in effect, a limbo in which they have nothing to hope for and nothing to fear, nothing to gain and nothing to lose. It is a life emptied of meaning.

"On the whole," said one Filipino doctor to me, "life is preferable in the slums of Manila." He said it without any illusions as to the quality of life in Manila.

These doctors have made the same journey as I, but in the reverse direction. Arriving as a young doctor in Africa twenty-five years ago, I was horrified at first by the physical conditions, the like of which I had never experienced before. Patients with heart failure walked fifty miles in the broiling sun, with panting breath and swollen legs, to obtain treatment—and then walked home again. Ulcerating and suppurating cancers were common. Barefoot men contracted tetanus from the wounds inflicted by a sand flea that laid its eggs between their toes. Tuberculosis reduced people to animated skeletons. Children were bitten by puff adders and adults mauled by leopards. I saw lepers with noses that had rotted away and madmen who wandered naked in the torrential rains.

Even the accidents were spectacular. I treated the survivors of one in Tanzania in which a truck—having no brakes, as was perfectly normal and expected in the circumstances—began to slide backward down a hill it had been climbing. It was laden with bags of corn, upon which twenty passengers, including many children, were riding. As the truck slid backward, first the passengers, then the corn, fell off. By the time I arrived, ten dead children were lined up by the side of the road, arranged in ascending order as neatly as organ pipes. They had been crushed or suffocated by the bags of corn that fell on top of them: a grimly ironic death in a country chronically short of food.

Moreover, political authority in the countries in which I worked was arbitrary, capricious, and corrupt. In Tanzania, for example, you could tell the representative of the sole and omnipotent political party, the Party of the Revolution, by his girth alone. Tanzanians were thin, but party men were fat. The party representative in my village sent a man to prison because the man's wife refused to sleep with him. In Nigeria the police hired out their guns by night to the armed robbers.

Yet nothing I saw—neither the poverty nor the overt oppression—ever had the same devastating effect on the human personality as the undiscriminating welfare state. I never saw the loss of dignity, the self-centeredness, the spiritual and emotional vacuity, or the sheer ignorance of how to live that I see daily in England. In a kind of pincer movement, therefore, I and the doctors from India and the Philippines have come to the same terrible conclusion: that the worst poverty is in England—and it is not material poverty but poverty of soul.

*1999*

# Do Sties Make Pigs?

UNTIL QUITE RECENTLY I had assumed that the extreme ugliness of the city in which I live was attributable to the Luftwaffe. I imagined that the cheap and charmless high-rise buildings that so disfigure the cityscape had been erected of necessity in great gaping holes left by Heinkel bombers. I had spent much of my childhood playing in deserted bomb shelters in public parks: and although I was born some years after the end of the war, that great conflagration still exerted a powerful hold on the imagination of British children of my generation.

I discovered how wrong I was not long ago when I entered a store whose walls were decorated with large photographs of the city as it had been before the war. It was then a fine place, in a grandiloquent, Victorian kind of way. Every building had spoken of a bulging, no doubt slightly pompous and ridiculous, municipal pride. Industry and labor were glorified in statuary, and a leavening of Greek temples and Italian Renaissance palaces lightened the prevailing mock-Venetian Gothic architecture.

"A great shame about the war," I said to the store assistant, who was of an age to remember the old days. "Look at the city now."

"The war?" she said. "The war had nothing to do with it. It was the council."

The City Council—the people's elected representatives—it

144

transpired, had done far more damage to the fabric of the city in the 1950s and 1960s than had Göring's air force. Indeed, they had managed to turn it into a terrible visual ordeal for anyone with the most minimal visual sensibility.

First among the reasons for this large-scale architectural vandalism was the prolonged revulsion against all things Victorian. In Britain this was particularly pronounced after the war because for the first time it was unmistakably clear just how far the country had declined from its Victorian apogee of world power and influence: a decline made somewhat easier to bear, psychologically speaking, by the consistent, unabashed denigration not only of the Victorians themselves but of all their ideas and works as well.

I witnessed a striking example of this revulsion in my own household. My father, a communist and therefore predisposed to view the past in a lurid light, especially by comparison with the inevitable postrevolutionary glories to come, had bought several Victorian paintings at Sotheby's during the war for ten shillings each. (Communists are not necessarily opposed to taking advantage of a temporary depression in prices.) He kept them in the loft of the house. Then, one day in 1960, quite arbitrarily, he decided that they were taking up too much space—unlike the tins of fruit he had stockpiled during the Korean War in the expectation that it would escalate into the Third World War, and which were now beginning to explode, but which he kept forever. He took all the paintings except one and put them on a bonfire, an act that I knew even at the age of ten to be one of terrible barbarism. I begged him not to do it—to give the paintings away if he didn't like them—but no, they had to be destroyed.

Then there was the modernist arrogance about not only the Victorian past but all the centuries that had gone before—my city swept away many eighteenth-century buildings along with Victorian and Edwardian ones. British architects finally caught up with the Italian futurist Marinetti, who condemned the past without exception, who demanded a clean break with all that had gone before, who ridiculed all previous styles, and who worshipped only those attributes of modernity: speed and size. Among other schemes, he wanted to fill in the canals of Venice and replace the *palazzi* with modern factories.

But just as the Italy of his day was technologically backward, so the Britain of the modernizing architects was no longer in the vanguard, the palm for modernity having long since passed to America. The architects thought that modernity was a value that transcended all other virtues; they thought they could wake the country from its nostalgic slumber, dragging it into the twentieth century by pouring what seemed to them the most modern of building materials—reinforced concrete—all over it. Hence, among many other crimes, they tore down the elegant Victorian wrought-iron tracery of my city's main railway station, with its splendid arched roof over platforms and tracks, and built instead a brutalist construction of steel and soon-discolored concrete to a plan that proved no more practical or functional than the old.

My city was far from alone in having suffered the Bakuninite demolishing fervor of the modernizers (as Bakunin said, the urge to destroy is also a creative urge). Even small country towns have not escaped their notice: Huntingdon, Oliver Cromwell's birthplace, was provided with a ring road of such hideous and dysfunctional design, simultaneously rendering exit from and entry into the town difficult and dangerous, that architects and town planners around the world now study it as a warning. Shrewsbury, Darwin's birthplace and a town that for several centuries managed to combine the most diverse architectural styles, so that its townscape as a whole was greater than the sum of its parts, has been ruined as an aesthetic experience by a few visually inescapable modern office blocks and multistory car parks. It would be too depressing to list the English towns and cities marred by this treatment.

But it is public housing that exemplifies most clearly the

ideas of those who transformed the British urban landscape during the 1950s and 1960s. Here the new aesthetics combined with socialist reforming zeal to produce a multi-layered disaster.

After the war, *bien pensants* universally agreed that prewar British society had been grossly unjust. The working class, it was said, had been shamelessly exploited, as was manifest principally in Britain's great inequalities of income and its overcrowded housing. A sharply progressive income tax (which at one point reached 95 percent) would redress the inequalities of income while slum clearance and the construction of large-scale housing projects would alleviate the housing problem.

The middle-class reformers thought of poverty wholly in physical terms: an insufficiency of food and warmth, a lack of space. How, they asked, could people come to the finer things in life if their basic requirements were so inadequately met? What could freedom mean (I remember my father asking) in the absence of decent housing conditions? Since social problems such as crime and delinquency (which we were soon to discover were in their infancy) were attributable to physical deprivation—to the environment rather than the criminal or delinquent—the construction of decent housing would solve all problems at once.

But what was decent housing? A civil servant, Parker Morris, provided the answer: a certain number of cubic yards of living space per inhabitant. The Ministry of Housing adopted the Parker Morris standards for all public housing; they governed the size and number of rooms—and that was all.

In the circumstances, who can be surprised that the architectural style, if style it can be called, of Le Corbusier came to dominate the construction of public housing, even though it had already proved disastrous in the one place, Marseilles, where Le Corbusier had been given full rein? It was the simplest and cheapest means of complying with the now-sacrosanct Parker Morris standards. Besides, Le Corbusier was a kindred spirit to bureaucrats and town planners—not just an architect but a visionary and would-be social reformer. Of Paris he wrote: "Imagine all this junk, which until now has lain spread out over the soil like a dry crust, cleaned off and carted away, and replaced by immense clear crystals of glass, rising to a height of over six hundred feet!" In this spirit, much of my city, especially the terraced housing of the working class, was cleaned off and carted away, to be replaced by Le Corbusier's "vertical city . . . bathed in light and air." Some light, some air!

It occurred to no authority that perhaps more was being swept away than a mere dry crust. If the reformers had been right, the people who lived in such poor housing should remember the conditions with bitterness: but they don't. Even allowing for the roseate glow that the passage of time lends to experience, what my patients tell me of the streets where they grew up does not vindicate the reformers.

True, the houses in which my patients lived often lacked the basic amenities now taken for granted: proper indoor plumbing, for example. They were cramped. And much of the terraced housing—known as two-up-two-down—was aesthetically undistinguished. But with imaginative adaptation and improvement (now belatedly under way in what remains of such housing), more than adequate, even pleasing accommodation could have been produced without the wholesale destruction of communities that resulted from the indiscriminate demolitions of the fifties and sixties.

For, as my patients tell me, a sense of community did exist in these streets of little red houses, to such an extent that people who came from more than a few streets away were regarded as strangers, almost as foreigners. No doubt the community feeling resulted in a certain small-mindedness, but it also meant that life was not then the war of permanently inflamed egos to be found in Corbusian housing projects—egos inflamed by the fact that the inhabitants have been, and continue to be, treated so transparently by social policymakers as faceless, interchange-

able, passive ciphers that the only way to assert their individual-
ity is to behave anti-socially. I fight, therefore I am.

This sense of community, now destroyed, allowed people
to withstand genuine hardship—hardship that wasn't self-
inflicted, like so much of today's. I remember a patient who described with great warmth the street on which he had lived as a
child—"until," he added, "Adolf Hitler moved us on." What an
admirable depth of character, uncomplaining in the face of misfortune, those few words convey! Nowadays the victim of such
a bombing would be more likely to blame the government for
having declared war on the Nazis in the first place.

The housing projects were built at what (for Britain) was
record speed, and whoever wants to see for himself the *reductio
ad absurdum* of the materialist and rationalist conception of
human life cannot do better than to visit one of these projects.
The idea that happiness and well-being consist of the satisfaction of a few simple physical needs, and can therefore be
planned on behalf of society by benevolent administrators, is
here bleakly mocked.

As the architects failed to foresee, the spaces between the
vast, geometric shapes of the Corbusian apartment blocks act as
wind tunnels, turning the slightest breeze into a hurricane. I
know an old lady who has been blown over so many times that
she no longer dares to do her own shopping. Nature itself is
turned into one more source of hostility. Walkways are isolated
and ill-lit, so that rapists may safely abduct: two of my patients
were raped en route to my clinic in a walkway not a hundred
yards away. Notices planted in the grass around the apartment
blocks of one housing project added to the Orwellian spirit of
the place before they were ripped out by residents: DO NOT WALK
ON THE GRASS. IT IS AN AMENITY TO BE ENJOYED BY EVERYONE.

As for the buildings themselves, they are, with a vengeance,
Le Corbusier's "machines for living in"—though perhaps "existing in" would be more accurate. The straight line and the

right angle reign supreme: no curves, no frivolous decorative touches, no softening materials add warmth to the steel, glass, and concrete. There is nothing that Mies van der Rohe, another dictator in architect's clothing, would have condemned as "aesthetic speculation."

What do the tenants think of their apartment blocks? They vote with their urine. The public spaces and elevators of all public housing blocks I know are so deeply impregnated with urine that the odor is ineradicable. And anything smashable has been smashed.

The people who inhabit these apartments are utterly isolated. All that connects them is the noise they make, often considerable, which permeates the flimsy walls, ceilings, and floors. They are likely to be unemployed and poorly educated, socialized neither by work nor by pastimes. Single mothers are housed here, guaranteeing the impoverishment of their children's social environment: and in Britain we are now into the second generation of children who know no other environment.

No civic or collective life is possible in such conditions, and so there are no standards of conduct: every man's whim is law, and the most physically powerful and ruthless is the one who sets the tone and makes the rules. When a patient of mine was suspended by her ankles from the window of her eleventh-floor apartment by her jealous boyfriend, no one noticed or considered it his duty to intervene. She herself was unaware that there was anything morally reprehensible (as against merely unpleasant) about her boyfriend's conduct.

It is true that when another patient of mine mountaineered down his apartment block from his fourteenth-floor apartment, the police asked me to visit to determine whether there was a medical explanation of his behavior. But what I found convinced me that no desert hermit was ever more alone than the inhabitant of an English housing project.

My patient had spent the last few years of his life sniffing glue in his apartment. The water and electricity had been cut off for nonpayment. He lived in permanent darkness, his filthy curtains always drawn. His apartment no longer contained a stick of furniture, but in the middle of his living room—Parker Morris standard—was an old oil drum that he had used as a brazier to burn his furniture to keep warm. The embers of the last of his bed glowed faintly.

Why, I asked, had he taken to the rope and climbed down the outer wall of his building?

Because, he replied, he feared that his brazier might set fire to his apartment, and he wanted to test his escape route.

And the other tenants of the block? I inquired.

A slightly puzzled look flitted across his face. What did I mean?

A dim apprehension that perhaps the Parker Morris standards were not sufficient for gracious urban living eventually filtered into the minds of British officialdom. Their response? Community centers.

These too were built of concrete. Their large grey cheerless rooms were radically unheatable, unpleasantly cool even in summer. Their basements, which could have served as torture chambers, housed Ping-Pong tables. Anything stealable was stolen, whether it was of use to the thief or not: more for the practice, really. What, after all, does one do with a table-tennis net in the absence of a table-tennis table? It soon became clear that the formula Parker Morris plus Ping-Pong did not work either. The community centers became places where unemployed young men and chronic schizophrenics went to exchange social security for marijuana.

When I aired my thoughts about public housing to a British architect—to whom, in my heart, I ascribed some of the collective blame for the calamitous situation—he at once shot back, "Yes, but do sties make pigs, or do pigs make sties?"

A profound question, perhaps the profoundest that can be asked. After all, you can lead a mugger to a victim, but you can't make him rob.

In the midst of one particularly grim housing project to which I once was called—a single mother was threatening to immolate her infant—stood an apartment block conspicuously less disgusting than the rest. It was inhabited entirely by old-age pensioners: either they no longer had the energy for vandalism, or they had not the inclination for it. If the Parker Morris standards were not a sufficient condition of decent living, neither were they a sufficient condition of its opposite.

What really made the difference, I concluded, was the policy by which public housing, of which there was a limited supply despite the building boom of three decades, was allocated. In conditions of shortage, justice demanded that such housing as existed should be allocated according to need: and what greater proof of need could there be than social pathology?

An unemployed single woman with three children by three fathers, none of whom supported his offspring in any way, could be said to be in greater need than a fully employed married couple with one child, who might reasonably be expected to look after themselves. Mirabile dictu, there was soon more than enough social pathology to fill the space available for it. Indeed, a kind of arms race in social pathology developed: my violence towards others outguns your attempts to kill yourself.

The results of this policy have been truly bizarre. Because public housing is subsidized, many desire it. Traditionally, city councils as landlords have been reluctant to evict their tenants, no matter what their behavior is or if they fail to pay their rent, in part to draw attention to the ideological difference between the public and the private sectors, to the gain of the former. Unlike the hard-hearted, exploitative private landlord struggling for private advantage, the city council landlord benevolently provides a social service. Thus a public housing tenancy is to psychopaths what tenure is to academics: no better invitation to irresponsibility could possibly be imagined.

Oddly enough, this encouragement of what was hitherto

considered anti-social behavior was given in the name of a sup-posedly tolerant refusal to make moral judgments. But since those who put themselves in a position of need by their own be-havior were favored over those who failed to do so, an implicit judgment was in fact made: a judgment whose perversity is evi-dent from the requests I receive from my patients for letters to the housing authorities to strengthen their case for receiving the tenancy of an apartment.

In these missives, my patients tell me, I should emphasize their alcoholism or drug addiction, their bad temper and ten-dency to assault those around them—the consequence, plainly, of a lack of proper accommodation. I should mention their re-peated overdoses, the fact that they resort to tranquilizers ob-tained illegally, that they have had several abortions and are now pregnant for the fifth time, that they have had three violent and drunken boyfriends in succession, that they gamble their money uncontrollably (or uncontrolledly). In not a single case has anyone ever asked me to write that he is a decent, hard-working, honorable citizen who would make a good tenant. That would send him straight to the bottom of the waiting list.

Indeed, the perverse criteria by which public housing has been allocated during the past two or three decades has rein-forced the inexorable rise in the proportion of the young adult population living alone, a tendency that many powerful cur-rents in our culture have encouraged. In the Thatcher years, the number of nonelderly adults living alone or as single parents doubled in absolute terms and almost as a proportion of total households as well. Hardly a day passes when I do not meet an eighteen- or nineteen-year-old without a job, without financial resources, without skills or training, without family support, without mental accomplishments, who has been given an apart-ment at public expense. Housing is a right, and the government therefore has a duty to provide it. The possibility that it will do so if only one behaves badly or impulsively enough acts as an irritant in domestic relations: for if a move elsewhere is a real possibility, you can afford to let a minor disagreement escalate into an irreparable breakdown.

So do pigs make sties, or do sties make pigs? I suspect that there is, as my father used to say, a dialectical relationship.

*1995*

# Lost in the Ghetto

◈ ONE OF THE terrible fates that can befall a human being is to be born intelligent or sensitive in an English slum. It is like a long, slow, exquisite torture devised by a sadistic deity from whose malevolent clutches escape is almost impossible.

Such was not always the case. My father was born in an English slum in the years before the First World War. In the borough in which he was born, one in every eight children died in his first year. But in those benighted times, when some London children, too poor to buy shoes, went to school barefoot, the "vicious cycle of poverty" had yet to be discovered. It had not yet occurred to the rulers of the land that the circumstances of a person's birth should seal his destiny. And so my father, having been found intelligent by his teachers, was taught Latin, French, German, mathematics, science, English literature, and history, as if he were fully capable of entry into the stream of higher civilization.

When he died, I found his school textbooks still among his possessions, and they were of a rigor and difficulty that would terrify a modern teacher, let alone child. But he, who was never generous in his praise of others and often imputed the worst of motives to his fellow beings, remembered his teachers with the deepest respect and affection: for they had not only taught him his lessons but had devoted much of their spare time to taking their intelligent slum children, himself included, to museums and concerts, to demonstrate to them that the life of the slum was not the only life there was. In this way my father was awakened to the very possibility of possibility.

A child born in a slum today with the same high intelligence as my father would be vanishingly unlikely ever to find such mentors. After all, today's teachers, steeped in the idea that it is wrong to order civilizations, cultures, or ways of life hierarchically, would deny either the existence or the value of a higher civilization, and would in any case be incapable of imparting it. For them, there is no height or depth, superiority or inferiority, profundity or shallowness; there is only difference. They even doubt that there is a right and wrong way to spell a word or construct a sentence—a view buttressed by such popular and supposedly authoritative works as Professor Steven Pinker's *The Language Instinct* (written, of course, with neither orthographical nor grammatical errors). Today's teachers assume that the slum child is fully equipped culturally by the environment in which he lives. His speech is by definition adequate to his needs, his tastes by definition acceptable and no worse or lower than any others. There is no reason, therefore, to induct him into anything.

A slum child would find no mentors such as my father found also because the belief in the equality of cultures that is a long-established pedagogic orthodoxy has now seeped into the population at large. Today's slum dwellers are aggressively convinced of the sufficiency of their knowledge, however restricted it might be, and of their own cultural life, of whatever it might consist. My older patients use the word "educated" as a term of approbation; my younger patients, never. When my father was a child, no one doubted what it was to be educated, or questioned the value of an education such as the one he received; but since teachers and parents now regard all cultural manifestations and fields of human knowledge as of equal worth, why waste the effort either to impart or to receive as rigorous, difficult, and unnatural an education as my father received, when any other training (or none at all) would be as good? Worse, such an effort would be to impose an arbitrary standard of worth—a mere disguise for the continuation of the hegemony of a traditional elite—and would thereby undermine the self-confidence of the majority and reinforce social divisions.

Unfortunately the culture of the slums is deeply unsatisfying to intelligent people in the long run. The tragedy is that, even though the average level of intelligence in the slums is probably lower than elsewhere, very many intelligent people have the misfortune to be born in them. And we do everything possible to ensure that that is where they stay.

They come to realize at different stages of their lives that something is wrong with the culture by which they are surrounded. Some realize it when they reach their teens, others only when their own children go to school. Many are unable to put their finger on what exactly is wrong: at thirty, they are aware only of an absence. This absence turns out to be a lack of any subject for their minds to work upon other than the day-to-day flux of their existence.

It is well recognized that intelligent children who are not sufficiently challenged in school, and who are made to repeat lessons they have already understood merely because others in the class, slower to learn than they, have not yet mastered them, frequently become disruptive, badly behaved, and even delinquent; it is less well recognized that this destructive pattern persists well into adult life. The bored—among whom are those whose level of intelligence is grossly mismatched with the requirements of their cultural environment—frequently solve the problem by fomenting easily avoided and completely foreseeable crises in their personal lives. The mind, like nature, abhors a vacuum: and if no absorbing interest has developed in childhood and adolescence, such an interest is soon manufactured from the materials at hand. Man is at least as much a problem-creating as a problem-solving animal. Better a crisis than the permanent boredom of meaninglessness.

Despite official genuflections in the direction of diversity and tolerance, the sad fact is that the culture of the slums is monolithic and deeply intolerant. Any child who tries to resist the blandishments of that culture can count on no support or defense from teachers or any other adult, who now equate both freedom and democracy with the tyranny of the majority. Many of my intelligent patients from the slums recount how, in school, they expressed a desire to learn, only to suffer mockery, excommunication, and in some instances outright violence from their peers. One intelligent child of fifteen, who had taken an overdose as a suicidal gesture, said she was subjected to constant teasing and abuse by her peers. "They say I'm stupid," she told me, "because I'm clever."

Teachers rarely protect such children or encourage them to resist absorption into the culture that will all too clearly imprison them in the social condition into which they were born: for teachers have themselves generally absorbed uncritically the notion that social justice—meaning little more than an equal distribution of income—is the *summum bonum* of human existence. I have heard two teachers expound the theory that, as social mobility reinforces the existing social structure, it delays the achievement of social justice by depriving the lower classes of militants and potential leaders. Thus to encourage an individual child to escape his heritage of continual soap opera and pop music, tabloid newspapers, poverty, squalor, and domestic violence is, in the eyes of many teachers, to encourage class treachery. It also conveniently absolves teachers of the tedious responsibility for the welfare of individual pupils.

Still, children arise in the unlikeliest places with ambitions very different from their peers, and fortunately not all teachers believe that no child can escape the slums unless all do. One of my patients, for example, early conceived a passion for French culture and literature (she never arrives in the hospital without a volume of Hugo, Balzac, or Baudelaire, which is a little like seeing a polar bear in the jungle). She decided at an early age that she would study French at university and was fortunate, considering the school she attended, to find a teacher who did not actively discourage her. But the cost to her in ordinary social relations with her peers was incalculable: she had to sit apart from them in the classroom and create her own enclosed little world in the midst of constant disorder and noise; she was mocked, teased, threatened, and humiliated; she was jeered at when standing at the bus stop to go home; she was deprived of friends and sexually assaulted by boys who despised, and perhaps secretly feared, her evident devotion to books; excrement was put through her mailbox at home (a common expression of social disapproval in our brave New Britain). As for her parents—of whom she was fortunate enough to have two—they did not understand her. Why could she not be like everyone else—and leave them in peace? It wasn't even as if a taste for French literature led automatically to highly paid employment.

She went to university and was happy for three years. For the first time in her life she met people whose mental world extended beyond their own very restricted experience. Her performance at university was creditable, though not brilliant, for by her own admission she lacked originality. She had always wanted to teach, thinking there was no nobler calling than to awaken the minds of the young to the cultural riches of which they would otherwise remain unaware; but on graduation, lacking savings, she returned to her parents for the sake of economy.

She found a job teaching French nearby, in the kind of school in which she herself had been educated. She was back in a world in which knowledge was no better than ignorance, and correction, whether of spelling or of conduct, was by definition a personal insult, an outrage to the ego. Who was she—who was any adult, in fact—to tell children what they should learn or do (a sensible enough question, impossible to answer, if you believe in the equal worth of all human activity)? Once more she found herself mocked, teased, and humiliated, and was powerless to prevent it. Eventually one of her pupils—if that is quite the word to describe the youth in question—tried to rape her, and she brought her career as a teacher to a premature end.

Now she would consider any paid employment that would take her away from the area in which she was born, or any area like it: that is to say, at least a third of Great Britain. Until her escape, however, she remains trapped in her parents' home, with no one to talk to about those things that interest her, either inside the house or out. Perhaps, she mused, it would have been better had she surrendered to the majority while she was still at school: for her heroic struggle had brought her little but three years' respite from misery.

Hers is not an isolated case by any means. With Britain's immense apparatus of welfare, which consumes about a fifth of the national income, there is little or nothing to spare for an eighteen-year-old girl such as the one who consulted me last week, who is making the most valiant efforts to escape her dismal background. Her father was a drunk who beat her mother every day of his married life, and quite often the three children as well, until finally he decided that enough was enough and deserted them altogether. Unfortunately my patient's younger brother stepped into the breach and became just as violent as the father had been. He beat his mother and one day broke a glass and used its jagged edge to inflict an extremely serious wound on my patient's left arm, from which she still, two years later, has not entirely recovered and probably never will.

Endowed apparently by nature with a forceful personality, my patient insisted not only on calling the police but in pressing charges against her brother, who was fourteen at the time. The magistrates gave him a conditional discharge. So appalled was my patient's mother at her lack of family solidarity that she threw her out of the house, at the age of sixteen, to fend for herself. This put an end to her plan—formulated under the most inauspicious circumstances—to continue her education and become a lawyer.

At sixteen, as she then was, she was deemed by social services to be too old for an orphanage but not old enough to receive any welfare benefits, and the only accommodation that the local apparatus of welfare could find for her was a room in a house used to resettle criminals. While her brother received every attention from social workers, she received none at all, since there was nothing wrong with her. Her criminal roommate in the halfway house was what she called "a baghead"—a heroin addict—and also a professional thief.

As intelligent as she was forceful, my patient found herself a job as a clerk in a local law office and has worked there ever since. She was thenceforth charged the full economic rent for her miserable room, and all pleas to the authorities on her part to be relocated in public housing were turned down on the grounds that she was already adequately accommodated and in any case was unfit yet to manage her own affairs. As to public assistance for further full-time education, that was out of the question, since in order to pursue such full-time education she would have to give up her job: and she would then be considered to have made herself voluntarily unemployed and thus unentitled to public assistance. But if she cared to become pregnant, why then, public assistance was at hand, in generous quantities.

The morals of her story could hardly have been clearer. First, the inhabitants of the milieu from which she came considered that her duty not to inform the authorities far outweighed her right not to be maltreated. Second, the authorities themselves considered the attack upon her as unworthy of serious attention. Third, she would receive no public help at all in escaping from the circumstances into which she had been born. To treat her as an especially deserving case, after all, would be to imply that there were undeserving cases; and to say that there were undeserving cases would be tantamount to admitting that one way of living is preferable—morally, economically, culturally, spiritually—to another. This is a thought that must at all costs be kept at bay, or the whole ideology of modern education and welfare collapses in a heap. It might be argued, of course, that it was precisely the lack of public assistance that put iron in my patient's soul in the first place (she was still determined one day to qualify as a lawyer): but that is the answer to a different question, and is besides a little harsh for my taste.

But at least these two girls, each remarkable in her way, had somehow glimpsed the existence of another world, even if neither had yet succeeded in fully entering it. Their awareness that the culture of the slums was insufficient to sustain an intelligent person came to them early in life—how or why they could no longer remember.

This realization comes considerably later to most of my intelligent patients, however, who complain in their thirties of a vague, persistent, and severe dissatisfaction with their present existence. The excitements of their youth are over: in the culture of the slums, men and women are past their prime by the age of twenty-five. Their personal lives are in disarray, to put it kindly: the men have fathered children with whom they have little or no contact; the women, preoccupied with meeting the increasingly imperious demands of these same children, drudge at ill-paid, boring, and impermanent jobs. (The illegitimacy rate in Britain has recently passed the 40 percent mark, and while most births are still registered in the names of two parents, relations between the sexes grow ever more unstable.) The entertainments that once seemed so compelling to both men and women—indeed, the whole purpose of life—seem so no longer. These patients are listless, irritable, and disgruntled. They indulge in self-destructive, anti-social, or irrational behavior: they drink too much, involve themselves in meaningless quarrels, quit their jobs when they can't afford to, run up debts on trifles, pursue obviously disastrous relationships, and move their home as if the problem were in the walls that surround them.

The diagnosis is boredom, a much underestimated factor in the explanation of undesirable human conduct. As soon as the word is mentioned, they pounce upon it, almost with relief: recognition of the problem is instant, though they had not thought of it before. Yes, they are bored—bored to the very depths of their being.

But why are they bored, they ask me. The answer, of course, is that they have never applied their intelligence either to their work, their personal lives, or their leisure, and intelligence is a distinct disadvantage when it is not used: it bites back. Reviewing their life stories, they see for the first time that at every point they have chosen the line of least resistance, the least strenuous path. They never received any guidance, because all agreed that one path was as good as another. They never awoke to the fact that a life is a biography, not a series of disconnected moments, more or less pleasurable but increasingly tedious and unsatisfying unless one imposes a purposive pattern upon them.

Their education was an enforced and seemingly interminable irrelevance: nothing their parents or their teachers told them, nothing they absorbed from the culture around them, led them to suppose that their early efforts at school, or lack of them, would have any effect upon their subsequent lives. The jobs they took as soon as they were able were purely to fund their pleasures of the moment. They formed relationships with the opposite sex whimsically, without thought of the future. Their children were born as instruments, either to repair troubled relations or to fill an emotional and spiritual void, and were soon found wanting in either capacity. Their friends—for the first time perceived as of lesser intelligence—now bore them. And, for the first time wishing to escape the artificial, self-stimulated crises that amuse them no longer, they suffer the undisguised *taedium vitae* of the slums.

Intelligence is not the only quality that the modern culture of the slums penalizes, of course. Almost any manifestation of finer feeling, any sign of weakness, any attempt at withdrawal into a private world is mercilessly preyed upon and exploited. A cultivated manner, a refusal to swear in public, an intellectual interest, a distaste for coarseness, a protest against littering are the objects of mockery and obloquy: and so it takes courage, even heroism, to behave with common decency.

One of my patients is a stout woman, aged fifty, who would once have been called an old maid. She is completely harmless and is in fact a woman of the most delicate sensibility. She is so timid that a harsh word is sufficient to reduce her to tears. She always apologizes to me for the inconvenience she believes that she causes me by her very existence; I have never been able to reassure her completely on that score. She is the Miss Flite of our times.

Needless to say, the life of such a person in a modern British slum is a living nightmare. The children in her street mock her unceasingly when she leaves her house; they push excrement through her mailbox as a joke. She has long since given up appealing to their mothers for help, since they always side with their children and consider any adverse comment on their behavior as an insult to them personally. Far from correcting their children, they threaten her with further violence. The relentless, gleeful revelations in the press, radio, and television of any wrongdoing by the authorities and the professions, unbalanced by any criticism whatever of members of the general public, have caused an atrophy of the faculty of self-criticism and prepare the mind always to look outward, never inward, for the source of dissatisfaction and malfeasance. *Vox populi, vox dei*—with every person a god in his own pantheon.

My patient is, of course, an easy target for burglars and robbers. Her house has been broken into five times in the last year, and she has been robbed in the street three times in the same period, twice in the presence of passersby.

Such a person can expect no sympathy from the authorities. The police have told her more than once that the fault is hers: someone like her should not live somewhere like this. The streets, in other words, should be left to the hooligans, the vandals, and the robbers, to ply their inevitable trades in peace, and it is the duty of citizens to avoid them. It is no part of the state's duty to secure the streets against them.

In such circumstances, decency is almost synonymous with vulnerability: a quality with which the authorities have no sympathy. Another patient of mine, a younger woman of respectable working-class background and unblemished character, despaired of finding a compatible man, her experience in that sphere having been uniformly disastrous. She decided thenceforth to live as a spinster, devoting her life to the rescue of stray animals. Her house, unfortunately, was in a street in a public housing project, in which all the other houses had been gradually abandoned after repeated vandalism and were now boarded up. The street then became a rendezvous and pickup point for drug dealers, who did not hesitate to break into my patient's house to make use of her telephone (saving expenses on their own cellular phones) and help themselves to whatever food was present. They broke into her house even when she was in it, mocking her fear and taunting her with her inability to do anything about it. Her largest expense soon became the telephone bills they ran up. They threatened her with death if she went to the police.

She did go to the police, however, and also to the housing authorities. Their advice was the same: she should buy a guard dog. She followed their advice, but it made little difference, because the dog soon grew used to the drug dealers, who fed it tidbits. But my patient grew to love her dog.

My patient asked the housing authorities to move her elsewhere. At first—that is to say, for two years—her request was turned down, because she was deemed to have insufficient reasons for wishing to move. When finally the authorities agreed to find her somewhere else to live, they offered her an apartment, in which, however, it was forbidden to keep animals. My patient pointed out that she had a dog, a creature upon which she now lavished all her capacity for affection, a fact perfectly obvious to anyone who spoke to her about her life for even a few moments. The housing authorities were adamant: take it or leave it. In vain did she point out that it was the housing authorities who had advised her to get the dog in the first place. The argument of the housing authorities was that if she were really serious about moving from her current inferno, she would take whatever she was given. After all, hundreds of thousands of British fathers abandoned their offspring without a moment's thought: what was all this sentimental fuss about a brute animal?

Life in the British slums demonstrates what happens when the population at large, and the authorities as well, lose all faith in a hierarchy of values. All kinds of pathology result: where knowledge is not preferable to ignorance and high culture to low, the intelligent and the sensitive suffer a complete loss of meaning. The intelligent self-destruct; the sensitive despair. And where decent sensitivity is not nurtured, encouraged, supported, or protected, brutality abounds. The absence of standards, as Ortega y Gasset remarked, is the beginning of barbarism: and modern Britain is well past the beginning.

*2000*

# And Dying Thus
# Around Us Every Day

◈ THE TRIAL IN January of Marie Therese Kouao and her
lover, Carl Manning, for the murder of their eight-year-old
ward, Anna Climbie, caused a sensation in England: not merely
because the pathologist who performed the postmortem on the
child said in court that it was the worst case of child abuse he
had ever seen, but because of the depths of incompetence and
pusillanimity it revealed among the public servants charged
with detecting, preventing, and responding to such abuse.

Perhaps it shouldn't be surprising that the competence of
our public servants has declined along with our nation's general
level of education; but in this case the authorities conducted
themselves with so stunning a lack of common sense that something more must account for it than mere ignorance. To para-
phrase Dr. Johnson slightly, such stupidity is not in nature. It
has to be worked for or achieved. As usual, one must look to
the baleful influence of mistaken ideas to explain it.

Anna Climbie died of hypothermia in February 1999. Her
body after death showed 128 marks of violence, inflicted with
leather belts, metal coat hangers, a bicycle chain, and a hammer. She was burned with cigarettes and scalded with hot water.
Her fingers were cut with razors. For six months she had been
made to sleep in a black plastic garbage bag (in place of clothes)

in a bathtub: sometimes she had been left in cold water, bound hand and foot, for 24 hours. She was emaciated to the point of starvation; her legs were so rigidly flexed that when she was admitted to the hospital the day before her death, they could not be straightened.

It was not as if there had been no warnings of Anna's terrible fate. She was admitted to the hospital twice during the months before she died; doctors alerted the social service authorities to the abuse she was suffering at least six times; and the police also were alerted more than once. No one did anything whatsoever.

Marie Therese Kouao came originally from the Ivory Coast, though she was a French citizen and lived in France for most of her life. She would return to the Ivory Coast from time to time to persuade relatives there to hand over their children to her, so that she could bring them up in Europe, assuring them a brighter future than West Africa offered, she said. She claimed to have a highly paid job at the Charles de Gaulle Airport in Paris.

She used the children successively entrusted to her care to claim benefits from the welfare system, first in France and then in England. She moved to England with Anna because the French authorities were demanding the reimbursement of $3,000 of benefits to which she had not been entitled. On her arrival in England, she was at once granted benefits worth, coincidentally, a further $3,000.

When the benefits ran out, she met the driver of a bus in which she traveled, a strange and isolated young West Indian called Carl Manning. He was almost autistic, a social misfit, whose main interests were bus routes and Internet pornography. She moved in with him at once.

It is possible that they then developed together the strange psychiatric condition known as *folie à deux* first described by two French psychiatrists in the nineteenth century. In this condition, two people who are mutually dependent and in unusually close association come to share the same delusion. Usually the person with the stronger character and greater intelligence is the originator of the delusion, which he or she believes with unshakable conviction; the other, weaker and less intelligent, character goes along with it because he or she has not the strength to resist. When the weaker character is separated from the stronger, he or she ceases to believe in the delusion.

Kouao—the stronger character of the two by far—needed Manning because he had an apartment, and she had nowhere else to stay; Manning needed Kouao because she was the only woman, other than a prostitute, with whom he had ever had a sexual relationship. When Kouao began to believe that Anna was possessed by the devil, Manning accepted what she said and joined in her efforts to abuse Satan out of Anna. They took her to several fundamentalist churches, whose pastors performed exorcisms: indeed, on the very day before Anna's death, it was the taxi driver who was taking them to one such church for an exorcism who noticed that Anna was scarcely conscious, and who insisted upon taking her to an ambulance station, from whence she was taken to the hospital in which she died.

The conduct of the two defendants in court supports the diagnosis of *folie à deux*. Manning was subdued and accepted his guilt. Kouao, however, kept a Bible in her hand always and frequently had to be removed from the dock because of her religious outbursts. She behaved as if truly mad.

Two distant relatives of Kouao's who lived in England testified that they drew the attention of the welfare authorities to Anna's condition. Nothing happened. A baby-sitter who looked after Anna when Kouao found work was so worried by her general condition, her incontinence of urine, and the marks on her skin that she took her to a hospital. There Kouao managed to convince an experienced doctor that Anna's main problem was scabies, from which everything else about her followed. Kouao claimed that the marks on her skin were the result of her own scratching to relieve the irritation of scabies.

Nine days later, however, Kouao herself took Anna to another hospital. There she claimed that the scalds from hot water
to the child's head had been caused by Anna's having poured
the water over herself in her frantic attempts to relieve the itch-
ing of scabies. This time, however, the doctors and nurses were
not deceived. Not only did they note Anna's injuries but also
her state of malnutrition and the gross discrepancy between the
rags she was wearing and the immaculate smartness of the
woman they assumed to be her mother. She ate ravenously, as if
unaccustomed to plentiful food—as indeed she was. Hospital
staff noted that she became incontinent at the prospect of this
woman's visits to the hospital, and a nurse reported that she
stood at attention and trembled when Kouao arrived.

The doctor in charge of the case duly informed the social
worker and the police of her well-founded suspicions. The social worker and the policewoman deputed to the case, both of
them black themselves, dismissed these suspicions out of hand,
however, without proper investigation, once again believing
Kouao's account of the case—namely that Anna had scabies,
from which everything else followed. The social worker and the
policewoman neither looked at the child themselves nor at the
hospital photographs of the child's condition. They insisted that
Anna be released back into the care (if that is quite the word) of
Kouao—the social worker explaining Anna's evident fear of
Kouao as a manifestation of the deep respect in which Afro-
Caribbean children hold their elders and betters. The fact that
the Ivory Coast is in West Africa, not the West Indies, did not
occur to the social worker, whose multi-culturalism obviously
consisted of the most rigid stereotypes.

On discovering that Anna had been returned to Kouao, the
doctor in charge of the case wrote twice to express her grave
concern about the child's safety to the welfare authorities, who
dispatched the same social worker to Manning's apartment,
which she found cramped but clean. That was all she saw fit to
comment upon. By then, Anna was kept in the bathtub at night

and beaten regularly, with (among other things) a hammer to the toes. Manning was writing in his diary that Anna's injuries were self-inflicted, a consequence of her "witchcraft."

The social worker and the policewoman never went back. They feebly pleaded fear of catching scabies from Anna. Finally Kouao visited the social worker and claimed that Manning was sexually abusing Anna, withdrawing the claim soon afterward. The social worker and the policewoman assumed that the claim was just a ploy on Kouao's part to obtain more spacious accommodations for herself, and their investigations evidently did not involve examining Anna.

Two months later, Anna was dead.

The case naturally provoked a lot of commentary, much of it beside the point. The social worker and the policewoman had been made into scapegoats, correspondents to the *Guardian*—the great organ of left-liberal thinking in Britain—suggested; the real problem was a lack of resources: social workers were too overworked and poorly paid to do their job properly. It is amazing how anything can be turned these days into a pay claim.

A former social worker, however, wrote to the *Guardian* and suggested that ideology, particularly in the training of social workers, was the fundamental problem. Here, of course, he went to the heart of the matter. The theme of race, and official attitudes towards it, ran through the Anna Climbie case like a threnody.

So rapidly has political correctness pervaded our institutions that today virtually no one can keep a clear head about race. The institutions of social welfare are concerned to the point of obsession with race. Official anti-racism has given to racial questions a cardinal importance that they never had before. Welfare agencies divide people into racial groups for statistical purposes with a punctiliousness I have not experienced since I lived, briefly, in apartheid South Africa a quarter of a century ago. It is no longer possible, or even thought desirable, for people involved in welfare services to do their best on a case-by-case basis, without (as far as is humanly feasible) racial bias. Indeed, not long ago I received an invitation from my hospital to participate in a race-awareness course, which was based upon the assumption that the worst and most dangerous kind of racist was the doctor who deluded himself that he treated all patients equally, to the best of his ability. At least the racial awareness course was not (yet) compulsory: a lawyer friend of mine, elevated recently to the bench, was obliged to go through one such exercise for newly appointed judges, and was holed up for a weekend in a wretched provincial hotel with accusatory representatives of every major "community." Come the final dinner, a Muslim representative refused to sit next to one of the newly appointed judges because he was Jewish.

The outcome of the Anna Climbie case would almost certainly not have been different had the policeman and the social worker at its center been white, but the reasons for the outcome would have been slightly different. As blacks who represented authority—in a society in which all serious thinkers believe oppressed blacks to be in permanent struggle with oppressing whites—these functionaries had joined forces with the aggressor, at least in the minds of those who believe in such simple-minded dichotomies. Under the circumstances, it would hardly be surprising if they exhibited, when dealing with other black people, a reluctance to enforce regulations with vigor, for fear of appearing to be Uncle Toms, doing the white man's work for him. In a world divided into Them and Us (and it would have been difficult, given the temper of the times, for the social worker and the policewoman to have escaped this way of thinking altogether), We are indissolubly united against Them: therefore, if one of us treats another one of us badly, it is a scandal that we must conceal for our own collective good. A black African friend of mine, who had been a refugee in Zambia, once published an article in which he exposed the corruption of the regime there. His African friends told him that, while nothing he said in the article was untrue, he should not have published it, because it exposed Africa's dirty linen to the racist gaze of Europeans.

In other words, the social worker and the policewoman believed Marie Therese Kouao because they wanted to avoid having to take action against a black woman, for fear of appearing too "white" in the eyes of other blacks. Thus they resorted to the preposterous rationalizations that the Ivory Coast is an island in the West Indies and that West Indian children stand at attention when their mothers visit them in the hospital.

The white doctor who was taken in by Kouao's ridiculous story of scabies (a diagnosis contradicted both by a dermatologist at the time and at postmortem) was afraid to appear too harsh in her assessment of Kouao, to avoid the accusation, so easily made in these times of easy outrage, of being a racist. Had she not affected to believe Kouao, she would have had to take action to protect Anna, at the risk of Kouao's accusing her of being racially motivated. And since (to quote another memo from my hospital) "racial harassment is that action which is perceived by the victim to be such," it seemed safer to leave Kouao to her coat hangers, hammers, boiling water, and so forth. For this reason, also, the outcome of the case would have been no different had the social worker and the policewoman been white: their fears would have been different from those of their black colleagues, but the ultimate effects of those fears would have been the same.

Kouao, Manning, and Anna Climbie were treated not as individual human beings but as members of a collectivity: a purely theoretical collectivity, moreover, whose correspondence to reality was extremely slight. No out-and-out racist could have suggested a less flattering picture of the relations between black children and black adults than that which the social worker and the policewoman appeared to accept as normal in the case of Kouao and Anna Climbie. And had the first doctor, the social worker, and the policewoman been less fixated on the problem of race and more concerned to do their best on a case-by-case basis, Anna Climbie would still have been alive, and Kouao and Manning would be spending less of their lives in prison.

I have seen such "racial awareness"—the belief that racial considerations trump all others—often enough. A little while ago I was asked to stand in for a doctor who was going on prolonged leave and who was well known for his ideological sympathy for blacks of Jamaican origin. For him, the high rates both of imprisonment and psychosis of young Jamaican males are evidence of what has come to be known in England, since a notorious official report into the conduct of London's Metropolitan Police, as "institutionalized racism."

A nurse asked me to visit one of the doctor's patients, a young black man living in a terraced house near the hospital. He had a long history of psychosis and was refusing to take his medication. I read his hospital notes and went to his house.

When I arrived, his next-door neighbor, a middle-aged black man, said, "Doctor, you've got to do something; otherwise someone's going to be killed." The young man, floridly mad, believed that he had been cheated by his family of an inheritance that would have made him extremely rich.

Only later did I learn of this young man's history of violence. The last time the doctor for whom I was standing in visited the home, the young man chased him away, wielding a machete. The young man had attacked several of his relatives and had driven his mother out of the house, which she owned. She had been obliged by his threats to seek accommodation elsewhere.

None of his propensity to violence, not even the incident with the machete, appeared in the medical notes. The doctor felt that to record the incidents would "stigmatize" the patient and add to the harm he chronically suffered as a member of an already stigmatized group. Furthermore, to treat him against his will for his dangerous madness—which English law permits—would simply be to swell the already excessive numbers of young black men requiring such compulsory treatment for psychoses caused (my colleague would say) by English racism.

No such delicacy of feeling was wasted upon the young man's mother, however, she who had spent many blameless years as a nurse, paying for the house from which her son had now driven her. Sympathy went out only to the son, who fitted the mold of someone in need of protection from an uncomprehending and hostile society. The fact that, if no one intervened, he might well kill or seriously injure someone and end up in an institution for the criminally insane for life was of no particular concern. My colleague would interpret it as further evidence of the oppressive, racist nature of society, and of the need to treat such as he with even more delicacy of feeling. There are no episodes from which the wrong conclusions cannot be drawn.

Even I, despite my staunch opposition to racialized thinking or actions, have found it difficult to resist the spirit of the age entirely. One of the worst mistakes I ever made was because I allowed myself to give consideration to race where none should have been given.

A young black man, who still lived with his mother, began to withdraw, as if into a shell. Never very communicative or outgoing, he continued to work but not to speak. On one occasion he did speak to his mother—about the disposal of his belongings if he should die.

One day his mother returned to find the house barricaded. Her son was inside, having propped furniture against the doors and windows. His mother called the fire department, who had difficulty entering. They found the son unconscious, with his wrists cut and blood everywhere. He had taken an overdose of pills also.

He had lost so much blood that he required a transfusion before the surgery to repair his tendons could begin. A more determined effort to kill oneself could hardly be imagined. I suggested to his mother that, after his recovery from the operation, he be transferred to a psychiatric ward.

At first she agreed, relieved at the suggestion. But then another of her sons and a friend arrived in the hospital, and the atmosphere changed at once. You might have supposed from their attitude towards me that it was I who had cut the young man's wrists, barricaded him in the house, and nearly done him to death. My argument that his conduct over the past weeks suggested that he had become mentally disturbed in some way that required further investigation, and that he was in grave danger of killing himself, was called racist: I wouldn't have argued thus if my patient had been white. The hospital was racist; the doctors were racist; I in particular was racist.

Unfortunately the mother, with whom my relations until the arrival of the two other men had been cordial, now took their part. Under no circumstances would she allow her son to go to a psychiatric ward, where they routinely (and purposely) drugged young black men to death. The brother and the friend warned me that if I insisted, they would get their friends to create a disturbance in the hospital.

The law allowed me to overrule the young man's mother, brother, and friend, but the scene was becoming ugly. I arranged to meet them the following day, in the hope that their attitude was but a manifestation of passing anxiety, but by then their attitude had hardened. I caved in: but before doing so, I made the mother sign a statement that I had warned her of the consequences of refusing further investigation and treatment of her son, for which she would hold neither me nor the hospital responsible. The document was of no legal validity whatsoever; whatever force it had was strictly moral.

I did not quite give up. I sent a nurse to the young man's home, but she was several times denied entry on the grounds that her (racist) services were not required. A few weeks later the young man killed himself by hanging.

At least the family did not have the gall to sue me for not having invoked the full force of the law (as, on reflection, I should have). They did not argue that I had failed to hospitalize him against his will for racist reasons, not caring about the fate of a mere black man—an argument that doubtless would have struck some people as entirely plausible. Indeed, I did not invoke the law for reasons of race, though not for racist reasons: for had the family been white, I would certainly have overruled them. But I had capitulated to the orthodoxy that avoiding race conflict must trump all other considerations, including the mere welfare of individuals. For in our current climate of opinion, every white man is a racist until proved otherwise.

No one doubts the survival of racist sentiment. The other day, for example, I was in a taxi driven by a young Indian who disliked the way a young Jamaican was driving. "Throw that man a banana!" he exclaimed unself-consciously. His spontaneous outburst spoke volumes about his real feelings.

But the survival of such sentiment hardly requires or justifies the presumption that all public services are inherently and malignantly racist, and that therefore considerations of racial justice should play a bigger part in the provision of services than considerations of individual need. In this situation, black and white are united by their own kind of *folie à deux*, the blacks fearing that all whites are racist, the whites fearing that all blacks will accuse them of racism.

And while we are locked in this folly, innocents like Anna Climbie die.

*2001*

# GRIMMER THEORY

# The Rush from Judgment

NOT LONG AGO I asked a patient of mine how he would describe his own character. He paused for a moment, as if savoring a delicious morsel.

"I take people as they come," he replied in due course. "I'm very nonjudgmental."

As his two roommates had recently decamped, stealing his prize possessions and leaving him with ruinous debts to pay, his neutrality towards human character seemed not generous but stupid, a kind of prophylactic against learning from experience. Yet nonjudgmentalism has become so universally accepted as the highest, indeed the only, virtue that he spoke of his own character as if pinning a medal for exceptional merit on his own chest.

That same week I was consulted by another patient who had experienced even worse consequences of nonjudgmentalism, though this time not entirely her own. Her life had been that of the modern slum dweller: three children by different fathers, none of whom supported her in any way and the last of whom was a vicious, violent drunk. She had separated from him by fleeing with their two-year-old to a hostel for battered women; soon afterward she found herself an apartment whose whereabouts he did not know.

Unfortunately, sometime later she was admitted to the hospital for an operation. As she had no one to whom she could entrust the child, she turned to Social Services for help. The social workers insisted, against her desperate pleas, that the child should stay with his biological father while she was in the hospital. They were deaf to her argument that he was an unsuitable guardian, even for two weeks: he would regard the child as an encumbrance, an intolerable interference with his daily routine of drinking, whoring, and fighting. They said it was wrong to pass judgment on a man like this and threatened her with dire consequences if she did not agree to their plan. So the two-year-old was sent to his father as they demanded.

Within the week he and his new girlfriend had killed the child by swinging him against the wall repeatedly by his ankles and smashing his head. At this somewhat belated juncture, society did reluctantly make a judgment: the murderers both received life sentences.

Of course, the rush to nonjudgment is in part a reaction against the cruel or unthinking application of moral codes in the past. A friend of mine recently discovered a woman in her nineties who had lived as a "patient" in a large lunatic asylum for more than seventy years but whose only illness—as far as he was able to discover—had been to give birth to an illegitimate child in the 1920s. No one, surely, would wish to see the return of such monstrous incarceration and cavalier destruction of women's lives: but it does not follow from this that mass illegitimacy (33 percent in the country as a whole, 70 percent in my hospital) is a good thing, or at least not a bad thing. Judgment is precisely that—judgment. It is not the measure of every action by an infallible and rigid instrument.

Apologists for nonjudgmentalism point, above all, to its supposed quality of compassion. A man who judges others will sometimes condemn them and therefore deny them aid and assistance, whereas the man who refuses to judge excludes no one from his all-embracing compassion. He never asks where his fellow man's suffering comes from, whether it be self-inflicted or no: for whatever its source, he sympathizes with it and succors the sufferer.

The housing department of my city holds fast to this doctrine. It allocates scarce public housing, it says in its self-congratulatory leaflets, solely on the basis of need (give or take a nepotistic connection or two—after all, even the nonjudgmental are human). It never asks how the need arose in the first place: it is there to care, not to condemn.

In practice, of course, things are a little different. It is true that the housing department makes no judgments as to the deserts of the applicants for its largesse, but that is precisely why it cannot express any human compassion whatever. Its estimation of need is mathematical, based on a perverse algebra of sociopathology.

To return to the case of my patient whose child had been murdered: she was driven from her home by her neighbors, who felt that she was responsible for the death of her child and therefore acted as good, outraged citizens by twice attempting to burn down her apartment. Thereafter she found cheap lodgings in a house where there also lodged a violent drug addict, who forced his attentions upon her. When she applied to the housing department for help, it refused her on the grounds that she was already adequately housed, in the sense of having four walls around her and a roof over her head (and it would be wholly wrong to stigmatize drug addicts as undesirable neighbors), and also because she had no young dependents—her only young dependent having been murdered and therefore not part of the equation. Stones might have wept at my patient's predicament, but not the housing department: it is far too nonjudgmental to do so.

Curiously enough, my patient was perfectly able—with a little encouragement—to accept that her misfortunes did not come entirely out of the blue, that she had contributed to them by her own conduct and was therefore not a pure or immaculate victim. Taking the line of least resistance, as she had done throughout her life, she had consented to have a child by a man whom she knew to be thoroughly unsuitable as a parent. Indeed, she had known him to be violent and drunken even before she went to live with him, but she still found him attractive; and she lived in a society that promotes its own version of the Sermon on the Mount—Sufficient unto the day is the attraction thereof. She had learned now from experience (better late than never)—which she could never have done had she refrained from making judgments about both herself and others. As a result, she had rejected another violent lover, abjured her own habitual drunkenness, and decided to go to college.

In the clinic, of course, a kind of nonjudgmentalism does and should hold sway: doctors ought never to refuse treatment on the grounds of moral deficiency. Moses Maimonides, the twelfth-century rabbi and doctor, wrote: "May I never see in the patient anything but a fellow creature in pain"—surely a noble aspiration, if somewhat difficult of achievement in practice.

But medicine is not just the passive contemplation of suffering: it is the attempt, by no means always successful, to alleviate it. And it cannot have escaped the attention of doctors that much modern suffering has a distinct flavor of self-infliction. I am not talking now of the physical illnesses that derive from habits such as smoking, but rather of the chronic suffering caused by not knowing how to live, or rather by imagining that life can be lived as an entertainment, as an extended video, as nothing but a series of pleasures of the moment. The whirligig of time brings in its revenges—at least in a cold climate such as ours.

If the doctor has a duty to relieve the suffering of his patients, he must have some idea where that suffering comes from, and this involves the retention of judgment, including moral judgment. And if, as far as he can tell in good faith, the misery of his patients derives from the way they live, he has a duty to tell them so—which often involves a more or less explicit condemnation of their way of life as completely incompatible with a satisfying existence. By avoiding the issue, the doctor is not being kind to his patients; he is being cowardly. Moreover, by refusing to place the onus on the patients to improve their lot, he is likely to mislead them into supposing that he has some purely technical or pharmacological answer to their problems, thus helping to perpetuate them.

For example, I am consulted at least once or twice a day—week in, week out; year in, year out—by women who complain of anxiety and depression, whose biographies contain obvious explanations for these unpleasant feelings. The women have often endured more than one violent sexual relationship, sometimes as many as four in succession, and have more than one young child to bring up. While they fear the loneliness of managing on their own, without help from another adult, they have come to the conclusion that all men are unreliable, even psychopathic. They are in an apparently insoluble dilemma: are they better off battered or alone?

Aided by a few simple questions, it doesn't take them long to analyze their situation, though at the outset they invariably ascribe their unhappiness to bad luck or fate. Such is the power of self-deception that even the most obvious considerations escape them. A few weeks ago a woman came to see me complaining of having been miserable and dissatisfied with her life for twenty years. Her husband treated her like a slave, and when he was not obeyed, he became aggressive, either throwing things about the room, smashing windows, or beating her.

"Why don't you leave him?" I asked.

"I feel sorry for him."

"Why?"

"Well, because he's not very bright, doctor, and he doesn't know how to read or write. He couldn't manage on his own; he can't do anything for himself. I even have to dial the telephone for him because he can't read the numbers."

"Does he work?"

"Yes, he's always worked."

"What does he do?"

"He's in charge of security at the Hall"—a large Elizabethan stately home on the outskirts of the city, owned by the municipality.

"How many people work in the security department there?" I asked her.

"Sixteen."

"You mean, every time he has to make a telephone call there, he asks one of his staff to do it for him because he can't read the numbers? Or every time he receives a letter, he has to have someone read it out to him?"

My patient looked at me wide-eyed. Obvious as this was, she hadn't thought of it.

"It's not very likely, is it, that such a man would be made the boss," I added.

She had failed, through cowardice and self-indulgence, to think about the clear discrepancy between her husband's career and his supposed helplessness at home: for had she recognized it, she could no longer think of herself as a victim (with all the psychological comfort that victimhood brings) but rather as the co-author of her own misery. She wanted to avoid a painful dilemma: either to accept the situation as it was or to do something about it.

After two more conversations with me, she did something about it. She delivered an ultimatum to her husband: either he must modify his behavior or she would leave him. Further, if ever he laid a finger upon her again, she would call the police and press charges against him. Since then he has behaved and even done what for twenty years she believed him incapable of doing: he made a cup of tea for himself. Meanwhile she has gone to art classes instead of imprisoning herself in their apartment, awaiting his arbitrary orders.

This patient had only one violent man to contend with;

many of my patients have had a succession of them. I ask where they met them, and almost without exception it was in a bar or a nightclub when they were both at a loose end, a previous relationship having broken up the week, or even the day, before. I ask what they had in common, apart from loss and loneliness. The invariable answer: sexual attraction and the desire for a good night out.

These are not contemptible in themselves, of course, but as the foundation of long-term relationships and parenthood they are a little thin and soon wear even thinner. I ask what other interests the women and their lovers have in common, and invariably there are none. The day-to-day flux is their whole world: a little shopping, a little cooking, a little tidying up, a lot of television, a visit to the social security office, and a few hours in the pub while the money lasts. This aimless routine soon palls but nevertheless remains a subject for continual and acrimonious disagreement. Moreover, there is no pressure—either moral pressure from the community or economic pressure from the system of taxation and social security benefits—to keep couples together. Before long, neither necessity nor desire cements relationships—only inertia, punctuated by violence. For the violent man, to have a woman trembling in fear of him is his only guarantee of personal significance.

But how, the women ask, are they to meet men who are not like this? How is a woman to find someone who will not exploit her alternately as a meal ticket and an object for the relief of sexual tension, who will not spend his own social security money in a single night out and then demand to be given hers as well, despite the fact that this money is needed to feed the children? How is she to find a man who will actually provide something in return, such as companionship and unconditional support?

The answer necessarily involves an examination of how they have lived, from their childhood onward. For if, as I contend and they agree, it is necessary to have interests in common in

LIFE AT THE BOTTOM

order to achieve some depth in a relationship, how are such interests generated in the first place?

The woeful inadequacy of their upbringing, education, and
outlook becomes apparent to them, perhaps for the first time.

"What are you interested in?" I ask. The question comes
like a warning shot.

"Well . . . nothing, really," they reply. They recognize the
unsatisfactory nature of their answer—which is all too truth-
ful—at once.

"Did you try hard at school?"

"No."

"What did you do instead?"

"Messed around, like everyone else."

Their peers discouraged, sometimes by physical violence,
those few who showed some inclination to work. To have resis-
ted the prevailing ethos would have required exceptional
courage, as well as parental backing, which was invariably
missing. It was better to go along with the crowd and enjoy the
illicit pleasures of the moment. It didn't really matter: after all,
there would always be enough to eat, a roof over one's head,
and a television to watch, thanks to subventions from the state.
Besides which, it is a truth universally acknowledged in the
slums that there is nothing to be gained by individual effort,
since the world is so unjustly organized. And in the absence of
either fear or hope, only the present moment has any reality:
you do what is most amusing, or least boring, at each passing
moment.

In the absence of an interest or career, motherhood seems a
good choice: only later does it become clear just how entrap-
ping it is, especially when the father—predictably, but not pre-
dictedly—takes no share of parental duties.

With no experience or knowledge of the worlds of science,
art, or literature, and deprived of the sheer necessity to earn
their subsistence, my patients are rich in nothing but time on
their hands, and so they embark upon the *Liaisons Dangereuses*

of the slums. But the relationships in which they thus embroil themselves are incapable for long of sustaining the burden placed upon them, and the descent into misery, drudgery, squalor, and fear is almost immediate.

In their late twenties the most intelligent among them say to me, "There's something missing in my life, but I don't know what it is." They remind me of the young people I met behind the Iron Curtain, who had never known any other life than that under the Communists, who knew little of the outside world and yet knew that their way of life was both abnormal and intolerable.

My patients medicalize both their own misery and the terrible conduct of their violent lovers, a way of explaining their existential dissatisfaction that absolves them of responsibility. It takes little time, however, to disabuse them of their misconceptions, and the fact that I am often able to predict from very near the outset of our consultation how their lovers have behaved towards them astonishes them. Last week I saw a patient who had taken an overdose after her boyfriend beat her up. Our dialogue followed a set pattern.

"And, of course, he sometimes grabs you round the throat and squeezes and tries to strangle you?" I ask.

"How did you know, doctor?"

"Because I've heard it practically every day for the last seven years. And you have marks on your neck."

"He doesn't do it all the time, doctor." This is the universal extenuation offered.

"And, of course, he apologizes afterward and tells you it won't happen again. And you believe him."

"Yes. I really think he needs help, doctor."

"Why do you say that?"

"Well, when he does it, he changes completely; he becomes another person; his eyes stare; it's like he has a fit. I really think he can't help it; he's got no control over it."

"Would he do it in front of me, here, now, in this room?"

"No, of course not."

"Then he *can* help it, can't he?"

The woman's desire to avoid a painful dilemma—love him and be beaten, or leave him and miss him—prevented her from asking herself the very obvious question as to why the "fits" happened only in the privacy of their apartment. Suddenly, inescapably, the responsibility for alleviating her misery became hers: she had to make a choice.

"But I love him, doctor."

The triumph of the doctrine of the sovereignty of sentiment over sense would have delighted the Romantics, no doubt, but it has promoted an unconscionable amount of misery.

"Your boyfriend is unlikely to change. He strangles you because he enjoys it and gets a feeling of power from doing so. It makes him feel big: 'I strangle her, but she still loves me, so I must be really wonderful.' If you leave him, he'll find someone else to strangle within the week."

"But it's difficult, doctor."

"I didn't say it was easy; I said it was necessary. There's no reason why what is necessary should also be easy. But you can't expect doctors to make you happy while your lover is still strangling you, or to make him stop strangling you. Neither of these things is possible. You must make a choice. There is simply no way round it."

To tell such a patient that she is responsible, both practically and morally, for her own life is not to deny her help; it is to tell her the truth. To force her to face her complicity in her misery is not to abandon her to her fate. On many occasions I have put such women in touch with lawyers, I have found them safe accommodation, I have found them places in colleges. Nor do I demand an immediate decision; what has taken years to develop is rarely undone in an hour or two. But I stick to the fundamental truth: that no doctor, no social worker, no policeman can improve the quality of such a woman's life unless she is willing to forgo whatever gratification she derives from her violent boyfriend. There is no painless way of resolving the dilemma.

In almost all cases the women return a few weeks later much improved in their mood. The love they thought they felt for their tormentors has evaporated; they find it difficult in retrospect to distinguish it from the fear they felt.

What should we do now? they ask me.

How am I to answer them? Should I pretend to an agnosticism about what might constitute a better life for them and their children? Should I pretend that a promiscuous granting of their favors to the first man they meet in a pub is as good as taking a little care over such matters? Wouldn't that be the ultimate betrayal?

I advise them that their first responsibility is to do everything in their power to prevent their children from following in their footsteps; they should try to open horizons to them beyond the miserable and sordid ones visible from the slums. This will involve spending time with them, taking an interest in their schoolwork, learning to say no to them when the occasion arises, and, above all, ensuring that they never again witness scenes of domestic violence.

As for themselves, they should try to go to college: for even if it fails to render them more employable, they will at least gain a sense of achievement and possibly an enduring interest. And if that means they have to break the rules governing social security—which decree that they should be theoretically available for work and therefore not engaged in full-time education—well, I am not going to inform the authorities, who (it seems) prefer their dependents utterly passive.

They often take my suggestions. (One of my patients, beaten for twenty years, has since become a nurse, and many others work as assistants in nursing homes, the desire to help others being a corollary of their desire to help themselves.) I am probably the only person they have ever met to whom the violence of their lives is not as natural as the air they breathe but the result of human choices; I am the only person who has ever suggested to them that they can behave otherwise than they do behave.

It would be vain to suggest that this approach works in every case. Judgment is necessary, too, in selecting the cases; there are those who are too old, too psychologically fragile, or too young to bear the pain of accepting partial responsibility for their own misery. Alas, there is a period during the downward spiral of self-destruction when little can be done, as if self-destruction has a natural course of its own. Just as alcoholics and drug addicts may take years to accept first, that they are addicted, and second, that addiction is neither an excuse for their conduct nor a fate imposed upon them by circumstances, so the willful self-destruction that I see around me often runs a prolonged course, thanks to the powers of human self-deception.

It can rarely be nipped in the bud. For example, in the week in which the woman whose child had been murdered consulted me, two young women came to my notice, neither of whom gave any thought to the future or to the past, and both of whom sleepwalked through the present.

The first was barely sixteen, a white girl two months pregnant by a Muslim burglar. She was covered in bruises. They had met when he burgled her house, where she had been left alone for the night by her single mother, with whom she fought like a cat and a dog tied up in a sack over the time she should come home at night from clubs and discotheques (her mother suggesting the abominably early hour of midnight). The burglar asked her to come with him, and she did; thenceforth he locked her up, never allowed her out of the apartment, forbade all contact with others, beat her black and blue, kicked her regularly in the stomach, demanded her conversion to Islam (he himself was a drunk), and in general expected her to be his slave.

When he went into the hospital for a small operation—the repair of a tendon in his arm, injured in the course of house-breaking—she had an opportunity to escape. I offered her every facility to do so, from a safe house to the services of a lawyer paid for by the public purse.

"I can't leave him," she said. "I love him, and he said he'd kill himself if I leave him."

I know from experience that such a man might take an overdose as a form of emotional blackmail: the vast majority of male overdoses in my ward are of men who have beaten their women—the overdoses serve the dual function of blackmailing the women into remaining with them and of presenting themselves as the victims rather than the perpetrators of their own violence. I also know from experience that the Muslim burglar would never actually kill himself. But when a young woman says she fears the suicide of her lover, she is in effect saying that she will not yet leave him, and nothing will induce her to change her mind.

While the Muslim burglar remained in the hospital, she appeared every day, dressed in Punjabi costume, to tend her tormentor-lover, to bring him his Indian delicacies and all the little comforts he lacked.

The second young patient was a black girl, now aged seventeen, whose parents first knew of her liaison with a white boy a year older than she when her teacher brought her home from school at the age of fourteen, having been beaten up by the boy in the schoolyard. A few months later she gave birth to his child, and they went to live together. (No doubt future social historians will find the contradiction between our concern about sexual abuse, on the one hand, and our connivance at and indifference to precocious sexual activity, on the other, as curious as we find the contrast between Victorian sexual prudery and the vast size of the Victorian demimonde.) Fatherhood did not improve the young man's conduct: he broke her jaw, fractured her ribs, partially strangled her, punched her regularly, and used her head to break a closed window before pushing her out of it altogether. He did not work, took her money for drink, went to spend nights with other girls, and demanded his meals be ready for him to suit his convenience.

I offered her, too, every opportunity to leave, every legal protection it was possible to provide, but her cup of bitterness, like the first girl's, was not yet full ("It's all right for you; you don't love him!") and therefore not yet ready to be drained. All one could do was offer to help whenever she was ready to ask for it.

Neither of these young women was deficient in intelligence, far from it; and in a few years, when they appear again in my hospital, as inevitably they will, they'll be ready to examine the source of their suffering, having wasted so much time. I hope someone will have the courage and compassion to guide them to that source: for only if the veil of self-deception is torn from their eyes can they improve the quality of their lives.

Experience has taught me that it is wrong and cruel to suspend judgment, that nonjudgmentalism is at best indifference to the suffering of others, at worst a disguised form of sadism. How can one respect people as members of the human race unless one holds them to a standard of conduct and truthfulness? How can people learn from experience unless they are told that they can and should change? One doesn't demand of laboratory mice that they do better: but man is not a mouse, and I can think of no more contemptuous way of treating people than to ascribe to them no more responsibility than such mice.

In any case, nonjudgmentalism is not really nonjudgmental. It is the judgment that, in the words of a bitter Argentinean tango, "todo es igual, nada es mejor": everything is the same, nothing is better. This is as barbaric and untruthful a doctrine as has yet emerged from the fertile mind of man.

*1997*

# *What Causes Crime?*

◈ AS I BROWSED in a bookshop shortly after my arrival in New Zealand on a recent visit, I came upon a volume of national statistics in which I discovered, to my amazement, that New Zealand's prison population is half as large again, per capita, as Britain's. And suddenly that remote nation, so far from Britain geographically and so close culturally, seemed an enormous conundrum for someone like me, with an interest in crime.

After all, for more than a century we British have thought of our former colony as a better, cleaner Britain. By 1900, New Zealand was already the healthiest place in the world. Almost the same size as Great Britain, it has a population equal to greater Manchester's alone. It is free of the squalor and decay so prominent in all English cities and towns, and if there is no great wealth there, neither is there much poverty. With one of the earliest welfare states in the world, it has an egalitarian ethos, and one can't readily tell a mechanic from a neurosurgeon from his manner of speech or of dress. The way of life is informal, the pace relaxed. Add all this to the impressive per capita GDP figures, and New Zealand has one of the highest standards of living in the world.

Such a society—prosperous, democratic, egalitarian—should be virtually free of crime, if the commonplace liberal explanations of criminality were true. But they aren't, and New

Zealand is now almost as crime-ridden as its mother country, itself the most crime-ridden nation in western Europe (along with prosperous, democratic, egalitarian Holland). Indeed, in the ever upward trend in the crime figures, New Zealand is only a handful of years behind Britain and, in point of homicide, a few years in advance of it. This fact is of great theoretical interest, or ought to be: it is an overwhelming refutation of the standard liberal explanations of crime.

Browsing further in the bookshop, I wasn't in the least amazed to turn up a book by a liberal criminologist who explained the startling imprisonment statistics by what he called the New Zealand criminal justice system's "obsession" with punishment. In fact, since the number of serious crimes in New Zealand (as everywhere else) has increased at a vastly greater rate than the number of prisoners, it would be more accurate to accuse the system of an obsession with lax enforcement, pleas of mitigation, excuse finding, and leniency—anything but punishment.

Shortly after my visit to the bookshop, my hostess in Wellington recalled over dinner a curious episode from her Christchurch childhood. When she was six, she recounted, her mother had taken her on a kind of pilgrimage to see the very spot in a park where the famous Parker-Hulme murder had taken place six years earlier, in 1954. This murder is the subject of the recent celebrated New Zealand film *Heavenly Creatures*, and in the last two decades it has been the subject of much liberal—that is to say, unctuously nonjudgmental—reinterpretation, which the New Zealand intelligentsia now almost universally, and unthinkingly, accepts. This acceptance is a phenomenon of great cultural significance, and it begins to answer the conundrum that so fascinated me throughout my New Zealand visit.

Gifted and intelligent, Juliet Hulme (pronounced "hume") and Pauline Parker had just finished their studies at Christchurch's most prestigious girls' high school. Their relationship was exceptionally close, but the Hulme family's impending return to England threatened them with separation. When Parker's mother refused to allow her daughter to follow Hulme, the girls decided to kill her. They bashed her repeatedly over the head with a brick wrapped in a stocking, having met her in the park ostensibly for a cup of tea and a stroll. The murder was premeditated, as the jocular tone in which Parker anticipated the happy event in her diary proved.

The case transfixed New Zealand and a large part of the world. My hostess's mother took her daughter to the site of this extraordinary murder because of the fascination that evil holds for those who have little personal contact with it. Christchurch in those days was a quiet, prosperous, provincial city that prided itself on its English gentility, that did not have a single restaurant outside the hotels, and that approached nearest to the excitement of wrongdoing in the daily enactment of the "six o'clock swill," that strange institution brought about by a law forbidding the sale of alcohol in public bars after six in the evening. Men would drink as much and as fast as they were able between leaving their offices and six o'clock, with sometimes unedifying results. So uneventful was life in Christchurch that to this day all its inhabitants over a certain age can point to the exact site of the murder, despite the explosion of serious crime in the intervening period.

The shift in the interpretation of the Parker-Hulme case signals a sea change in New Zealand's attitude toward crime in general, a change that has occurred everywhere else in the Western world. Public opinion at the time universally regarded the Parker-Hulme murder as the evil act of evil girls acting in the grip of an evil passion. Nowadays a different interpretation is almost as universal. A well-known book on the case, *Parker and Hulme: A Lesbian View*, by two lesbian academics, Julie Glamuzina and Alison Laurie, sums up today's prevailing opinion.

According to the reinterpretation, the Parker-Hulme case

was not a brutal and pointless murder but the natural, inevitable outcome of a grand passion thwarted by narrow-minded social prejudice and intolerance. New Zealand was then a repressed and repressive society, and something had to give. The authors unquestioningly accept the hydraulic model of human desire, according to which passion is like the pus in an abscess, which, if not drained, causes blood poisoning, delirium, and death. If society prevented two lesbian adolescents from acting upon their passion, therefore, it was only to be expected that they should have done to death the mother of one of them. The primordial wrongness of bashing people with bricks has vanished altogether.

In support of their hypothesis, the two authors asked a number of lesbians who grew up at the time of the case for their reaction to it. Yes, they replied, they understood the girls only too well, for they themselves had sometimes harbored murderous feelings towards their parents. Both the authors and the respondents overlooked the significant moral difference between occasionally wishing one's mother would drop dead and causing her actually to do so. Nor is this obtuseness exclusive to lesbians. The *Los Angeles Times* reported the film's director, Peter Jackson, as regarding his own film as nonjudgmental. This, of course, lays bare the curious moral stance of our age: it is not wrong to bash an innocent woman to death with a brick, but it is wrong to condemn the deed and its perpetrators.

From being branded monsters of depravity, Parker and Hulme now appear almost martyrs to a cause. Public opinion admires them—not because they managed after their release from five years' imprisonment to make successful new lives for themselves, thus pointing to the hope and possibility of redemption (Juliet Hulme has become an internationally acclaimed crime novelist, under the name Ann Perry). Instead it's because they are thought to have engaged in a lesbian affair at a time of extreme primness and propriety in New Zealand—though Hulme explicitly denies that this was the case. They are believed to have acted upon forbidden desires, the greatest feat of heroism that the *bien-pensants* of our age can imagine.

But of course, if repression of desire were truly the cause of crime, one would have expected the crime rate to fall as social and legal obstacles to the expression of desire were removed. And there can be little doubt that New Zealand has become much less straitlaced than it was in the 1950s. It is far more tolerant of people doing their own thing than it was then. It is thus a natural experiment for the verification or refutation of the hydraulic model of desire.

When Parker and Hulme committed their murder, the whole of New Zealand recorded annually about a hundred serious violent offenses. Indeed, it was the extreme contrast between the brutality of the crime and the placidity of the country that made it so startling: had it occurred in Colombia, no one would have given it a moment's thought. Forty years later, after continued loosening of restraints upon the expression of desire, the number of violent offenses in New Zealand has increased by four to five hundred times. The population has not quite doubled in the interval.

Perhaps reporting practices have also changed, but no one could seriously doubt that violent offenses had increased enormously (by 400 percent between 1978 and 1995 alone), and increased in viciousness as well. There is no genre of modern crime—from serial rape to mass killing—from which New Zealand is now immune. Gone forever are the days (within the memory of people by no means old) when everyone left his house unlocked and deliveries of cash to banks in country towns could be left untouched overnight on the pavement outside.

The Parker-Hulme case is far from the only case in New Zealand in which explanation has slid inexorably into moral neutrality and then total exculpation of crime. This moral neutrality, which begins with intellectuals, soon diffuses into the rest of society and provides an absolution in advance for those inclined to act upon their impulses. It acts as a solvent of any remaining restraint. Criminals learn to regard their crimes not as the result of decisions they themselves have taken but as the vector of abstract and impersonal forces upon which they exert no influence.

The most prominent New Zealand case now undergoing exculpatory reinterpretation is that of a woman called Gay Oakes, currently serving a life sentence for the murder of her common-law husband, Doug Garden, father of four of her six children. She poisoned his coffee one day in 1994, and he died. She buried him in her backyard: ashes to ashes, dust to dust, and Doug Garden to dug garden, as it were.

The case has become a cause célèbre because Doug Garden was by most (though not all) accounts a very nasty man who unmercifully battered and abused Gay Oakes for the ten years of their liaison. Oakes has now written and published her autobiography, to which is appended a brief essay by her lawyer, one of the best-known advocates in New Zealand, Judith Ablett-Kerr. The lawyer, who is fighting to get her client's sentence reduced, argues that Oakes was suffering from what she calls "battered-woman syndrome" and therefore could not be held fully responsible for her acts, including poisoning. Women who undergo abuse over so long a period, the argument goes, do not think clearly or rationally and must therefore be held to a different standard of conduct from the rest of us.

There is no doubt, of course, that women abused over a long period are often in a confused state of mind. At least one such woman consults me every working day of my life. But the idea that a battered woman suffers from a syndrome that excuses her conduct, no matter what, has a disastrous logical consequence: that battering men also suffer from a syndrome and cannot be held accountable for their actions. No one, then, is individually responsible for what is done. This is no mere theoretical danger: I have male patients who claim precisely this and ask for help in overcoming their battering syndrome. Of the many indications that their behavior is under voluntary control, one is that they ask for help only when threatened with a court case or a separation, and resume their destructive conduct once the danger has passed.

The battered-woman-syndrome concept is uncompromising in its rejection of personal responsibility. The truth is that most (though not all) battered women have contributed to their unhappy situation by the way they have chosen to live. Gay Oakes's autobiography clearly, if unwittingly, illustrates her complicity in her fate, though she artlessly records the sordid and largely self-provoked crises of her own life as though they had no connection either with one another or with anything she has ever done or omitted to do. Even in prison, with a lot of time at her disposal, she has proved incapable of reflection on the meaning of her own past; she lives as she has always lived, in an eternal, crisis-ridden, unutterably wretched present moment. Her life story reads like a soap opera written by Ingmar Bergman. And the more that people choose—and are financially enabled by the state—to live as she has lived, the more violence of the kind she has experienced will there be. The lessons to be drawn from her case are myriad, but they are not those that the liberals draw.

Born in England, Oakes went to live in Australia in early adolescence. Though not devoid of intelligence, she chose to follow the crowd in not taking school seriously, and she married thoughtlessly at the age of sixteen. The marriage didn't last ("we weren't ready for it"), and by the age of twenty she had two children by different men. She claimed to love the second of the men but nevertheless alienated him by a casual affair with yet another man: her whim was law. Then, still in Australia, she met her future victim. One of her first experiences of him was watching him smash up a bar in a drunken rage.

Before long, by her own account, he was habitually drunk, jealous, and violent towards her. He repeatedly cheated her of her money so that he could gamble, told outrageous and transparent lies, and was lazy even as a petty criminal. He broke his promises to reform time out of number. Nevertheless, the question did not occur to her (nor has it yet occurred to her, to judge from her memoirs) whether such a man was a suitable father for her children.

Four years into their relationship, by which time she had had two of his children, he abandoned her for his native New Zealand. Some time later he wrote to say that he had abjured alcohol and to acknowledge that he had treated her very badly. Would she now rejoin him in New Zealand?

Although she had received innumerable such promises before, although he had abundantly proved himself to be worthless, lazy, unreliable, dishonest, and cruel—if her own account of him is to be believed—she nevertheless entertained his proposal. "All this time, Doug had blamed me for his behaviour and his admission that he was responsible for his own actions had me fooled," she wrote. "I still loved him and I really believed he had finally realised that the way he had treated me was wrong. I struggled with myself over whether to go to New Zealand. . . . In the end, I had to admit to myself that I missed Doug and wanted to be with him."

Having poisoned her loved one six years and two children later, she found he was too heavy to bury without help from a friend. Halfway through the burial (which she revealed to no one else, until the police found the body fourteen months later), she feared that she and her friend might be caught in *flagrante* and was seized with misgivings. "I was terribly sorry that I had got Jo [her friend] involved," she recalled. "I had thought we should be just pushing him over a cliff somewhere."

This is the woman whom we (and the New Zealand courts) are seriously invited to believe is a helpless victim, a woman who, though not mentally deficient, seems never once in her life to have thought more than ten minutes ahead, even about such matters as bringing a child into the world. And in this, of course, she was a true child of modern culture, with its worship of spontaneity and authenticity and its insistence that the for-swearing of instant gratification is unnecessary, even an evil to be avoided. In this sense—and in this sense alone—was she a victim.

While liberal intellectuals in New Zealand explain away such crimes as hers in this frivolous fashion, the entire New Zealand criminal justice system has come under attack in a kind of pincer movement. Miscarriage of justice of two kinds—one that liberals use for inflammatory and destructive ends, and the other that casts doubt on the sanity of the courts—undermines confidence that the enterprise of distinguishing guilt from inno-cence is even worth undertaking. If guilt and innocence are so easily confounded, so difficult to distinguish both in theory and in practice, what is the point of self-restraint?

The miscarriage of justice that liberals wave as a banner is the case of David Bain, a young man who languishes in jail, having been found guilty of murdering his entire family one morning in 1994. An Auckland businessman, Joe Karam, has since devoted his life and wealth to exposing the sloppy police work, the weaknesses in the prosecution's case, the incompe-tence of the legal defense, and the immobility of the appeal sys-tem that have resulted in the young man's life sentence. Karam has quite plausibly convinced many New Zealanders that he is right, and that his alternative theory of the death of Bain's fam-ily—namely, that his father shot them and then himself—is far more credible than the official police version.

Karam himself comes to the conclusion in the book he wrote about it that the verdict proves the essential inadequacy of the criminal justice system. This is an understandable, though mistaken, reaction by a man who has immersed himself for years in a single case of injustice. But his good-faith conclu-sion is echoed and amplified in bad faith by liberals.

They maintain on the basis of the Bain case (and one or two others) that New Zealand wrongfully locks up thousands of people, and that therefore it must change its criminal justice system completely. What they know full well and artfully suppress, however, is that any system that deals with a large number of cases will occasionally make mistakes, even bad ones, since all human institutions are imperfect. The new system that would replace the old would likewise make mistakes, and not necessarily fewer. What liberals object to in their hearts, therefore, is not this system of criminal justice but any system of criminal justice. For in the liberal view, we are all equally guilty and therefore all equally innocent. Any attempt to distinguish between us is ipso facto unjust. Parker and Hulme were just innocent schoolgirls, after all, who did what any such innocent schoolgirls would have done in their circumstances.

Another case of injustice, even more destructive in its effects than the Bain case, is the case of Peter Ellis, a young man accused and found guilty in 1996 of horrific sexual abuse of children in a municipal day-care center in Christchurch. The case has many, and eerie, parallels with a notorious case that took place in the town of Wenatchee, Washington.

It was alleged and supposedly proved in court that Ellis had strung children up, sodomized them, and made them drink urine and have oral sex with him. This continued for a prolonged period, without any physical evidence of his activities ever having come to light. No parent suspected that anything was wrong until the initial accusation was made, and then accusations followed in epidemic fashion.

It now emerges that much of the evidence was tainted. The woman who made the first accusation was a fanatic who possessed and had read a great deal of literature about satanic abuse. The detective in charge of the investigation (who has since resigned from the police) had an affair with her and with another of the accusing mothers. The foreman of the jury was related to one of the accusers. Many of the children have since retracted their testimonies, which social workers had obtained by lengthy interrogation. And now the homosexual lobby has alleged that Ellis was accused in the first place because he was a homosexual, and because it was unusual for a man to work in a day-care center. The controversy over the case threatens to degenerate into an argument as to who is most politically correct.

A New Zealand court has given credence to accusations that even the Spanish Inquisition might have found preposterous, a sign oddly enough of how far the courts have come under the influence of the *bien-pensants*, and how much they fear their censure and crave their approbation. For sexual abuse is the one crime that escapes the all-embracing understanding and forgiveness of such liberals, being a crime whose supposed pervasiveness in all ages exposes as hypocritical the pretensions of bourgeois society to decency and morality and makes clear, as well, that any one of us, in the hands of a sufficiently sensitive therapist, might discover his own secret victimhood, absolving him of responsibility for his life and actions. Sexual abuse is thus an intellectual battering ram with which to discredit the traditional edifice of self-restraint and to wipe away the personal responsibility of individuals, and no judge can do himself harm in the eyes of the right-thinking by taking the hardest and most punitive of lines towards it, whether it actually occurred in any particular instance or not.

Where crime is concerned, then, New Zealand presents a curiously familiar pattern to a visitor from Britain (and would, no doubt, to an American visitor as well): a dramatically elevated crime rate, a liberal willingness to explain away the worst crimes except those relating to sexual abuse, and an assiduously cultivated decline in public confidence in the justice system's ability to distinguish guilt from innocence. New Zealand, distant but no longer isolated, is now fully incorporated in the main current of modern culture.

Of course, New Zealand liberals still bang the old drums, too, blaming crime on poverty and inequality. At first sight, the disproportionate share of New Zealand crime committed by

Maoris and migrants from the Pacific Islands seems to come to the rescue. The Maoris and islanders are relatively (though not absolutely) poor, and they suffer discrimination (though not at the hands of the government). Only an eighth of the population, they commit half the crime. Ergo, poverty and discrimination cause crime.

But this won't wash. If the Maoris and islanders had the same crime rate as the whites, total crime in New Zealand would still be only one-third lower than it is today. Such a total would still represent a dramatic rise in the rate over the last few decades. Indeed, the removal of Maori and islander crime from the equation would represent a delay of only a few years in the upward trend.

Moreover, there were almost as many Maoris, proportionately, in the years when the crime rate was very low, and they were poorer then and suffered more open discrimination. Poverty and discrimination thus don't account for the rise in New Zealand's crime rate.

This rise provides no support for liberal theories of crime, no sustenance for the kind of person who proves the strength of his compassion by conceiving of those less law-abiding than himself as automata, mere executors of the dictates of circumstance. It is true, of course, that the decision of criminals to commit their crimes must have antecedents; but they are not to be found in New Zealand's poverty, unemployment, or inequality. Rather, they are to be found in the prudential calculations such criminals make (the likelihood of being caught, imprisoned, and so forth) and also in the characteristics of the culture, particularly the popular culture, from which they construct their thoughts about the world. And this is a culture that not only despises the achievements of past ages, inflaming ignorant egotism by teaching that we need no connection with them, but is profoundly antinomian—of which there could be no better illustration than the name of a rock band, hundreds of posters for whose concerts were plastered everywhere in Wellington and Christchurch during my visit: Ben Harper and the Innocent Criminals.

*1998*

# How Criminologists
# Foster Crime

◈  LAST WEEK in the prison I asked a young man why he was there.

"Just normal burglaries," he replied.

"Normal for whom?" I asked.

"You know, just normal."

He meant, I think, that burglaries were like grey skies in an English winter: unavoidable and to be expected. In an actuarial sense, he was right: Britain is now the burglary capital of the world, as almost every householder here will attest. But there was also a deeper sense to his words, for statistical normality slides rapidly in our minds into moral normality. The wives of burglars often talk to me of their husband's "work," as if breaking into other people's homes were merely a late shift in a factory. Nor is only burglary "normal" in the estimation of its perpetrators. "Just a normal assault," is another frequent answer prisoners give to my question, the little word "just" emphasizing the innocuousness of the crime.

But how has crime come to seem normal to its perpetrators? Is it merely a recognition of the brute fact of a vastly increased crime rate? Or could it be, on the contrary, one of the very causes of that increase, inasmuch as it represents a weakening of the inhibition against criminality?

As usual, one must look first to the academy when tracing the origins of a change in the Zeitgeist. What starts out as a career-promoting academic hypothesis ends up as an idea so widely accepted that it becomes not only an unchallengeable orthodoxy but a cliché even among the untutored. Academics have used two closely linked arguments to establish the statistical and moral normality of crime and the consequent illegitimacy of the criminal justice system's sanctions. First, they claim, we are all criminal anyway; and when everyone is guilty, everyone is innocent. Their second argument, Marxist in inspiration, is that the law has no moral content, being merely the expression of the power of certain interest groups—of the rich against the poor, for example, or the capitalist against the worker. Since the law is an expression of raw power, there is no essential moral distinction between criminal and noncriminal behavior. It is simply a question of whose foot the boot is on.

Criminologists are the mirror image of Hamlet, who exclaimed that if each man received his deserts, none should escape whipping. On the contrary, say the criminologists, more liberal than the prince (no doubt because of their humbler social origins): none should be punished. These ideas resonate in the criminal's mind. If his illegal conduct is so very normal, he thinks, what's all the fuss about in his case, or why should he be where he is—in prison? It is patently unjust for him to be incarcerated for what everyone still at liberty does. He is the victim of illegitimate and unfair discrimination, rather like an African under apartheid, and it is only reasonable that, on his release, he should take his revenge upon so unjust a society by continuing, or expanding, his criminal activity.

It is impossible to state precisely when the Zeitgeist changed and the criminal became a victim in the minds of intellectuals: not only history, but also the history of an idea, is a seamless robe. Let me quote one example, though, now more than a third of a century old. In 1966 (at about the time when Norman Mailer in America, and Jean-Paul Sartre in Europe, portrayed

criminals as existential heroes in revolt against a heartless, inau-
thentic world), the psychiatrist Karl Menninger published a
book with the revealing title *The Crime of Punishment*. It was
based upon the Isaac Ray lectures he had given three years earlier—Isaac Ray having been the first American psychiatrist who
concerned himself with the problems of crime. Menninger
wrote: "Crime is everybody's temptation. It is easy to look with
proud disdain upon those people who get caught—the stupid
ones, the unlucky ones, the blatant ones. But who does not get
nervous when a police car follows closely? We squirm over our
income tax statements and make some adjustments. We tell the
customs official we have nothing to declare—well, practically
nothing. Some of us who have never been convicted of crime
picked up over two billion dollars' worth of merchandise last
year from the stores we patronize. Over a billion dollars was
embezzled by employees last year."

The moral of the story is that those who go to court and to
prison are victims of chance at best and of prejudice at worst:
prejudice against the lowly, the unwashed, the uneducated, the
poor—those whom literary critics portentously call the Other.
This is precisely what many of my patients in the prison tell me.
Even when they have been caught *in flagrante*, loot in hand or
blood on fist, they believe the police are unfairly picking on
them. Such an attitude, of course, prevents them from reflecting
upon their own contribution to their predicament: for chance
and prejudice are not forces over which an individual has much
personal control. When I ask prisoners whether they'll be coming back after their release, a few say no with an entirely credible vehemence; they are the ones who make the mental
connection between their conduct and their fate. But most say
they don't know, that no one can foresee the future, that it's up
to the courts, that it all depends—on others, never on themselves.

It didn't take long for Menninger's attitude to permeate official thinking. A 1968 British government document on juvenile

delinquency, *Children in Trouble*, declared: "It is probably a minority of children who grow up without ever misbehaving in ways which may be contrary to the law. Frequently, such behavior is no more than an incident in the pattern of a child's normal development."

In a sense this is perfectly true, for in the absence of proper guidance and control, the default setting of human beings is surely to crime and anti-social conduct, and everyone breaks the rules at some time. But in a period of increasing permissiveness, many draw precisely the wrong conclusion from human nature's universal potential for delinquency: indeed, the only reason commentators mention that potential at all is to draw a predetermined liberal conclusion from it—that acts of delinquency, being normal, should not give rise to sanctions.

In this spirit, *Children in Trouble* treats the delinquency of normal children as if its transience were the result of a purely biological or natural process rather than of a social one. Delinquency is like baby teeth: predetermined to come and go at a certain stage of a child's development.

Not so very long ago, such an attitude would have struck almost everyone as absurd. Everyone knew, as if by instinct, that human behavior is a product of consciousness, and the consciousness of a child must be molded. I can best illustrate what I mean by my own experience. At the age of eight, I stole a penny bar of chocolate from the corner store. It gave me a thrill to do so, and I enjoyed the chocolate all the more for the fact that it had not made an inroad into my weekly pocket money (sixpence). Unwisely, however, I confided my exploit to my elder brother, in an attempt to win his respect for my bravery, which was much in question at the time. Even more unwisely, I forgot that he knew this incriminating story when, furious at him because of his habitual teasing, I told my mother that he had uttered a word that at that time was never heard in respectable households. In retaliation, he told my mother that I had stolen the chocolate.

My mother did not take the view that this was a transient episode of delinquency that would pass of its own accord. She knew instinctively (for, at that time, no one had yet befuddled minds by suggesting otherwise) that all that was necessary for delinquency to triumph was for her to do nothing. She did not think that my theft was a natural act of self-expression, or a revolt against the inequality between the power and wealth of children and that of adults, or indeed of anything other than my desire to have the chocolate without paying for it. She was right, of course. What I had done was morally wrong, and to impress the fact upon me she marched me round to Mrs. Marks, the owner of the store, where I confessed my sin and paid her tuppence by way of restitution. It was the end of my shoplifting career.

Since then, of course, our understanding of theft and other criminal activity has grown more complex, if not necessarily more accurate or realistic. It has been the effect, and quite possibly the intention, of criminologists to shed new obscurity on the matter of crime: the opacity of their writing sometimes leads one to wonder whether they have actually ever met a criminal or a crime victim. Certainly it is in their professional interest that the wellsprings of crime should remain an unfathomed mystery, for how else is one to convince governments that what a crime-ridden country (such as Britain) needs is further research done by ever more criminologists?

It is probably no coincidence that the profession of criminology underwent a vast expansion at about the same time that criminal activity began the steepest part of its exponential rise. Criminologists in Britain once numbered in the low dozens; and criminology, considered unfit for undergraduates, was taught only in one or two institutes. Today hardly a city or town in the country is without its academic criminology department. Half of the eight hundred criminologists now working in Britain got their training (mostly in sociology) in the late sixties and early seventies, during the heyday of radical activism, and they trained the other half.

Of course, it might have been that the problem of crime called forth its students. But since social problems are often of a dialectical nature, could it not also have been that the students called forth their problem? (British economist John Vaizey once wrote that any problem that became the subject of an ology was destined to grow serious.) Since the cause of crime is the decision of criminals to commit it, what goes on in their minds is not irrelevant. Ideas filter down selectively from the academy into the population at large, through discussions (and often bowdlerizations) in the papers and on TV, and become intellectual currency. In this way the ideas of criminologists could actually become a cause of crime. In addition, these ideas deleteriously affect the thinking of the police. In our hospital, for example, the police have posted notices everywhere warning staff, patients, and visitors about car theft. *Motorists!* proclaims the notice. *Your car is at risk!* This is a very criminological locution, implying as it does a mysterious force—like, say, gravity—against which mere human will, such as that exercised by thieves and policemen, can be expected to avail nothing.

In the process of transmission from academy to populace, ideas may change in subtle ways. When the well-known criminologist Jock Young wrote that "the normalization of drug use is paralleled by the normalization of crime," and, because of this normalization, criminal behavior in individuals no longer required special explanation, he surely didn't mean that he wouldn't mind if his own children started to shoot up heroin or rob old ladies in the street. Nor would he be indifferent to the intrusion of burglars into his own house, ascribing it merely to the temper of the times and regarding it as a morally neutral event. But that, of course, is precisely how "just" shoplifters, "just" burglars, "just" assaulters, "just" attempted murderers, taking their cue from him and others like him, would view (or at least say they viewed) their own actions: they have simply moved with the times and therefore done no wrong. And, not surprisingly, the crimes that now attract the deprecatory qualification "just" have escalated in seriousness even in the ten years I have attended the prison as a doctor, so that I have even heard a prisoner wave away "just a poxy little murder charge." The same is true of the drugs that prisoners use: where once they replied that they smoked "just" cannabis, they now say that they take "just" crack cocaine, as if by confining themselves thus they were paragons of self-denial and self-discipline.

Of course, the tendency of liberal intellectuals such as Jock Young not to mean quite what they say, and to express themselves more to flaunt the magnanimity of their intentions than to propagate truth, is a general one. Not long ago I was involved in a radio discussion with a distinguished film critic about the social (or anti-social) effects of the constant exposure of children to depictions of violence. He strenuously denied that any ill effects occurred or were likely to occur, but admitted *en passant* that he would not permit a diet of violence for his own children. He perhaps did not notice that, underscoring his contradictory attitude, was an unutterable contempt for half of mankind. In effect he was saying that the proles were so beyond redemption, so immoral by nature, that nothing could make them either better or worse. They did not make choices; they did not respond to moral or immoral influences; they were violent and criminal by essence. His own children, by contrast, would respond appropriately to his careful guidance.

Criminologists, needless to say, are not monolithic in their explanations of criminality: an academic discipline needs theoretical disputes as armed forces need potential enemies. But above the cacophony of explanations offered, one idea makes itself heard loud and clear, at least to criminals: to explain all is to excuse all. Criminological writing generally conceives of criminals as objects, like billiard balls responding mechanically to other billiard balls that impinge upon them. But even when they are conceived of as subjects, whose actions are the result of their ideas, criminals remain innocent: for their ideas, criminologists contend, are reasonable and natural in the circumstances in which they find themselves. What more natural than that a poor man should want material goods, especially in as materialistic a society as ours?

Recently, biological theories of crime have come back into fashion. Such theories go way back: nineteenth-century Italian and French criminologists and forensic psychiatrists elaborated a theory of hereditary degeneration to account for the criminal's inability to conform to the law. But until recently, biological theories of crime—usually spiced with a strong dose of bogus genetics—were the province of the illiberal right, leading directly to forced sterilization and other eugenic measures.

The latest biological theories of crime, however, stress that criminals cannot help what they do: it is all in their genes, their neurochemistry, or their temporal lobes. Such factors provide no answer to why the mere increase in recorded crime in Britain between 1990 and 1991 was greater than the total of all recorded crime in 1950 (to say nothing of the accelerating increases since 1991), but that failure does not deter researchers in the least. Scholarly books with titles such as *Genetics of Criminal and Antisocial Behavior* proliferate and do not evoke the outrage among intellectuals that greeted the publication of H. J. Eysenck's *Crime and Personality* in 1964, a book suggesting that criminality is an hereditary trait. For many years, liberals viewed Eysenck, professor of psychology at London University, as virtually a fascist for suggesting the heritability of almost every human characteristic, but they have since realized that genetic explanations of crime can just as readily be grist for their exculpatory and all-forgiving mills as they can be for the mills of conservatives.

Recently an entire television series in Britain focused on the idea that crime is the result of brain dysfunction. The book that accompanied the series states that the two authors "believe that—because we accept the findings of clinicians with no penal axe to grind—many criminals act as they do because of the way their brains are made. The past two decades have vastly extended the horizons of knowledge, and we believe it is time to benefit from that knowledge—the result of the work of endocrinologists, bio-physiologists, neurophysiologists, biostatisticians, geneticists and many others."

But despite the alleged lack of penal axe to grind, the ultimate message is all too familiar: "What stands out from literally hundreds of papers and studies of the various types of criminal is widespread and cogent evidence of disordered minds resulting from dysfunctional brains. . . . But we do not recognize; we merely condemn. Incarceration is an expensive and wasteful reaction."

Both parts of this message are welcome to my patients in the prison: that they are ill and in need of treatment, and that imprisonment is not only pointless but cruel and morally unjustified—less justified, indeed, than their crimes. After all, the judges who sentence them to imprisonment cannot exculpate themselves by virtue of their dysfunctional brains.

No wonder that each week prisoners tell me, "Prison's no good to me, doctor; prison's not what I need." I ask them what they do need, then.

Help, treatment, therapy.

The idea that prison is principally a therapeutic institution is now virtually ineradicable. The emphasis on recidivism rates as a measure of its success or failure in the press coverage of prison ("Research by criminologists shows . . ." etc.) reinforces this view, as does the theory put forward by criminologists that crime is a mental disorder. *The Psychopathology of Crime* by Adrian Raine of the University of Southern California claims that recidivism is a mental disorder like any other, often accompanied by cerebral dysfunction. *Addicted to Crime?*, a volume edited by psychologists working in one of Britain's few institutions for the criminally insane, contains the work of eight academics. The answer to the question of their title is, of course, yes; addiction being—falsely—conceived as a compulsion that it is futile to expect anyone to resist. (If there is a second edition of the book, the question mark will no doubt disappear from its title, just as it vanished from the second edition of Beatrice and Sidney Webb's book about the Soviet Union, *The Soviet Union: A New Civilisation?*—which included everything about Russia except the truth.)

Is it surprising that recidivist burglars and car thieves now ask for therapy for their addiction, secure in the knowledge that no such therapy can or will be forthcoming, thereby justifying the continuation of their habit? "I asked for help," they often complain to me, "but didn't get none." One young man aged twenty-one, serving a sentence of six months (three months with time off for good behavior) for having stolen sixty cars, told me that in reality he had stolen more than five hundred and had made some $160,000 doing so. It is surely an unnecessary mystification to construct an elaborate neuropsychological explanation of his conduct.

Burglars who tell me that they are addicted to their craft, thereby implying that the fault will be mine for not having treated them successfully if they continue to burgle after their release, always react in the same way when I ask them how many burglaries they committed for which they were not caught: with a happy but not (from the householder's point of view) an altogether reassuring smile, as if they were recalling the happiest times of their life—soon to return.

Criminals call for therapy for all anti-social behavior—curiously, though, only after it has led to imprisonment, not before. For example, last week a young man finally imprisoned for repeated assaults on his girlfriend and his mother, among others, told me that prison was not doing him any good, that what he needed was anger management therapy. I remarked that his behavior in prison had been exemplary: he was always polite and did as he was told.

"I don't want to be taken down the block [the punishment floor], do I?" he replied, rather giving the game away. He had been violent to his girlfriend and his mother because hitherto there were advantages, but no disadvantages, to his violence. Now that the equation was different, he had no problem "managing" his anger.

The great majority of the theories criminologists propound lead to the exculpation of criminals, and criminals eagerly take up these theories in their desire to present themselves as victims rather than as victimizers. For example, not long ago "labeling theory" took criminology by storm. According to these theorists, the quantity of crime, the type of person and offense selected to be criminalized, and the categories used to describe and explain the deviant are social constructions. Crime, or deviance, is not an objective "thing" out there. So far, I haven't tried this theory out on my noncriminal patients whose houses have been burgled three times in a year—or who have been attacked in the street more than once, as is common among these patients—but I think I can imagine their response. For criminals, of course, a theory that suggests that crime is an entirely arbitrary social category without justified moral content is highly gratifying—except when they themselves have been the victim of a crime, when they react like everyone else.

Since criminologists and sociologists can no longer plausibly attribute crime to raw poverty, they now look to "relative deprivation" to explain its rise in times of prosperity. In this light they see crime as a quasi-political protest against an unjust distribution of the goods of the world. Several criminological commentators have lamented the apparently contradictory fact that it is the poor who suffer most, including loss of property, from criminals, implying that it would be more acceptable if the criminals robbed the rich.

In discussing the policy of zero tolerance, criminologist Jock Young avers that it could be used selectively for "progressive" ends: "one can," he says, "be zero-tolerant of violence against women and tolerant about the activities of the dispossessed." One might suppose from this that among those tolerable activities of the dispossessed there was never any violence against women.

Moreover, the very term "dispossessed" carries its own emotional and ideological connotations. The poor have not failed to earn, the term implies, but instead have been robbed of what is rightfully theirs. Crime is thus the expropriation of the expropriators—and so not crime at all, in the moral sense. And this is an attitude I have encountered many times among burglars and car thieves. They believe that anyone who possesses something can, ipso facto, afford to lose it, while someone who does not possess it is, ipso facto, justified in taking it. Crime is but a form of redistributive taxation from below.

Or—when committed by women—crime could be seen "as a way, perhaps of celebrating women as independent of men," to quote Elizabeth Stanko, an American feminist criminologist teaching in a British university. Here we are paddling in the murky waters of Frantz Fanon, the West Indian psychiatrist who believed that a little murder did wonders for the psyche of the downtrodden, and who achieved iconic status precisely at the time of criminology's great expansion as a university discipline.

"Justice" in the writings of many criminologists does not refer to the means by which an individual is either rewarded or punished for his conduct in life. It refers to social justice. Most criminologists can't distinguish between unfairness and injustice, and they conclude that any society in which unfairness continues to exist (as it must) is therefore unjust. And the question of social justice usually boils down to the question of equality: as Jock Young puts it starkly: "Zero tolerance of crime must mean zero tolerance of inequality if it is to mean anything." Since one of the inhibitions against crime (as crime is commonly understood, by people who have suffered it or are likely to suffer it) is the perceived legitimacy of the legal system under which the potential criminal lives, those who propagate the idea that we live in a fundamentally unjust society also propagate crime. The poor reap what the intellectual sows.

No one gains kudos in the criminological fraternity by suggesting that police and punishment are necessary in a civilized society. To do so would be to appear illiberal and lacking faith in man's primordial goodness. It is much better for one's reputation, for example, to refer to the large number of American prisoners as "the American gulag," as if there were no relevant differences between the former Soviet Union and the United States.

In fact, criminals know all about the power of punishment: both its deterrent and rehabilitative effect. For prison is a society divided clearly in two, between wardens and prisoners. Prisoners maintain the rigid division by their own extremely severe code of punishment. Should an individual prisoner try to break down this division, other prisoners will inflict immediate, severe, and public punishment. The division therefore holds, even though many prisoners would prefer to side with the wardens than with their peers.

Criminology is not monolithic, and there are more dissenters now than there once were, as Jock Young recognizes. "This recent pattern [of criminologists who believe in detection and punishment] is in contrast to a generation of liberal opinion and scholarship whose aim was to minimize police intervention and lower police numbers. One might even say that this has been the hidden agenda of academic criminology since the Nineteenth Century."

From the criminal's point of view, criminology has served him proud.

*1999*

# Policemen in Wonderland

◈ THE LONG MARCH through the institutions—by which radical intellectuals have sought to remake society surreptitiously, without resort to the barricades—has succeeded so completely in Britain that it sometimes seems that a Nietzschean transvaluation of all values has taken place. The police are a prime case in point. Their leaders are now so desperate for the approval of liberal critics that they often seem more focused on public relations than on crime prevention and detection—on protecting their reputation rather than protecting the public. As a result, Britain is suffering a crime wave that is affecting areas hitherto spared, such as the West End of London—street robbery in the capital having increased by a fifth in the last twelve months alone.

For fear of criticism by liberals, the actions of the police now often are the mirror image of what they should be—and of what they have been in New York and other American cities, with dramatic reductions in the crime rate as a result. Yet however imbued with, or affected by, liberal values the police become, liberals will never accept them as full members of the human race or cease their carping, because it is, at base, the mere existence of the police that offends the liberal conscience, not any of their particular acts. For the permanent necessity of a police force suggests that the default setting of humanity is not to virtue and social harmony, that externally applied pressure to conform to decent behavior is a necessary component of any civilized society. And the admission that this is so (surely obvious to anyone not still in thrall to adolescent utopian dreams) undermines the very suppositions upon which the modern liberal desire to remove all external restraints upon behavior rests. We hate nothing so much as the living refutation of our cherished ideas.

Of course, one must not exaggerate the degree to which the police have been undermined: one's perception depends in part upon which end of the telescope one looks down. Seen from prison, for example, the police must still be doing a lot of their traditional work: why else are so many malefactors behind bars? Every day a new harvest, undiminished in size, comes in through the gates. Rare indeed are the cases of the wrongfully imprisoned—though the press trumpets the few that come to light in order to destroy public confidence in "the system." By means of the old rhetorical devices of *suppressio veri* and *suggestio falsi*, the predators on society appear its victims, and sympathy for the criminal becomes, in elite orthodoxy, the touchstone of a tender heart. But of the guilt of the vast majority of prisoners there can be no doubt, and it is the police who have been key in bringing them to justice.

But seen down the other end of the telescope, from the world outside prison, things look very different. Here it is not the wrongfully imprisoned but the wrongfully free who give rise to concern. For every person wrongfully imprisoned, there are literally hundreds who manifestly deserve to lose their liberty. Not only is this also an injustice (I have never understood the liberal assumption that if there were justice in the world, there would be fewer rather than more prisoners), but it makes life a torment for millions of people.

For those who live in the world of impunity—that is to say, the poorer half of the population—the police are not merely impotent but positively unwilling to do anything to rectify the situation. To err is human, to forgive divine: and the police have now taken up the role of divinities, making allowances for wrongdoers instead of apprehending them. The police forgive them, for they know not what they do.

Working in a hospital in an area where the police take a purely abstract, sociological view of crime—it is the natural consequence of deprivation and therefore neither blameworthy nor reducible by means of the application of the law—I quite often catch glimpses of police reluctance to deal with criminal offenses, even when committed in the presence of several reliable witnesses. The allowances they make for the offender (he had a bad upbringing, he once saw a psychiatrist and must therefore be psychologically disturbed, he is unemployed, he is an addict) reinforce their reluctance to undertake the paperwork nowadays consequent upon any arrest—paperwork imposed upon them, of course, by the attempt to answer the continual criticisms of the civil libertarians. The net effect has been to imprison the poor and old in their houses after dark and sometimes before it as well.

For example, a man in his late twenties was admitted to our ward one day, having taken an overdose of illegally obtained drugs. He was also an habitual inhaler of butane gas. I had known him a long time and suspected him of having stolen a piece of equipment from my office. He had a substantial criminal record—burglaries and assaults—and I knew him also from the prison.

He asked one of the senior physicians for a prescription of drugs that he wanted merely for pleasure. The physician quite properly refused, whereupon the patient became angry and abusive. He refused to calm down, and when he pinned the physician against the wall, the nurses called the police.

Having extricated the physician from his immediate predicament, the police considered their task ended. There was, in their view, no point in arresting a man so clearly out of his head as the patient—a man who knew not what he did and was therefore not answerable for his crime. What admirable compassion, and what a saving of time on paperwork, so that they might spread their compassion elsewhere!

Four weeks later the same young man broke into the house of an aged priest at night and, on being interrupted by him, battered him brutally to death. On this occasion, of course, he was arrested, butane gas or no butane gas.

I know of many other, lesser instances of police refusal to do anything about clear infringements of the law, in cases where the evidence is undoubted and where the infringement is an obvious sign of things to come.

A prostitute was a patient in our ward, and her pimp arrived to visit her. He was a man of evil appearance and demeanor: gold front teeth glistened menacingly in his mouth; his shaven head bore the marks of more than one machete attack (or defense). In the past he had broken his prostitute's jaw and ribs; he had a long criminal record. He demanded of a nurse to know the diagnosis, treatment, and expected period of hospitalization of the patient; when the nurse refused to tell him on the grounds that the information was confidential, he backed her into a corner (in the presence of another nurse) and threatened to follow her home and set fire to her house, with her, her husband, and her children in it.

The police came and escorted the pimp out but otherwise took no action, though what he had said and how he had behaved were clearly criminal offenses. The nurse did not return to work and has not been seen since on our ward.

To take one more example: a young man arrived in our emergency department having taken a small overdose. As is usually the case in such incidents, he had just had a violent quarrel with his girlfriend. (The purpose of the subsequent overdose is threefold: first, to induce the girlfriend to call an ambulance rather than the police; second, to warn her not to leave him because he might kill himself, "and then you'll be sorry, you bitch"; and third, to present himself as the victim of his own behavior—and therefore not responsible for it—and in need of treatment.) His girlfriend arrived shortly afterward with the things that he would need for a hospital stay. He at once resumed the quarrel and began to beat her again, this time in front of the nurses. They called the police, who claimed that, because the assault had been so minor—the girlfriend was not yet badly injured—there was nothing they could do, especially as they were busy elsewhere. The police evidently did not care to speculate what this man must have been capable of in private if he behaved in this fashion in a public place in front of several reliable witnesses. And the effect of this example on those who saw it—particularly young men—must have been profound.

A young man went to a local family doctor and demanded addictive drugs for which there was no medical indication. The doctor—rather unusually in the circumstances—refused, and the patient became abusive and threatening. The doctor's receptionist called the police, who took the young man into custody. But instead of taking him to the police station and charging him, they brought him to the emergency department of our hospital, where they left him, as if they were merely a delivery service.

Once again he demanded drugs, and once again, on refusal, he became abusive and threatening. The nurses called the hospital security staff; but when, instead of leaving the hospital as they requested, he took a swing at one of them, the police were again called. This time they took him out and dumped him in the street around the corner.

I was myself the victim of a minor assault, significant because it was quite likely the harbinger of a future murder. It took place in the prison in which I work. A young prisoner asked me when he would receive his ration of tobacco, to which I replied, truthfully, that I did not know. He thereupon reached out of the hatch in his cell door and tried to hit me, in the process scratching my face slightly and grabbing my glasses, which he then broke into pieces and threw out of his window.

He had been imprisoned for assault on the police, who had

been called after he had assaulted his girlfriend. Since his arrival in the prison, he had assaulted almost everyone with whom he had come into contact. He had attacked a warden so badly that he couldn't come to work for six weeks afterward. The warden informed the police of that assault, but they told him that assaults by prisoners on wardens were only to be expected and therefore they could—or rather would—do nothing. Naturally, assaults on the police themselves, however minor, are a completely different matter.

My attempts to have the prisoner charged with his assault on me came to naught. I was not really injured, and I have suffered no psychological ills from the assault. My motive in trying to have the prisoner charged and further imprisoned was to protect the public, for however inadequate a period, from a very dangerous man. But the police told me that they considered it not in the public interest to bring a prosecution, for clearly the offender was psychologically disturbed. In vain did I point out that it was therefore even more imperative that charges be brought. How could it be in the public interest for such a man to be walking the streets? And who would suffer? The poor, of course, among whom he moved.

This young man is now at liberty: but it is not at all unlikely that his liberty is someone else's imprisonment by terror.

I can only hope he will be rearrested before he kills, but I wouldn't bet on it.

No doubt it might be objected that these are just anecdotes: but scores of anecdotes of the same kind become a pattern. Besides, my experience is precisely that of all my patients, many thousands of them. One told me, for example, that her former boyfriend had broken into her home no fewer than ten times, with the drunken intention, sometimes carried out, of committing violence against her, and that on each occasion she had called the police. On each occasion they had simply given him a ride back to his own lodgings, thus acting as a free taxi service. The moral of the story seems to be that if you should find yourself without money in a British city and in need of a lift home, you should assault someone. It is quicker than walking.

But only if you already have a criminal record, are drug-addicted, drunk, or in some other way disreputable or reprehensible. For the police, so sluggish in dealing with real wrongdoing, are like avenging angels when it comes to the merest whiff of suspicion that respectable persons may have been up to no good. Then they pursue matters to the uttermost ends of the earth, like those breeds of dogs that, once they have sunk their teeth into flesh, never let go. In this way the police hope to demonstrate to the liberals that they are not prejudiced against the poor, as they are so often accused of being.

Recently, for example, a man was admitted to our hospital having taken an overdose of painkillers while he was very drunk. The hospital staff knew the patient well: he had been abusive to most of them at some time in his career as a recurrent patient. He had a very long criminal record. During a recent hospital admission, the nurses had called the police because he had assaulted a patient in the bed opposite his. As usual, the police did nothing, because, after all, he was a patient and therefore a suffering human being, and no decent person could arrest, much less charge, a sufferer. (The police, of course, didn't allow the source of his suffering to influence their indiscriminate compassion.)

During his last admission to my ward, he took himself to the lavatory to smoke and then refused to come out again. Since he needed an antidote to the pills he had taken and might otherwise die, the nurses tried to persuade him to return to his bed. He refused in no uncertain terms, and the nurses called the security staff. They hauled him, struggling, back to his bed, where the treatment was given, and his life was duly saved.

Two weeks later this same man took himself off to the local police station to accuse the security staff of assault. The police, of course, knew this man to be a recidivist criminal, a drunk, a liar, a general nuisance, and inclined to violence into the bargain: but they took his complaints seriously. Having refused to act when he assaulted the patient opposite him, they now interviewed the security men, not once but repeatedly, under caution that anything they said might be used in evidence against them. They interviewed other hospital staff to ferret out any evidence that might lead to the prosecution of the security men. As of this moment, the investigations continue, despite the fact that the only evidence is the man's word, and that in the meantime he has committed suicide while drunk, so that he can no longer be called as a witness. The police have hinted that they might still arrest the security staff.

The police have told the hospital authorities that they are duty bound to take every complaint seriously and investigate it thoroughly, but this they must know to be an unscrupulous and stupid lie, for in the ten years that I have worked in the hospital they have never taken any complaint by a member of the staff seriously. Instead they take the part of a drunken psychopath and ignore the safety of the hospital staff—to demonstrate that they have no social prejudices that might offend liberal opinion. As a result, the security staff are now understandably reluctant to lay a hand upon an obstreperous or violent patient, leaving the rest of the hospital staff completely unprotected at a time when assaults upon them are increasing.

This case is no isolated instance of the police pursuing the obviously innocent and respectable. I will relay just one more, out of many. A patient of mine, the son of Indian immigrants, came home from university, where he was studying physics, and helped his parents in their family business, a small convenience store. The young man was of unblemished character and pleasing personality. He was ambitious and had an excellent future.

Three white youths came into the shop while he was serving and demanded to buy some beer. They appeared to him to be underage, and he asked for identification. They began to abuse him with the racial slurs all Indian shopkeepers suffer at some point from modern Britain's new legions of ill-educated, uncouth, and depraved young men. Then one of them took some beer from a refrigerator, and the three of them walked out, laughing.

Perhaps foolishly, my patient followed them and demanded the return of the beer. The three set upon him, badly bruising him; but, in the process, one of them swung a punch at him and missed, his arm going through the store window. (A surprising proportion of British criminals have had the tendons of their forearms and wrists severed by plate-glass injuries: an "occupational hazard," as criminals openly call such injuries.) The youth was badly hurt and required a six-hour operation to repair his arm. As soon as the injury occurred, the fight stopped, and—with considerable forbearance—my patient invited the injured youth into the shop, where he called an ambulance and bound up the injury as best he could while waiting.

Not surprisingly, the police were soon involved, and a week later my patient was astonished to be arrested and charged with grievous bodily harm, a serious crime potentially carrying a long prison sentence. The three youths, all with long records of serious wrongdoing, had claimed that, for no reason at all, this hitherto law-abiding and even rather timid man had suddenly followed them out of the shop and set upon all three of them, in the process injuring one of them severely. The police treated this preposterous story in all seriousness, as if it might have been true. No person of minimal intelligence would have given it a moment's credence, yet my patient was being pursued through the courts with all rigor possible: and in the meantime, his life had been wrecked: he was a shell of his former self, he has twice tried to kill himself, and the law's delay is such that he might try again (and succeed) before the case is resolved, probably by the judge throwing it out as being utterly unworthy of his court.

It is not racism that explains this extraordinary episode but, on the contrary, another intrusion of liberal ideology into policing. The three youths, being vicious, dishonest, at best semi-literate, and probably unemployable, needed protection from

the ill will and prejudice of the respectable, who were responsible for their deprivation because of the unjust structure of
the society from which they, the respectable, had so unfairly
benefited. By taking the obviously bogus and conspiratorial
complaints of these three youths seriously, the police were
demonstrating to a liberal constituency that they did not automatically side with the respectable against those whom Labour
Party bigwigs call, as they cant their way through their next
bottle of champagne, the socially excluded.

The national priorities of the police can be seen in two revealing facts. The first is that the police are considering using an
expensive hi-tech satellite tracking system to catch speeding
drivers. The second is the fate of the chief of police of the northern city of Middlesborough.

I do not praise my fellow countrymen lightly, but there is
one aspect of their conduct that is markedly superior to that of
other nations: their driving habits. They drive, on the whole,
with reasonable consideration for others. Why their good manners should be confined to the road I do not know, but it is so.
For years our road accident rate has been by far the lowest of
any country with comparable levels of traffic; our road fatality
rate is far lower than France's, Germany's, or Italy's.

One might have supposed that the police would count themselves lucky to have a nation of relative law-abiders as far as
traffic regulations are concerned, allowing them to concentrate
on more important matters. But no. With ever increasing offi-
ciousness, they set up cameras in our streets and concentrate
their efforts on the least manifestation of speeding and other
minor infringements of traffic regulations. The expensive satellite system is the next stage in the campaign.

At the same time, the chief constable of Middlesborough, a
man called Ray Mallon, has been suspended from duty for the
last twenty-six months. At first his superiors alleged that he had
made false expense-account claims, but it turned out that if
anything he had underestimated the reimbursement he was

owed. His enemies in the police hierarchy instituted a desperate search for evidence of other wrongdoing by him, so far without success. As he himself has said, he has been treated worse than any criminal.

Why this persecution? Simple: Mallon is a charismatic policeman dedicated to the proposition that the police force can reduce the level of crime, even with all the obstructions those who imagine they are well-meaning place in its path. Having brought about a startling reduction of crime in the town of Hartlepool—a feat that made him into a local hero—he was promoted to the larger town of Middlesborough. There he said he would resign if he had not reduced the crime rate by a fifth within eighteen months. He did it in nine.

Mallon became the most famous policeman in the country. Clearly, he was the kind of leader who would not ask his men to do what he was not prepared to do himself. His drive was formidable and perhaps (even to someone like me) a little frightening. But he had brought an improvement in the quality of many people's lives, and no one has ever been able to show that he did it by illicit or foul means. He merely applied the law.

His suspension was the result of the terror he aroused, not in the public but in other senior police officers. If Mallon could do it in as tough a beat as Middlesborough—the very model of modern urban deprivation—why could the other chief constables not do it? He was setting a bad and dangerous example for them. If Ray Mallon were allowed to continue in his post, the general population would get the idea that a high crime rate was not an inevitable aspect of modern life or an act of God. Therefore he had to go, on any pretext that came to hand: and when he went, about a sixth of the population of Middlesborough signed a petition for his immediate reinstatement.

Looking down one end of the telescope, then, we see the police doing their job as they always have. Looking down the other, however, we see them subverting the purpose for which they were instituted, largely from fear of liberal criticism, which, as American readers well know, is impervious to fact. These liberals pride themselves on their tenderheartedness: but the warm glow it imparts to them comes at the expense of the poor, who as a practical consequence live in a torment of public and private disorder, which I have trembled to behold every day of the last ten years of my professional life.

*2000*

# Zero Intolerance

---

AMONG THE POOR, the police have never been popular. But interestingly, today the all-coppers-are-bastards view of the police has spread to a large section of the bourgeois intellectual class. Not long ago, for example, a journalist told me, *en passant*, that he hated the police. I asked him why: had they falsely arrested, unjustifiably manhandled, brutally interrogated him? No, he replied, he had no personal reason; he just hated them for what they were.

Well, as King Lear said, nothing comes of nothing: and the journalist's hatred of the police was unlikely to have sprung completely at random and fully formed from his consciousness. I suspected, as is so often the case with opinions lightly adopted but firmly held, that this one was forged from a combination of ignorance, dishonesty, and fashion. By expressing a dislike of the police, a bourgeois intellectual is thereby establishing his solidarity with the poor. In an age of empathy, you can't claim to wish anyone well unless you fully share his feelings.

But the bourgeois intellectual needs to find reasons for his opinions: rationalization is, after all, his métier. And it isn't difficult for him to think up such reasons with regard to the police. Their function is, after all, to defend the social order: and since the social order is widely held to be responsible for the poverty of the poor, it follows that the police are in part responsible for that poverty. They are a part not of the criminal justice system but of the social injustice system.

The intellectual never acknowledges how much of his liberty he owes to the existence of the police—a humiliating thought, to which he prefers the idea that the comparative peace and tranquility in which he lives, and that make his work possible, emerge spontaneously from the goodwill of his fellow men, requiring no external coercion to maintain them. Since—in the opinion of the intellectual—the poor hate the police, and moreover as victims can think no wrong, it follows that weak policing would be of benefit to the poor.

It so happens that something close to a natural experiment in weak policing is under way in my district of the city, where the police are a minimal presence and intervene only in the very gravest of situations. Far from having adopted a policy of zero tolerance, as in New York, they have adopted one of zero intolerance; and their approach to crime is almost as abstract—as ethereal—as that of liberal criminologists. It is therefore of some interest, both practical and theoretical, to examine whether the quality of life of the poor has improved or deteriorated under this lax police regime.

The policy of zero intolerance appears to have sprung from the brains of the city's most senior policemen, increasingly indistinguishable in their public pronouncements from senior social workers. Their constituency is not the people of the city but the liberal intelligentsia. A policeman on the beat who had occasion to visit my ward recently told me that he and his colleagues were under orders not to arrest and charge anyone who was previously unknown to the police for crimes up to and including attempted murder. As an old hand nearing an eagerly anticipated retirement from a job he had once loved, he found this instruction deeply demoralizing. It was, he knew, a virtual incitement to crime.

The policy of zero intolerance is no mere local aberration.

The chief of police of another force explained recently in an essay why it was necessary to keep arrests to a minimum. It takes four hours to process each one, he wrote, and therefore such arrests distracted the police from their other duties. He never explained what police duties could be more important than the apprehension of lawbreakers, nor did he call for a streamlining of the process of arrest (which requires, on average, forty-three forms). Besides, he added, mere repression of criminality, whenever the police chanced to catch a criminal, would never on its own put an end to crime. Much better, he seemed to imply, to let the criminals get on with it.

And get on with it they have, not surprisingly. I encounter instances of police inaction in the face of crime every day. For example, a man in his early thirties arrived in the emergency department of my hospital recently, having taken a deliberate but not life-threatening overdose of tablets. His wife arrived while he was awaiting further medical attention. The pair resumed the quarrel that had been the occasion of his overdose, and before long he employed his usual final, irrefutable argument: his fists. The sound of his blows raining down on her head alerted the nurses to the situation. By the time they came to the wife's rescue, she was on the floor, vainly trying to avoid his kicks to her face and stomach.

The nurses called the police, two of whom duly arrived (an eventuality by no means guaranteed). They left soon afterward, without even having requested the husband not to behave in this fashion again. They told the nurses that it was a domestic, and that therefore they were powerless to act. An Englishman's emergency room, apparently, is his castle—and his wife his property.

That a crime is domestic—or, in the words of those who commit such a crime, just a domestic—has long been the most frequently cited of many police excuses for folding their hands and doing nothing. Their habitual reluctance to intervene in what they regard as essentially private disputes is the result, no doubt, of several considerations: among them, a laudable, if imperfectly thought-out, desire to separate the realm of personal morality from that of law. There should be a limit to state supervision of the relations between people, and not every morally reprehensible act should draw a legal sanction. The police view intervention in domestics (quite apart from its practical futility, for victims often balk at testifying in court) as an almost totalitarian extension of their powers. But even on the most generous interpretation of the scope of the private—a senior British policeman once famously, or infamously, remarked that a certain murder was not serious: it was only a man killing his wife—what happened in the emergency room was not domestic, or even a domestic. It was an offense not merely against the victim but against public order. Yet still the police failed to act.

In one respect the police were correct in their understanding of the situation: the man's wife had forgiven him by the time she was picked up off the floor, and she would have refused to testify against him in court. She likewise refused all offers of help to obtain accommodation away from him (he would find her anyway, she said), and she didn't want a lawyer. Her only concern now was to bring him the things he said he would need during his stay in the hospital.

But the police didn't need the wife's testimony to bring a successful prosecution. The nurses had heard and seen enough to convict him twenty times over. The officers' final words of self-justification as they departed the scene were that they were too busy to deal with so trivial a matter. They did not mention what they were busy with.

The effect on the nurses of this dereliction of duty was—at least for a time, until further emergencies occupied their attention—profound and demoralizing. Not only did they feel, rightly, that the police considered valueless the evidence they could so easily have given, as if they were not trustworthy witnesses, but they felt that their position as law-abiding citizens anxious to do their duty was devalued too.

Moreover, many of the nurses inhabit a world not so far removed, physically or morally, from that of the abused wife in the emergency room. Many of them consult me about their problems: one of the nurses in the emergency room that day had a drug-taking daughter whose various boyfriends were violent towards her; another had asked me earlier what to do about her violent common-law husband. So when they see a man beat up a woman in a public place with complete impunity, indeed with what amounted almost to police protection, they catch a horrifying glimpse of their own vulnerability.

And finally, the incident took place in the emergency department of a large inner-city hospital, in which a considerable proportion of the patients present were, almost by definition, of the same cast of mind as the violent husband. They would have remarked on the impotence of the police in the face of this conduct and would have drawn the appropriate conclusion: that you can get away with anything short of murder.

In addition, the culprit himself would soon, no doubt, be spreading the good news in the pubs he frequented, embellishing the tale to present himself to his listeners as even more heroic in his defeat of the police than he already believed himself to be. When I spoke to him after the policemen left the emergency room, he told me that he was himself astonished that he had never once been called to account by the law for his numerous assaults, not only on his wife but upon many others. (His first assault on his wife had been at their wedding reception, in front of the guests.) One of the criteria for diagnosing psychopathy is an individual's failure to learn from experience: but thus far this man had not had the experience from which he might have failed to learn.

The police display perverse ingenuity in concocting reasons for nonintervention in domestic violence. A recent patient of mine had finally broken away from the jealous, drunken, and violent father of her three illegitimate children. She had found her own apartment and had lived there quietly for some time when she held a birthday party for one of her children. But somehow her former boyfriend had discovered where she lived and, on that very afternoon, had rung at her door. She answered; he barged his way in. He dragged her by the hair into the room where the party was taking place and punched her to the ground, kicking her in front of the terrified children. Then he left.

She called the police. She was battered and bruised, and the children who had seen the assault were still there. The police said there was nothing they could do, because she had opened the door to her assailant. And they left.

The police opinion in this case appeared to be that, once you let a man into your house, he is free thereafter to behave in any way he likes. Even after her physical recovery, my patient was in no position to dispute this extraordinary police doctrine: she belonged to that vast class never taught to read or write properly. Unable to set out a letter—not knowing even that the first-person singular pronoun is written in the upper case (I tested her)—she was obliged to take the police at their word.

When I put this case to the police force's second-in-command, he expressed surprise. The only explanation he could think of for his policemen's conduct was that the woman had taken out a restraining order against the man and in effect nullified it by opening the door to him. It was this nullification, he hypothesized, that led to the police's failure to act. That so high-ranking a policeman (transparently a decent man) could have so deficient an understanding should terrify the law-abiding and comfort the wrongdoer.

In their struggle to stay inactive, the police often make a point I hear with some sympathy: that prosecution isn't worth the effort because of the inadequate sentences that follow conviction. For example, a prisoner I know, who had many times beaten up and half-strangled his girlfriend—who had three times threatened to kill her and had once kidnapped her—received a sentence that meant he'd serve only fifteen months in jail (nine of them already served while awaiting trial) instead of the ten years' imprisonment the law allowed. He had made it crystal clear that he would keep pursuing his girlfriend, whatever sentence he received; and his previous record—he had burned the car of another girlfriend, then pregnant, who had tried to leave him—would have suggested to anyone except the judge that he would pose a threat to his former girlfriend and to any other woman he might meet in the future.

The judge's leniency was therefore callous in the extreme towards the well-being of society. But it would compound the damage to make the argument that, because a fifteen-month sentence was inadequate, it would have been better for this prisoner to have received no sentence at all. Nonetheless this is precisely what the police implicitly do argue, and it remains one of the cornerstones of their edifice of passivity.

A drunk deliberately stubbed out his cigarette on the face of a senior nurse in our emergency department, burning her cheek. The police came but, having inspected her injury, declared that it was not severe enough for the crime to be worth prosecuting. Perhaps they reasoned that the drunk, not remembering what he had done after he had sobered up, would therefore not learn a lesson. As agents of the state, however, they had made clear what value the state placed on the physical safety of the nurse: zero.

Another standard excuse for police inaction is that the offender is mad, or at least is a psychiatric patient (not quite the same thing, of course). The merest hint of a psychiatric history—a single consultation with a psychiatrist five years previously is enough—will explain and excuse almost anything in the eyes of the police, and justifies a failure to prosecute.

Not long ago I was called to a police station to examine a man arrested after attempting to kill his lawyer. He had a long history of psychosis—caused or exacerbated by taking drugs—

and lawbreaking. He had gone to his lawyer with a hammer with one end sharpened into a pick, had shouted, "You have to die!" and had aimed a blow at the lawyer's head. Fortunately the lawyer saw the blow coming, twisted out of the way, and received only a slight injury. His violent client tried again to hit him, but having missed, fled the office, after which the lawyer called the police.

It was clear that the man was mad; but I knew from experience that if I recommended he be admitted straight to the hospital, the police would forget the whole matter of the attempted murder. I insisted that charges be filed: but the police refused, saying—falsely, of course—that they were not permitted to prosecute madmen. They said that if he were not hospitalized, they would have to release him—which they did: first giving him back his hammer, for they had no right to deprive him of his property. Thus an attempted murder did not reach the crime statistics, and the police could congratulate themselves on the maintenance of public order.

Needless to say, the mad understand the impunity of madness well. Twice I have heard schizophrenics exclaim to the police, "You can't touch me, I'm a schizophrenic!" On the very day on which I wrote this, I interviewed a patient—an alcoholic—who sometime before had, while extremely drunk, tried to strangle his girlfriend. He had smashed her car, wrecked her apartment, and threatened to kill her daughter. By the time the police arrived, he had started to attack his girlfriend's neighbor, who had come to help. The police concluded that no sane man would behave like this, took him to the hospital, and left him there. As far as they were concerned, the incident was closed. And these crimes also did not reach the crime statistics. This is how we now control criminality in England.

Domestic crimes are not alone in getting such lighthearted treatment. In the last two weeks the following three cases have come to my notice. An acquaintance of mine, a dealer in antique jewelry, exhibited at an antiques fair. Overnight a thief broke into the exhibition hall and stole her jewelry, worth $32,000, as well as that of other exhibitors, worth a further $120,000. In this instance the police caught the thief the following day: he was on bail for eight country-house burglaries, itself a sign of police frivolity, for, had they objected strenuously enough to the setting of bail, he would still have been in custody. Despite their swift apprehension of the culprit, however, the police had not recovered a single piece of jewelry (something a private detective surely would have been able to do); indeed, they claim to be too busy to make the effort. Little wonder that the insurance premiums on antique jewelry are too high for most small dealers to pay. So my acquaintance must swallow the whole loss—to her, a catastrophe.

A patient of mine became severely depressed after some young thieves, well known in the area, broke into the shed in her garden and stole her children's new bicycles. Her neighbors, it so happened, were able to make a clear videotape of the thieves as they stole, but—two weeks later—the police still had not responded to either my patient's or her neighbors' request for assistance. Bicycle theft, after all, is not a serious crime.

A prisoner with a long history of violent crime as well as theft and burglary was coming to the end of his most recent prison sentence. He frankly admitted to me that he was much happier in prison than at liberty: the enforced discipline of prison life enabled him to live at peace. He came to me in desperation: could I do something to prevent his release, for he knew he would soon commit a dangerous offense again, possibly even a murder? He had gone to the prison warden, asking not to be released. The warden told him there was no legal way to do that. In an attempt to stay in prison, he then confessed to several serious crimes, with which he had never been charged. Corroboration of his confession would have been possible, and the warden called in the police. But they declined to take the matter further, saying that it was not in the public interest to do so. The prisoner then assaulted and seriously injured another inmate to receive more prison time. Again the police came but declined to take the matter further, saying that it was not in the public interest to do so. The prisoner was released June 12.

The loss of nerve or will on the part of the police has occurred at precisely the same time as a weakening, almost to the point of extinction, of the informal but strong social restraints upon personal behavior that once made England so civil a country—restraints such as fear of what the neighbors will say. The lack of either internal or external restraint has allowed "natural" man to emerge: and far from being a delight, he is a charmless psychopath. Man is a wolf to man, and more particularly to woman.

Naturally, social trends do not affect all sectors of society equally. Weak policing affects principally the poor—the very people whose welfare the intelligentsia claimed weak policing would benefit. It is true that the middle classes haven't been unscathed: they pay ever-higher insurance premiums for their homes and cars, and they worry as never before about burglary. There is scarcely anyone in the country—even among the burglars themselves—whose first thought on returning home is not, "Have I been burgled?"

But these are trifling concerns beside my patients' pervasive and permanent sense of personal insecurity wherever they may be. They fear lawbreakers because they know the police offer no protection. The degree to which fear of crime rules the lives of people in poor areas is something that my middle-class friends find hard to believe, let alone understand. Scores of my patients have told me that they leave their homes as rarely as possible for fear of being attacked or of having their homes broken into. Every week I meet patients who have been mugged or burgled three times or more in a year; last week I had a patient whom the children next door stone—literally shower with stones—whenever she leaves the house. They have broken her windows on innumerable occasions and have smeared the walls of her house with feces while she was out. No one has ever been apprehended for these offenses, and she has given up informing the police of them.

The pretense by intellectuals—which, alas, has not been without its practical effects in the real world—that the police are but the executive arm of a hypocritical bourgeoisie determined to preserve its ill-gotten gains at the expense of the poor, is terrifyingly shallow when tested against the experience of people who suffer weak policing. The idea that a juster social order would render the police redundant is utopian nonsense. A reliable and trustworthy police force is not a denial of freedom but a precondition of its exercise. For those who doubt it, I can only recommend the last lines of Pablo Neruda's poem of the Spanish Civil War:

> Come and see the blood
> running through the streets!
> Come and see the blood
> running through the streets!
> Come and see the blood
> running through the streets!

*1998*

# *Seeing Is Not Believing*

◆ THE FIRST DUTY of the modern intellectual, wrote George Orwell, is to state the obvious, to puncture "the smelly little orthodoxies . . . now contending for our souls." Orwell meant by these the totalitarian doctrines that mesmerized the intellectuals of his time and that prevented them from accepting the most obvious and evident truths about their own and other societies: but his admonition holds true even now, when fascism and communism are dead. The demise of totalitarianism has led not to a more straightforward or honest appreciation of reality but merely to a proliferation of distorting lenses through which people choose to look at the world. If humankind, as T. S. Eliot put it, cannot bear very much reality, it seems that it can bear any amount of unreality.

The intellectual's struggle to deny the obvious is never more desperate than when reality is unpleasant and at variance with his preconceptions and when full acknowledgment of it would undermine the foundations of his intellectual worldview. Given the social history of England in the last forty years, little wonder that collective denial should be one of the most salient characteristics of our national intellectual life.

I am in an unusual position: while I spend most of my professional life as a doctor working in the extensive lower reaches of society, I have, because of my writing, an entrée into literary society. The complacent disregard by the latter of the social catastrophe wrought in the former appalls me almost as much as the catastrophe itself. Never has so much indifference masqueraded as so much compassion; never has there been such willful blindness. The once pragmatic English have become a nation of sleepwalkers.

Recently, for example, I was invited to a lunch at a famous and venerable liberal publication, to which I occasionally contribute articles that go against its ideological grain. The publication's current owner is a bon vivant and excellent host who made several scores of millions in circumstances that still excite considerable public curiosity. Around the lunch table (from which, I am glad to say, British proletarian fare was strictly excluded) were gathered people of impeccable liberal credentials: the one exception being myself.

On my right sat a man in his late sixties, intelligent and cultivated, who had been a distinguished foreign correspondent for the BBC and who had spent much of his career in the United States. He said that for the last ten years he had read with interest my weekly dispatches—printed in a rival, conservative publication—depicting the spiritual, cultural, emotional, and moral chaos of modern urban life, and had always wanted to meet me to ask me a simple question: Did I make it all up?

Did I make it all up? It was a question I have been asked many times by middle-class liberal intellectuals, who presumably hope that the violence, neglect, and cruelty, the contorted thinking, the utter hopelessness, and the sheer nihilism that I describe week in and week out are but figments of a fevered imagination. In a way I am flattered that the people who ask this question should think that I am capable of inventing the absurd yet oddly poetic utterances of my patients—that I am capable, for example, of inventing the man who said he felt like the little boy with his finger in the dike, crying wolf. But at the same time the question alarms me and reminds me of what

Thackeray once said about the writings of Henry Mayhew, the chronicler of the London poor: we had but to go a hundred yards off and see for ourselves, but we never did.

On being asked whether I make it all up, I reply that, far from doing so, I downplay the dreadfulness of the situation and omit the worst cases that come to my attention so as not to distress the reader unduly. The reality of English lower-class life is far more terrible than I can, with propriety, depict. My interlocutors nod politely and move on to the next subject.

It is the custom at the lunches of that famous and venerable liberal publication, once the plates have been removed, for one of the guests to speak briefly to a subject that preoccupies him at the moment. And on this occasion it was the BBC's former correspondent in the United States who spoke: eloquently and well, as one might have expected.

And what was the subject upon which he dilated with such eloquence? The iniquity of the death penalty in the United States.

It is not easy to capture the contented mood that settled round the table as he spoke, a mixture of well-fed moral superiority (one of the pleasantest of all emotions) and righteous indignation (another very pleasant emotion). The consensus was that they were benighted savages over there, while we over here, guardians as ever of civilization itself, had not resorted to such primitive and barbaric methods for ages—that is to say, for thirty-five years.

Everyone agreed with the BBC man, and it was my turn to say something. I confess to not being an enthusiast for the death penalty: it seems to me that the possibility of error, and the historical fact of such errors having taken place (not only in the United States but in Britain and presumably in every other jurisdiction where true due process reigns) is a powerful, if not absolutely decisive, argument against the death penalty, whatever its deterrent effect might be. And having seen photographs of execution chambers, where fatal injections are administered,

246

decked out as if they were operating rooms in hospitals, I cannot help but feel that something sinister is going on: the pretense that execution is a therapeutic procedure. One begins to see the force of Dr. Johnson's argument that executions should be in public, in the open air, or not take place at all: at least there is no danger then that executions might be taken for something other than what they are.

But I was anxious to dispel the cozy atmosphere of rectitude, of sanctity so easily achieved without cost or effort. I said we should look closer to home, to the fact that, with the single (and admittedly important) exception of murder, crime rates in Britain were now higher, and in some cases much higher, than in the United States: and that the chief failing of our criminal justice system was not its excessive harshness or its liability to wrongful imprisonment but its patent failure to enforce the law or to protect citizens from the most blatant lawbreaking. The result was that for untold numbers of our compatriots, life was a living hell.

I briefly outlined my reasons for saying so: the vast numbers of people—thousands and possibly tens of thousands—who have told me about their lives, which are dominated by the possibility, or rather the high probability, of violence and other criminal acts being committed against them, and who quite rightly felt themselves to be totally unprotected by the police or by the courts.

Opposite me was a well-known pacifist, a man of the highest principle, who was by no means a puritan, however, at least with regard to food and wine. His shiny cheeks radiated bonhomie and self-satisfaction at the same time, and he spoke in the plummy tones of the English upper middle class.

"You know funny people," he said, leaning slightly toward me across the table.

I know funny people: I was reminded of a medical school friend of mine whose mother, when introduced to his girlfriend, whispered in his ear, "NQOCD," the acronym for Not Quite Our

Class, Dear. "Funny" those people whom I knew might be, I replied to the pacifist, but there were a lot of them, and moreover they lived in our country, often within walking—and burgling—distance of our front doors.

The man's complacency was by no means unusual. A few days earlier I had met my publisher for lunch, and the subject of the general level of culture and education in England came up. My publisher is a cultivated man, widely read and deeply attached to literature, but I had difficulty in convincing him that there were grounds for concern. That illiteracy and innumeracy were widespread did not worry him in the least, because—he claimed—they had always been just as widespread. (The fact that we now spent four times as much per head on education as we did fifty years ago and were therefore entitled to expect rising rates of literacy and numeracy at the very least did not in the slightest knock him off his perch.) He simply did not believe me when I told him that nine of ten young people between the ages of sixteen and twenty whom I met in my practice could not read with facility and were incapable of multiplying six by nine, or that out of several hundreds of them I had asked when the Second World War took place, only three knew the answer. He replied smoothly—almost without the need to think, as if he had rehearsed the argument many times—that his own son, age seven, already knew the dates of the war.

"The trouble is," he said in all seriousness, "your sample is biased."

And true enough: everyone's experience is founded upon a biased sample. But it didn't occur to him to doubt whether his sample—of one, the son of a publisher living in a neighborhood where houses usually cost more than $1.5 million—really constituted a refutation of my experience of hundreds of cases, an experience borne out by all serious research into the matter. He accused me of moral panic, as if the only alternative to his imperturbable complacency (he was so serene you might have thought him a monk from a contemplative order) were irrational, agitated alarmism.

"Have you actually ever met any of the kind of people I'm talking about?" I asked him. He replied not that he had, but that he supposed he must have done.

Complacency and denial dominate public as well as private discourse, and when a little of the unpleasant side of contemporary English reality is allowed an airing, a damage-control exercise swiftly ensues.

A newspaper recently asked me to go to Blackpool, a northern English resort town on the Irish Sea, to describe the conduct of the people who go there for a weekend. Blackpool has never been a place of great refinement and has long attracted people who cannot afford to go to more desirable places for their holidays. Boardinghouses rather than hotels predominate, presided over by formidable landladies. But Blackpool was, within living memory, a resort of innocent fun, with donkey rides and Punch-and-Judy shows on the beach, and a brisk sale of the mildly salacious comic postcards about which George Orwell once wrote with great sympathy and insight, in which weedy men are dominated by large, fat wives in bathing costumes, in which mothers-in-law are always battle-axes, in which unmarried men are always trying to escape the snares of marriage set for them by young women, and whose captions are always saucy double entendres. For example, a judge in the divorce court says to a co-respondent, "You are prevaricating, sir. Did you or did you not sleep with this woman?" to which the co-respondent replies, "Not a wink, my lord!"

This sophisticated innocence has departed. Without the institution of marriage, mother-in-law and divorce jokes are pointless and passé. Fun now means public drunkenness on a mass scale, screaming in the streets, and the frequent exposure of naked buttocks to passersby. Within moments of arriving on the street along the beach, which was ankle-deep in discarded fast-food wrappings (the smell of stale fat obliterates completely the salt smell of the sea), I saw a woman who had pulled down her slacks and tied a pair of plastic breasts to her bare buttocks, while a man crawled after her on the sidewalk, licking them. At midnight along this street—with the sound of rock music pounding insistently out of every club door, and each door presided over by a pair of steroid-inflated bouncers, among men vomiting into the gutters, and with untold numbers of empty bags of marijuana on the pavement—I saw children as young as six, unattended by adults, waiting for their parents to emerge from their nocturnal recreations.

On the day after the publication of my article, I appeared briefly on the BBC's main breakfast-time radio program, which has an audience of several million. The interviewer was an intelligent and cultivated woman, and having briefly and accurately summarized for the readers my account of what I saw in Blackpool, she then asked me, "Aren't you being a toff?"—that is to say, a social and cultural snob.

The question was, of course, a loaded one, with many layers of deeply derogatory implication. I in turn asked her whether she would herself bare her buttocks to passing strangers, and if she wouldn't, why not? She declined to answer this question, as if it were not serious—just as a future government minister with whom I once appeared on the radio, after asserting that one of the tragedies of some recent urban riots was that they had taken place in the rioters' poor inner-city neighborhood, refused to answer when I asked her if she would rather the riots had taken place in her own rich neighborhood.

Not long after the interview about my experiences in Blackpool, the BBC broadcast letters from a few listeners who charged that I had failed to understand the nature of working-class culture. They used the word "culture" here in the anthropological sense of the sum total of a way of life, but they were also taking cunning and dishonest advantage of the word's connotations of Bach and Shakespeare to insinuate that the wearing of plastic breasts on the Blackpool promenade is indistinguishable in value from the B-Minor Mass or the sonnets.

The liberal assumption, in this as in most things, is that to understand is to approve (or at least to pardon), and therefore my disapproval indicated a lack of understanding. But strangely enough, the letters that the BBC and the newspaper that published the original article forwarded to me—those they hadn't broadcast or published—wholly endorsed my comments. They were from Blackpool residents and from working-class people elsewhere who passionately denied that working-class culture had always consisted of nothing but mindless obscenity. Several writers spoke very movingly of enduring real poverty in childhood while maintaining self-respect and a striving for mental distinction. The deliberate exclusion of these voices from public expression provided a fine example of how the British intelligentsia goes about its self-appointed task of cultural destruction.

Violence, vulgarity, and educational failure: three aspects of modern English life that are so obvious and evident that it requires little observational power to discern them. Indeed, it requires far more mental effort and agility not to discern them, to screen them out of one's consciousness: the scenes in Blackpool, for example, being only slightly worse and more extreme than those to be seen in the center of every English town and city every Saturday night of the year.

It is worth examining the mental mechanisms that liberal intellectuals use to disguise the truth from themselves and others, and to ask why they do so.

First, there is outright denial. Increasing crime, for example, was long dismissed as a mere statistical artifact, before the sheer weight of the evidence overwhelmed the possibility of denial. It wasn't so much crime that was increasing, we were told, as people's willingness or ability to report it—via the spread of the telephone. As to educational failure, it was long denied by the production of statistics showing that more and more children

were passing public examinations, a classic half-truth that omitted to say that these examinations had deliberately been made
so easy that it was impossible to fail them (the concept of failure having been abolished), except by not turning up for them.
But even the most liberal of university professors has now noticed that his students can't spell or punctuate.

Second, there is the tendentious historical comparison or
precedent. Yes, it is admitted, violence and vulgarity are a large
part of modern British life; but they always were. When English
soccer fans ran amok in France during the European cup finals
(the kind of behavior now universally expected of them), even
the conservative *Daily Telegraph* ran an article to the effect that
it was ever thus, and that Hanoverian England was a riotous,
drunken era—thereby implying that there was nothing to be
alarmed about. For some reason not fully explained, it is supposed to be a comfort—even a justification—that anti-social behavior has persisted unabated over hundreds of years. In the
same way, intellectuals depict alarm over rising crime as unrea-
sonable (and those who express it as lacking in historical
knowledge), because it is not difficult to find historical epochs
when crime was worse than it is now. I have even seen worry
about a rising murder rate treated with mockery, because in me-
dieval England it was very much higher than it is now. Thus historical comparison with a period hundreds of years ago is held
up as more relevant than comparison with thirty or even ten
years ago, as long as that comparison fosters an attitude of
complacency towards undesirable social phenomena.

Third, once the facts are finally admitted under the duress of
accumulated evidence, their moral significance is denied or per-
verted. Do children emerge from school as ignorant of facts as
when they entered? Well, of course: this is because they are no
longer taught by rote but instead are taught how to go about
finding information for themselves. Their inability to write legi-
bly in no way lessens their ability to express themselves but

rather accentuates it. At least they have not been subjected to the learning of arbitrary rules. Vulgarity is liberty from unhealthy and psychologically deforming inhibition; it is merely the revival of popular bawdy, and those who oppose it are elitist killjoys. As to violence, any quantity of it can be explained away by reference to the "structural violence" of capitalist society.

A BBC television producer recently outlined the phases of liberal denial for me. His colleagues, he told me, regarded him as a maverick, a tilter at windmills, almost a madman. And what was his madness? He wanted the BBC to make unvarnished documentaries about life in the lower third of society: about the mass (and increasing) illiteracy, the mass (and increasing) illegitimacy and single parenthood, the mass (and increasing) hooliganism, violence, lawlessness, drug taking, welfare dependency, and hopelessness, so that the rest of the population might begin to take stock of what was happening on their very doorstep. And he wanted, in particular, to concentrate on the devastating effects of the fragmentation—no, the atomization—of the family that liberal legislation, social engineering, and cultural attitudes since the late 1950s have so powerfully promoted.

His BBC superiors greeted his proposals with condescension. First, they denied the facts. When he produced irrefutable evidence of their existence, they accused him of moral panic. When he proved that the phenomena to which the facts pointed were both serious and spreading rapidly up the social scale, they said that there was nothing that could be done about them, because they were an inevitable part of modern existence. When he said that they were the result of deliberate policy, they asked him whether he wanted to return to the bad old days when spouses who hated each other were forced to live together. And when he said that what had been done could be undone, at least in part, they produced their ace of trumps: the subject was not interesting, so there was no point in making programs about it. The British public would be left to sleepwalk its way undisturbed through the social disaster from which a fragile economic prosperity will certainly not protect it.

But why so insistent a denial of the obvious by the very class of people whose primary function, one might have supposed, was to be what the Russians called truth bearers?

The answer is to be sought in the causative relationship between the ideas that liberal intellectuals advocated and put into practice and every disastrous social development of the last four decades. They saw their society as being so unjust that nothing in it was worth preserving; and they thought that all human unhappiness arose from the arbitrary and artificial fetters that their society placed on the satisfaction of appetite. So dazzled were they by their vision of perfection that they could not see the possibility of deterioration.

And so if family life was less than blissful, with all its inevitable little prohibitions, frustrations, and hypocrisies, they called for the destruction of the family as an institution. The destigmatization of illegitimacy went hand in hand with easy divorce, the extension of marital rights to other forms of association between adults, and the removal of all the fiscal advantages of marriage. Marriage melted as snow in sunshine. The destruction of the family was, of course, an important component and consequence of sexual liberation, whose utopian program was to have increased the stock of innocent sensual pleasure, not least among the liberators themselves. It resulted instead in widespread violence consequent upon sexual insecurity and in the mass neglect of children, as people became ever more egotistical in their search for momentary pleasure.

If liberal intellectuals recalled their childhood experiences of education as less than an unalloyed joy, education had to become a form of childish entertainment: for who, in any case, were mere adults to impose their ideas on those equally sentient beings, their children? Were not grammar and arithmetic—indeed all disciplines—mere bourgeois (or, in America, racist) tools with which to maintain social hegemony? And self-respect being radically incompatible with failure, the very idea of failure itself had to go. The only way to achieve this was to do away with education altogether—an experiment that could be carried out in full only on that section of the population least concerned about education in the first place, thus creating a now hereditary caste of ineducables.

And if crime was a problem, it was only because an unjust society forced people into criminal activity, and therefore punishment constituted a double injustice, victimizing the real victim. By what right could an unjust society claim to impose its version of justice? Empathy and understanding were what was needed, provided they absolved the criminal of his responsibility. The creation of a universal disposition to do good, and not the creation of fear of the consequences of doing evil, was what was needed to extirpate crime. Not surprisingly, these were glad tidings to those tempted by the life of crime and demoralizing ones to those who upheld the law.

Every liberal prescription worsened the problem that it was ostensibly designed to solve. But every liberal intellectual had to deny that obvious consequence or lose his Weltanschauung: for what shall it profit an intellectual if he acknowledge a simple truth and lose his Weltanschauung? Let millions suffer so long as he can retain his sense of his own righteousness and moral superiority. Indeed, if millions suffer they are additional compassion fodder for him, and the more of their pain will he so generously feel.

And so the prescription is: more of the same. The Liberal Democrat Party, Britain's third party, which is dominated by the middle-class liberal intelligentsia and is gaining an unthinking popularity born of disillusionment with the government and of the patent incompetence of the official opposition, recently held

its annual conference. And what were the most important proposals put forward there? The legal recognition of homosexual
marriage and shorter prison sentences for criminals.

Nero was a committed firefighter by comparison.

*2000*

# Index

# Index

# Index

Karam, Joe, 203–204
Kinsey, Alfred, 40
Kouao, Marie Therese,
167–177

Labour Party, 230
Laing, R. D., 41, 125
Language and linguistics, ix,
xii, 156; BBC, 81; diction,
80, 81; impersonal language,
79; language of prisoners,
5–6; passive language, 5–6,
10; spelling, xiv, 71
*Language Instinct, The*
(Pinker), xii, 156
Laurie, Alison, 197–198
Le Corbusier, 147–149
Leach, Edmund, 40
Liberal Democrat Party, 255
Liberalism, 12, 13–14, 118,
125, 132, 245–247; denial,
249, 251–252, 254; middle
class and, 233–243; New
Zealand, 195–196, 203,
205–206; police and,
221–232; use of historical
comparison, 252; use of
moral significance, 252–253.
*See also* Intellectualism.
Liberation theology, 89
Life expectancy, 13. *See also*
Infant mortality rate.

Linguistics. *See* Language and
linguistics.
Littering, 140

Mailer, Norman, 40, 209
Maimonides, Moses, 184
Mallon, Ray, 230–231
Manning, Carl, 167–177
Maoris, 206
Marinetti, Filippo Tommaso,
145–146
Marxism, 13, 26, 97, 123
Mass media, 14
Mathematics, 70
Mayhew, Henry, 246
Mentally ill, 124–130,
239–240
Middle class, 78–88; liberal
ideology and, 233–243;
police policies and, 242
Middlesborough, England,
230–231
Mies van der Rohe, Ludwig,
150
Morris, Parker, 147, 151
Multiculturalism, 26–35, 170;
Indians, 31–33; Jamaicans,
32; Muslims, 28–29;
religious tolerance, 32–33;
Sikhs, 33
Music, 83
Muslims, 28–29, 122–123

# Index

Vulgarity, 249–250, 253

Wealth, English attitudes
  towards, 102
Welfare, viii–ix, 134–143,
  160–162, 168–169, 195
Weltanschauung (worldview),
  ix, 77, 255
Working-class culture, 249–251

Worldview (Weltanschauung),
  ix, 77, 255

Young, Jock, 213, 214, 219

Zero intolerance, 233–243
Zero tolerance, 219

## A NOTE ON THE AUTHOR

Theodore Dalrymple is a British doctor and writer, born in 1949, who has worked on four continents and now works in a British inner city hospital and a prison. He has written a column for the *London Spectator* for ten years and is a contributing editor of the *City Journal*. His work has appeared in the *Wall Street Journal*, the *Daily Telegraph*, the *Sunday Telegraph*, the *Guardian*, the *Daily Mail*, the *National Post* (Canada), *New Statesman*, *National Review*, and many other publications. He has published a novel entitled *So Little Done*, the philosophical self-justification of a fictional serial killer, and *Mass Listeria*, an investigation into the meaning of health scares.